FARAWAY WOMEN

AND

THE *ATLANTIC MONTHLY*

A VOLUME IN THE SERIES
Studies in Print Culture and the History of the Book

EDITED BY
Greg Barnhisel
Robert A. Gross
Joan Shelley Rubin
Michael Winship

FARAWAY WOMEN
AND
THE *ATLANTIC MONTHLY*

CATHRYN HALVERSON

University of Massachusetts Press
AMHERST AND BOSTON

Copyright © 2019 by University of Massachusetts Press
All rights reserved
Printed in the United States of America

ISBN 978-1-62534-455-7 (paper); 454-0 (hardcover)

Designed by Sally Nichols
Set in Palatino
Printed and bound by Maple Press, Inc.

Cover design by Frank Gutbrod
Cover photo by Florian Klauer/Unsplash

Library of Congress Cataloging-in-Publication Data

Names: Halverson, Cathryn, author.
Title: Faraway women and the Atlantic monthly / Cathryn Halverson.
Description: Amherst : University of Massachusetts Press, 2019. | Includes
bibliographical references and index. | Summary: "In the first decades
of the twentieth century, famed Atlantic Monthly editor Ellery Sedgwick
chose to publish a group of nontraditional writers he later referred to
as "Faraway Women," working-class authors living in the western United
States far from his base in Boston. Cathryn Halverson surveys these
enormously popular Atlantic contributors, among them a young woman
raised in Oregon lumber camps, homesteaders in Wyoming, Idaho, and
Alberta, and a world traveler who called Los Angeles and Honolulu home.
Faraway Women and the "Atlantic Monthly" examines gender and power as it
charts an archival journey connecting the least remembered writers and
readers of the time with one of its most renowned literary figures,
Gertrude Stein. It shows how distant friends, patrons, publishers, and
readers inspired, fostered, and consumed the innovative life narratives
of these unlikely authors, and it also tracks their own strategies for
seizing creative outlets and forging new protocols of public expression.
Troubling binary categories of east and west, national and regional, and
cosmopolitan and local, the book recasts the coordinates of early
twentieth-century American literature"—Provided by publisher.
Identifiers: LCCN 2019019870 | ISBN 9781625344557 (paperback) | ISBN
9781625344540 (hardcover) | ISBN 9781613766996 (ebook) | ISBN
9781613766989 (ebook)
Subjects: LCSH: American literature—Women authors—History and criticism.
| Women and literature—West (U.S.) —History—20th century. | American
literature—20th century—History and criticism. | Journalism and
literature—United States—History—20th century. | Atlantic monthly.
Classification: LCC PS151 .H35 2019 | DDC 813/.99287—dc23
LC record available at https://lccn.loc.gov/2019019870

British Library Cataloguing-in-Publication Data
A catalog record for this book is available from the British Library.

To Linda Karell

CONTENTS

ACKNOWLEDGMENTS

The final stages of this book were written under very different conditions than its initial ones. In 2016 the Danish government slashed funding for higher education, leading to the elimination of nearly five hundred permanent positions at the University of Copenhagen. My tenured associate professorship in English was one of them, as my department abruptly informed me, by email: given four months' notice, the offer of psychological counseling, and nothing else. The two-plus years between receiving that news and beginning my present job at Minot State University, North Dakota, were hard, as I sought to finish a book and find a job without an affiliation, library, or income.

I spent that time, in roughly equal measure, in Mexico, Japan, Wyoming, and the Netherlands. Throughout, in person and remotely, I relied on family, friends, colleagues, and strangers for all manner of assistance: logistical aid, financial advice, emotional counsel, and professional guidance. They petitioned their chairs, reviewed my applications, conducted mock interviews, and gave pep talks; they offered funding to conferences, feedback on drafts, passwords to library accounts, and rooms in their homes. Had I accepted all the offers of letters of support, I would have another book. I also cherish the fiery protest letter submitted by my first-year literature students at Copenhagen, some of the most talented I have had the privilege to teach.

While I cannot list everyone here, this generous group includes old friends: Erica Abrams Locklear, Stephanie Palmer, Laura Stevens, June

Howard, Dave Struthers, Zeljka Svrljuga, Emily Dolbear, and Paul Willen; new friends: Michael Brose, Wendy Harding, Alyson Hagy, and Renee Laegreid; and Western Literature Association colleagues, among others Kathy Boardman, Nancy Cook, Kerry Fine, Melody Graulich, Charles Johanningsmeier, Victoria Lamont, Will Lombardi, and Tara Penry. This book is dedicated to the most stalwart of them all, Linda Karell, for reasons that anyone who knows Linda will know.

I also thank my indefatigable letter writers: Christine Bold, Martyn Bone, Sue Maher, and Kerry Larson. Kerry was one of my advisers at the University of Michigan; his first recommendation letter for me dates back to 1997. It was also he who prompted this study, at a 2011 American studies conference in Oslo: on hearing my plans for an essay on the *Atlantic Monthly*'s surprising interest in western women, he said the subject warranted a book.

Research for this book was supported by a semester as an International Research Fellow for the Wyoming Institute for Humanities Research at the University of Wyoming, a research award from the Charles Redd Center for Western Studies at Brigham Young University, a grant from the American Heritage Center at the University of Wyoming, and a Ruth R. & Alyson R. Miller Fellowship at the Massachusetts Historical Society. I thank the MHS, my primary archive, for permission to quote from materials in the Ellery Sedgwick collection authored by Sedgwick. I relied as well on the assistance and goodwill of librarians and archivists at the New York Public Library Archives, Houghton Library, Harvard University Archives, University of Oregon Special Collections, the University of California–Los Angeles (UCLA), and the Sweetwater County Historical Museum in Green River, Wyoming. My special thanks to Susanne Bloomfield; it was a privilege to follow her research trail.

It was only as I was writing these acknowledgments that I realized how much the support network I describe reads as an updated twenty-first-century version of those I uncover for my main writers. I have long been aware, however, of how much succor I found in the perseverance with which these women pieced together writing lives, outside of institutional structures and distant from social worlds of power. Although my circumstances are far more privileged, I did share with them an urgent need to finish a book. I often reminded myself of the confident assertion that Hilda Rose made from Fort Vermillion, Alberta: "If I fix

ACKNOWLEDGMENTS   xi

up another book in the coming year and sell it all will be well" (and tried to overlook the fact that she never did).

In regard to fixing up the book, I am grateful to my editor at the University of Massachusetts Press, Brian Halley, for making the path to publication so straight and swift. The generously stringent counsel of my peer reviewers, including Melissa Homestead and two anonymous readers, not only strengthened this study but also set me up for the next one to come. For their many kindnesses, I am indebted to my brother, Peter, and his wife, Janice; my sister, Priscilla, and her husband, Odd-Even; my sister-in-law, Lauren; and my mother-in-law, Mary. I also thank new colleagues in North Dakota, including Eric Furuseth and my chair, Robert Kibler, as they helped me adjust to living and teaching in the United States once again, and both MSU's Division of Humanities and vice president for academic affairs Laurie Geller for kindly granting subventions for the book.

And finally my deepest gratitude to David, always an unflagging source of comfort, inspiration, and support.

ABBREVIATIONS

The following archival collections and primary sources, along with selected other works, are abbreviated in the text:

AABT Gertrude Stein, *The Autobiography of Alice B. Toklas* (1933; reprint, Stockholm/London: Continental, 1947)

AH Ellery Sedgwick, *Atlantic Harvest: Memoirs of the Atlantic* (Boston: Little, Brown, 1947)

AWH Susanne K. George [Bloomfield], *The Adventures of the Woman Homesteader: The Life and Letters of Elinore Pruitt Stewart* (Lincoln: University of Nebraska Press, 1993)

EFP Emerson Family Papers, Manuscripts and Archives Division, New York Public Library, Astor, Lenox, and Tilden Foundation

ESP Ellery Sedgwick Papers, Massachusetts Historical Society

FL1 Juanita Harrison to Alice M. Foster, January 9, 1931, Ann Cunningham Smith collection of letters from Juanita Harrison to Alice M. Foster, Charles E. Young Research Library, University of California Los Angeles

FL2 Juanita Harrison to Alice M. Foster, March 11, 1931, Ann

Cunningham Smith collection of letters from Juanita Harrison to Alice M. Foster, Charles E. Young Research Library, University of California Los Angeles

FL3   Juanita Harrison to Alice M. Foster, July 12, 1936, Ann Cunningham Smith collection of letters from Juanita Harrison to Alice M. Foster, Charles E. Young Research Library, University of California Los Angeles

GWBW Juanita Harrison, *My Great, Wide, Beautiful World* (New York: Macmillan, 1936; reprint, New York: G. K. Hall, 1996)

HP   Ellery Sedgwick, *The Happy Profession* (Boston: Little, Brown, 1946)

LEH   Elinore Pruitt Stewart, *Letters on an Elk Hunt* (Boston: Houghton Mifflin, 1915)

LWH   Elinore Pruitt Stewart, *Letters of a Woman Homesteader* (1914; reprint, Boston: Houghton Mifflin, 1988)

MP   Mildred Morris, preface to *My Great, Wide, Beautiful World*, by Juanita Harrison (1936)

SBC   Susanne Bloomfield Collection, Sweetwater County Historical Museum, Green River, Wyoming

SF   Hilda Rose, *The Stump Farm: A Chronicle of Pioneering* (1928; reprint, Boston: Little, Brown, 1935)

SO   Opal Whiteley, *The Story of Opal: The Journal of an Understanding Heart* (Boston: Atlantic Monthly Press, 1920)

TJ   Ellery Sedgwick, travel journal, *ESP*

FARAWAY WOMEN

AND

THE *ATLANTIC MONTHLY*

INTRODUCTION

"OUTLYING TERRITORIES OF LITERATURE"

n the summer of 1933, *Atlantic Monthly* editor Ellery Sedgwick ran "Letters of Two Women Farmers," a two-part serial that overlapped with another, longer, serial that was also generated by a women's partnership, "Autobiography of Alice B. Toklas." "Letters of Two Women Farmers" is composed of the letters that Evelyn Harris and Caroline Henderson exchanged about coping with drought and the Depression in Maryland and Oklahoma. These farmers scarcely knew each other: encouraged by the prominence of women's life narratives in the *Atlantic,* they had begun a long-distance correspondence with the express purpose of pitching it to Sedgwick. Thus, while Henderson's account of dust-bowl conditions is gripping, her and Harris's presumptive friendship is not, registered in stilted statements such as "You must have been writing to me on the very evening that I was thinking especially of you, and wondering whether farming in Maryland is as different as it is here on the great plains." "Letters of Two Women Farmers" attracted little attention and quickly faded from view, a fate that, of course, differs starkly from that of Gertrude Stein's memoir. A sensation on publication, *The Autobiography of Alice B. Toklas* is now entrenched (in its bound-volume version) in the canon of American modernism. Stein delineates, through the voice of the text's nominal author, her literary achievements in conjunction with her enduring relationship with

Toklas. "Only three times in my life have I met a genius," she has Toklas declare of her, "and each time a bell within me rang" (*AABT* 11).[1]

On first inspection, only chance periodic proximity links *The Autobiography of Alice B. Toklas* to "Letters of Two Women Farmers." However, such proximity assumes greater significance when viewed in light of the *Atlantic*'s commitment to women's life narratives. Often organized as serials, such narratives were a popular, widely recognized feature of Sedgwick's thirty-year editorship, which spanned 1908 to 1938. The collected letters of white women homesteaders in Wyoming, Idaho, and Alberta, the diary of a child in an Oregon lumber camp, and the seeming journal of an African American world traveler who called Los Angeles home were among those that achieved the greatest cultural traction. Implicitly contrasting them to the northeastern writers he also favored, Sedgwick dubbed these unlikely *Atlantic* authors "Faraway Women" in a chapter of the same name in his 1946 memoir, *The Happy Profession:* women who published accounts of unusual life experiences in Europe, Asia, the American South, and, most saliently, the American West. *Atlantic* readers were especially captivated by the western serials, which all went on to become best-selling books. Consequently, they played an important role in consolidating the "imagined community" of the *Atlantic Monthly,* to adapt Benedict Anderson's paradigm.[2]

In the "Faraway Women" chapter, Sedgwick recruits westering metaphor to discuss how the "unpremeditated record of interesting happenings by an interesting person" boosted circulation during his early *Atlantic* years (*HP* 197). "If only interest were there, and personality," he recollects of his tactics, "I could stake out an original *Atlantic* claim in the pleasantest of all the outlying territories of Literature." He identifies these territories as the genres especially associated with women—diary and letter—and in summing up the venture states, "It was to women then that my thoughts oftenest turned, and a score of lonely, self-dependent histories were woven into the texture of the Atlantic" (*HP* 200). Their conspicuous position in the *Atlantic* attests to his break with the dedication to "literature with a big 'L'" (*HP* 197) (to use his phrase) that had been central to the magazine's reputation since its 1857 inception, even as it demonstrates his continued investment in its equally long tradition of regional writing.

He could in good faith, then, apprise Stein in rejecting an early submission, "Here there is no group of literati or illuminati or cognoscenti or illustrissimi of any kind."[3] A fuller discussion of Stein awaits the epilogue, but I begin with this well-known author to suggest one way recovering the era's "faraway women" reshapes the critical contours of U.S. literary history. Once we situate *The Autobiography of Alice B. Toklas* in its original periodical context, Stein's text displays not just a modernist, European genealogy but also a gendered, regional American one. Her intentionally vernacular rendition of a relationship between two Californian women mirrors the productions of the other *Atlantic* writers, for whom the vernacular was the only register to hand.

Faraway Women and the "Atlantic Monthly" surveys four of Sedgwick's most popular life writers, all westerners, and their main texts: Elinore Pruitt Stewart and *Letters of a Woman Homesteader* (1914), Opal Whiteley and *The Story of Opal* (1920), Hilda Rose and *The Stump Farm* (1927), and Juanita Harrison and *My Great, Wide, Beautiful World* (1936). Sedgwick himself, as editor, publicist, and memoirist, is also a subject, and his words and acts structure this book. The study assembles sets of sometimes contradictory narratives and histories, including the authors' biographies, their published work, the social and institutional processes their texts underwent, and the stories that Sedgwick and others told about them. Official accounts of these texts—as written across correspondence, *Atlantic* framing materials, and reviews—are supplanted by more complex nuanced ones. *Faraway Women* tracks these westerners' authorial agency, even as it also tracks the ways in which distant friends, patrons, publishers, and readers inspired, advanced, and consumed their literary expression. My desire is to recast, through a sequence of microhistories, the coordinates of American literature, a remapping that not only challenges binary assumptions about East and West, national and regional, cosmopolitan and local, gender and power, but also charts an archival journey connecting the least remembered writers and readers of the time with one of its most famous literary figures. These connections are all routed through male editorial power, but, as the readings demonstrate, complicate and exceed its workings.

Elinore Pruitt Stewart, a homesteader in southwestern Wyoming, made for Sedgwick's first venture into "familiar letters," which he characterized as "the warmest and friendliest among the satellites of Literature" (*HP* 197). *Letters of a Woman Homesteader* comprised Stewart's correspondence with Juliet Coney, a woman who had once employed her as a housekeeper in Denver and became a friend and mentor after her move to

Wyoming. Stewart dramatizes her transformation from Coney's "wash-lady" into a "bloated landowner," to use her self-deprecating terms (*LWH* 44, 7). One of her textual challenges is making a case for herself as the intrepid, independent "woman homesteader" when she is actually a married mother of four, immersed in a family enterprise. A more immediate challenge, however, is that of managing a key personal relationship, as she navigates the shoals of writing about crude frontier conditions to a fastidious past employer whose affection and approval she was anxious to retain. Following *Atlantic* publication—and assisted by Sedgwick—she entered into a host of rewarding new epistolary friendships.

Opal Whiteley grew up poor in logging communities near Cottage Grove, Oregon, where she was known as a prodigy. At twenty-two she published *The Story of Opal: The Journal of an Understanding Heart,* purportedly the diary she wrote at the ages of six and seven but believed by some to be a hoax. Reconstructed under Sedgwick's supervision, the text describes Opal's travails at home and her sometimes comic, sometimes mystic, experiences in the Oregon woods. It also hints at her fantasy of being an orphaned French princess, "Françoise." "Now I sit here and I print," she writes. "The baby sleeps on. The wind comes creeping in under the door. It calls, 'Come, come, petite Françoise, come'" (*SO* 57). Whiteley was one of Sedgwick's most notorious contributors, as well as his most personally vexing, and *The Happy Profession* devotes a full chapter to her.

Hilda Rose's *The Stump Farm: A Chronicle of Pioneering* is set in Idaho and far northern Alberta, Canada. Formed from Rose's letters to benefactors and friends, it reads as a running debate over whether the rewards of farming and homesteading compensate for the attendant isolation and hardship. While Rose endorsed her husband's desire to take her "so far from the world that it would never spoil me," her decision to join him on a "stump farm" in the mountains of Idaho and to homestead in a remote region of Canada had profound social and psychic costs.[4] The prolific correspondence that ensued became her entrée to public authorship, with her arduous experiences routed through her acquaintances to the *Atlantic* and beyond. Funding her wilderness homesteading by writing about it, Rose entered into especially close relations with the *Atlantic* community, broadly conceived.

Juanita Harrison rounds out the overview. Originally from Mississippi, she traveled and lived overseas for much of her adult life, even as she established Los Angeles and Honolulu as American bases. *My Great, Wide, Beautiful World* records eight years of travel and itinerant domestic work, a composite of sojourns in Europe, the Middle East, and Asia. Published as a travel journal chronicling an around-the-world voyage, the book was actually assembled from Harrison's letters to friends and employers in Europe and the United States. Only disjointed elements, such as the dedication, register its epistolary origins: "To Mrs. Myra K. Dickinson Your great kindness to me have made my traveling much happier if You hadnt been interested in me I never would have tryed to explain my trips." Like Stewart and Rose, Harrison was a newly minted westerner. She identified California as her home state, and on her return to U.S. territory settled in Waikiki, where she met with Sedgwick on his way to Japan.

Sedgwick's view of these women as "faraway" depends on more, of course, than their physical distance from the *Atlantic* office that published their texts and distributed their royalties. It also stems from their socioeconomic distance from his personal milieu and that of the cultured readership usually associated with the magazine. But equally important, their own perception of distance drove their texts. Stewart's anxious sense of separation from middle-class lifestyles, Whiteley's yearning for her true family in France, Rose's dearth of female companionship, Harrison's exhaustive travels induced them to write. Their self-portraits are positioned in reference to faraway realms, whether conceived as actual distant sites, or their lost places of origins, or higher class standing, or mainstream America. Thus, we can understand their textual achievement as an outcome of persistent efforts to approach the geographic, cultural, or socioeconomic locations they craved. Their *Atlantic* showing was only the most conspicuous milestone in their life journeys of coming "closer." It was also only the most conspicuous return from their extended networks of friends, acquaintances, mentors, and benefactors, within and across lines of class, race, gender, and region. They exploited limited resources to their fullest extent, in pursuit of personal fulfillment and social and economic advance.

The other faraway women whom Sedgwick names as such (including Jean Kenyon Mackenzie, Africa missionary; L. Adams Beck, Asia scholar; and Eleanor Risley, Alabama walker) also published intriguing life narratives in the *Atlantic*. However, the faraway texts that riveted the magazine's readers and swelled its subscription rates, and which

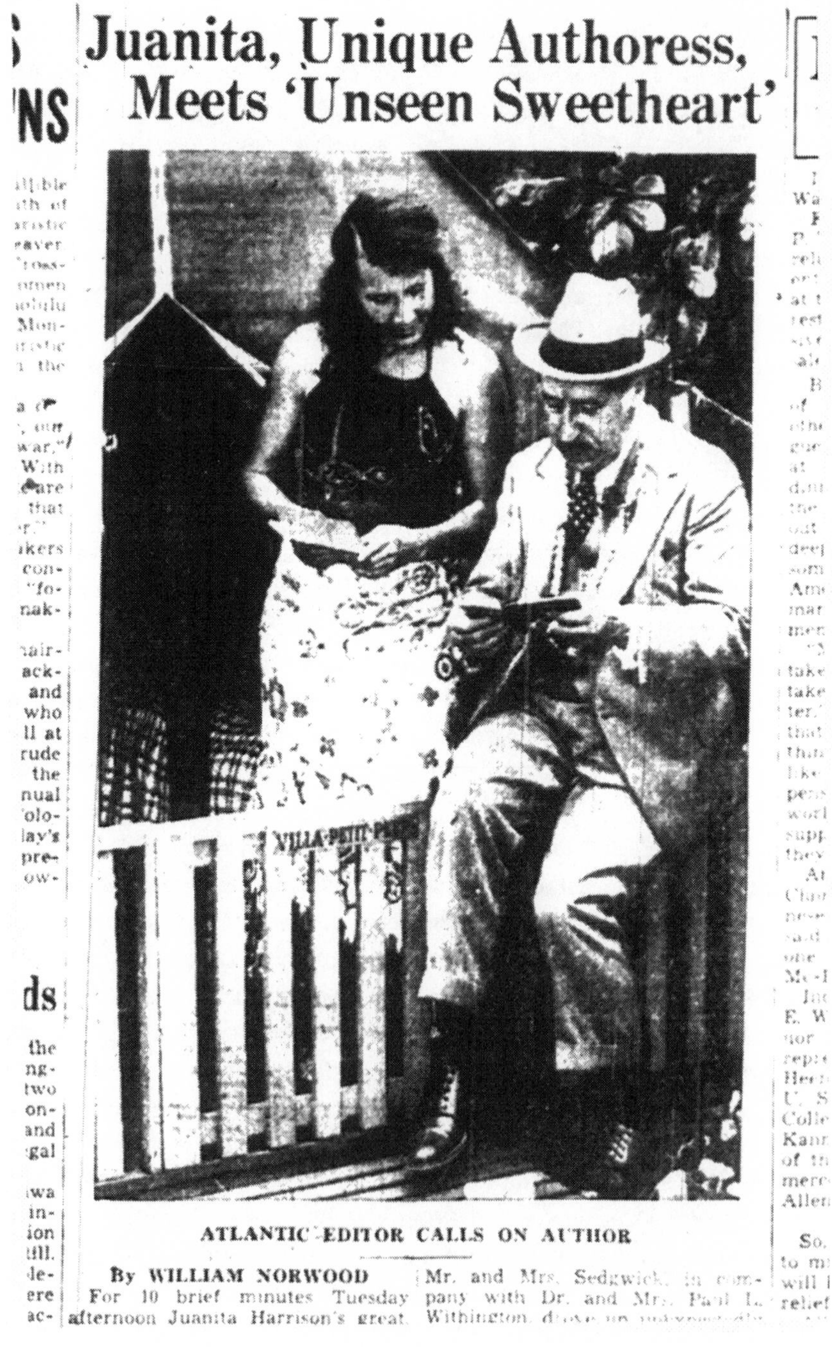

Juanita, Unique Authoress, Meets 'Unseen Sweetheart'

ATLANTIC EDITOR CALLS ON AUTHOR

By WILLIAM NORWOOD

For 10 brief minutes Tuesday afternoon Juanita Harrison's great

Mr. and Mrs. Sedgwick, in company with Dr. and Mrs. Paul L. Withington, drove up unexpectedly

FIGURE 1. Juanita Harrison and Ellery Sedgwick meet in Honolulu. *Honolulu Star-Bulletin.*

were expanded into popular books that ran to multiple printings, were all authored by westerners. They were faraway women, but not *that* faraway, still embedded in American networks despite their mobility, and as such people with whom the magazine's increasingly diverse readership could identify. Reflecting his personal enthusiasm, it was also the westerners who were most often referenced in profiles of Sedgwick, and it was they who left the most visible trails.

I came to these writers through my long-standing research on women's autobiography of the American West. Rose aside, they feature in my study of the surprising domestic arguments that link western writers across generations, *Playing House in the American West: Western Women's Life Narratives, 1839–1987* (one of its footnotes conveys the germ of *Faraway Women*), while my earlier *Maverick Autobiographies: Women Writers and the American West, 1902–1936* includes chapters on Whiteley and Harrison. Hence, some of the critical views I look to amend are my own, as I deepen my research perspective and more purposely build a full print-culture and archival context. I like to think that Clifford Geertz's observation applies to this progression: "Studies do build on other studies, not in the sense that they take up where the others leave off, but in the sense that, better informed and better conceptualized, they plunge more deeply into the same things."[5]

In what may initially seem like incongruous identities, *Faraway Women and the "Atlantic Monthly"* is both the first critical investigation of the early-twentieth-century *Atlantic* and the first monograph devoted to the era's working-class western women writers. "The frameworks for reading women's periodical writings are still very much in the making," Jean Lutes observes, and this study develops one such framework.[6] In featuring the strategies of unprivileged westerners for seizing creative outlets and forging new protocols of public expression, it dislodges established origin tales of American literature, and it also redresses a critical blind spot about regional writing. Mainstream versions of U.S. literary history position regionalism as a subset of realism that gives way before modernism, even though, of course, it endured. *Faraway Women* explores one of the genre's new guises, both familiar and fresh.

Signposting the numerous women and men who contributed to these textual projects, I travel the path Holly Laird's *Women Co-authors* has cleared. In her study of the collaborative alliances formed by writers like Harriet Jacobs and Lydia Maria Child or Stein and Toklas, Laird eschews the work of a literary detective (intent on who wrote what) to instead read such shared projects as "the realization of relationships," with all the mixed currents of obligation, affection, recalcitrance, and calculation that compose them.[7] On the one hand, I uncover these women's agency as writers and authors, agency that has been unacknowledged or even denied. On the other hand, I demonstrate the resolutely communal and intersubjective nature of their careers and actual texts, as the outcome of repeated encounters—sometimes in person but more often in writing—with the supporters who propped them up economically, instructed them culturally, and spurred them narratively. My subject is social networks, but not networks as we have come to know them through nineteenth-century writers based in the East, preserved through personal contact. Largely structured and even engendered by long-distance print exchanges, these were far more diffuse.

Sedgwick, I suggest, was not only commissioner and editor but also a kind of coauthor. Crystallized life records filtered from a mass of text generated over months and years—diaries, letters, sketches, travel records—the texts he so enthusiastically hailed as artless demanded huge amounts of editorial labor. He and his staff oversaw the assembly of a (sometimes literal) jumble of manuscripts into books, manifold texts compressed into single riveting accounts. But I also recognize other, less readily apparent, silent partners hovering outside the frame of the final published versions: the more privileged, although now obscure, women to whom these writers directed their texts and who in some cases helped get them into print. This book tells their stories, too, tracing the relationships that inform the "lonely, self-dependent histories" Sedgwick profiled. As Jack Stillinger comments in *Multiple Authorship and the Myth of Solitary Genius*, "The better [interpretive] theories may turn out to be those that cover not only more facts but more authors."[8] Discovering further participants does more than just recover the material conditions of these texts. It unlocks the source of their generic identities.

To date, a writer's matrix of female influence and support has been far down the list of critical priorities in western studies. Linda Karell argues in *Writing Together/Writing Apart: Collaboration in Western American Literature* that the field perpetuates the American impulse to celebrate individual enterprise over collective endeavor, the pioneer over the commune. As a consequence, she observes, "Western

American literature, as well as the literary criticism of it, has been nearly untouched by the theoretical insights that question the author as an autonomous being."[9] The West's overdetermined association with masculinity, which of course operates in conjunction with this privileging of the individual, similarly suppresses critical inquiry into women's alliances.[10] If the masculine constitutes the West, then women can neither respond to nor work within conditions other women have shaped. The enduring position of male discourse as the reference point of western studies can occasion a rather dreary sense of critical déjà vu, with discussions of how some writers proffer western myths alternating with discussions of how others revise them.[11] Focusing on how faraway women drew equally on the West (with its economic opportunities and literary subjects) and the East (with its social opportunities and literary markets) makes for a new optic on western writing that displaces the usual attention to women's interventions in male traditions and the usual arguments about their limning of an alternative West defined by community, family, and home.

Finally, throughout these chapters I chart the permeable generic boundaries and intimate editor-writer-reader relations that constitute, I would submit, an operative poetics of the *Atlantic Monthly*. Prose so vernacular that it begins to resemble a modernist experiment. Diaries bleeding into letters into essays into letters once more. Texts as gifts made over into texts as commodities that lead to further gifts. Monthly serials contained in single volumes while still presenting as texts in process. Writers discussing their *Atlantic* relations within their *Atlantic* publications and later staging their *Atlantic* returns. Texts circulating in private, in reading communities, in commercial venues, and in private again. Intimating untold stories and unnarrated places, they are marked with traces of the women who as their original readers prompted them. Moreover, they invite in new readers for whom like texts are created, as the lives of authors and readers entwine in both narrative and actual encounters. All these generative, fluid relations are brokered by the rather staid institution of the *Atlantic Monthly* and the rather staid personage of Ellery Sedgwick. Mutual longing percolates among writers, readers, and editor: a longing for the faraway, in all its many forms.

My research draws extensively on the Ellery Sedgwick papers at the Massachusetts Historical Society, in concert with public records and smaller author collections at other libraries. I especially press personal letters into service, complementing the epistolary identities of the books they shed light on. Different chapters of the study have different structures and emphases, as the archives, critical histories, and the texts themselves allow. However, each of the main chapters centers on a single author and her work, her cast of supporters, and her *Atlantic* experiences. This attention extends to the material processes of her writing—often piecemeal and improvised—and the generic stages it underwent. By the turn of the twentieth century, a single text could be "circulated redundantly through different nodes," as print historians Carl Kaestle and Janice Radway formulate it, moving between periodicals, books, newspapers, and other media, and such redundancy is certainly true of my set of texts.[12] One methodological challenge is representing the full range of their iterations while maintaining distinctions between them: the privately circulating manuscripts, the *Atlantic* serials, and the bound books.

The project is in part an exploration of the "textual condition," to use Jerome McGann's paradigm, the "determinate sociohistorical conditions" under which "every text enters the world." McGann maintains, "Literary works cannot know themselves, and cannot be known, apart from their specific material modes of existence/resistance. They are not channels of transmission, they are particular forms of transmissive reaction." John Kevin Young usefully formulates the critical work this perspective fosters as attending to "the residue of the social processes through which texts pass on their way to publication." I examine presentation, too, not only "the insides of texts" but also "the outsides of books," as Gabrielle Dean puts it. A literary work only reaches us clad in the often ill-fitting garments of its paratexts, famously defined by Gérard Genette as the "productions, themselves verbal or not, like an author's name, a title, a preface, illustrations" that "ensure its presence in the world." I discuss how these publications were formally received, in reviews and other forums, and how they were registered by ordinary readers, as evinced in casual evaluations and fan mail. And throughout this study, region is never far from view, in accord with theorists who emphasize what regions do rather than what they are, and whose interests stories about them serve. The interplay of regions exhibited in these texts maps onto that of their human agents—writers, readers, editor—not identical but related.[13]

I begin with a chapter on Sedgwick, assessing him in respect to his work with women writers. While initially he favored the formally conservative, his editorial range broadened to encompass both relatively high-literary practitioners such as Amy Lowell, Willa Cather, and Gertrude Stein and the emerging authors considered here. It may seem problematic to have a powerful male authority contextualize women writers whose daring life choices and innovative life narratives clash with many of his professed views, but the choice does replicate the historical actuality of Sedgwick's position as their gateway to a public readership. Robert Scholes and Clifford Wulfman's comment about the function of Ezra Pound in their monograph, *Modernism in the Magazines: An Introduction,* could well describe that of Sedgwick in mine: "[He] is a thread that runs through all of these efforts. This did not happen because we loved him." Susan L. Johnson has commented on "the arrogance and condescension of those accustomed to uncontested narrative 'power,'" and Sedgwick is a prime example, this leader of a singularly prestigious literary institution who could wield his cultural authority like a club.[14]

Such authority need not be ineluctable. While I look to rehabilitate the reputation of a man whose name has become shorthand for a complacent New England elite, I also scrutinize his contradictory practice and probe his conspicuous investment in class, gender, and racial hierarchies. Paternalistic editor of a venerable "gentlemen's magazine," Sedgwick midwifed texts that were both generated by and exhibit women's friendship, labor, and aspiration, making for a host of narrative and situational ironies. And while his views on class and gender were often incongruous, his views on race could resemble those of his faraway women; with the salient exception of Harrison, shared racial ideologies bolstered relationships between writers and editor and with some readers, too. The following chapters contest Sedgwick's "narrative power"—in all its genteel, genial, affable, amiable, paternalistic articulations—even while giving full credit for his crucial role and showing the ways in which he and his writers were in accord. The dominant sentiment expressed by his faraway women was, after all, gratitude. He made not only their books possible but also this one, too, which extends his project of amplifying their voices.

The four core chapters, ordered chronologically, begin with Elinore Pruitt Stewart. Stewart is widely recognized in western studies, and there are many modern editions of *Letters of a Woman Homesteader*. Pushing back against its contemporary promotion as "genuine letters," critics often highlight the self-consciously literary qualities of the book. However, I work in the opposite direction to restore its original rhetorical life, as missives exchanged across space and over time for the consideration of their first reader, the woman born Sarah Juliet Graves on a Massachusetts farm who became the "Mrs. Coney" Stewart cherished in Denver. Stewart's published accounts of rural western exploit are undergirded by Coney's unwritten history of urban eastern striving, and *Letters of a Woman Homesteader*, I argue, is the by-product of not only the author's adopted Wyoming home but also her interlocutor's Massachusetts birthplace. Yet this chapter also shows how Stewart's view of her writing as a gift to bestow—and the *Atlantic* as the ideal medium for the exchange—checked the development of her career.

The Story of Opal is also still in print, enjoys a small cult following, and attracts periodic attention in the context of children's literature, diary, and the West. Opal Whiteley is the subject of four biographies (none scholarly) and several archival collections. Unlike the other texts in this study, her book did not originate in letters, but it is nonetheless implicitly directed at an internal readership, the author's mother and the small-town Oregon community who misjudged her. It is also profoundly collaborative, formed from the literally shredded manuscript Whiteley restored under Sedgwick's direction. The book that together they produced displays not only the family estrangement that kindled it but also the pair's conflict over what guise it should take, whether an expression of a transcendent "spirit of childhood," as Sedgwick wished, or of the exiled princess Whiteley believed herself to be. This disagreement reflects the regional and social relations that structured the project: the Boston editor had a precise vision of the story he craved from his Oregon ward.

Hilda Rose's name is now least heard. Although *The Stump Farm* was once a fixture in homes, schools, libraries, book clubs, and even church groups and offices across Canada and the United States, it is long out of print. Rose has attracted no critical attention beyond Lynn Z. Bloom's useful introduction in the context of women's homesteading narratives, and as far as I know I am the first to work with her unpublished letters. This chapter analyzes the social conditions of Rose's writing, which like Stewart's was brokered by more privileged friends, and discusses her struggle to attain the level of authorship she envisioned. It also investigates how ordinary men and women received *The Stump Farm*, extracting the bracing lessons they craved, and the nature of the support they in turn tendered Rose. During the Depression, the *Atlantic* institutionalized the charitable aid she had long received with a call to readers to help fund a new homestead. Even as she was promoted as a self-sufficient, intrepid pioneer, donations from a diverse, dispersed cast of well-wishers enabled her family to stay on the land. Yet similar to Stewart, despite the materially and emotionally remunerative *Atlantic* fellowship she cherished, Rose's loyalty to the magazine did not serve her writing career.

Of the life narratives I discuss, in my view Juanita Harrison's *My Great, Wide, Beautiful World* is the most absorbing. Nevertheless, I work to displace the celebratory discourse it typically attracts with a more critical analysis, in part through redirecting attention from Harrison's cosmopolitan accomplishments to the actual composition of her text. While the book was reprinted in 1996 in Henry Louis Gates and Jennifer Burton's important series, "African-American Women Writers, 1910–1940," discussions about it are still largely confined to anthologies and encyclopedias (often recycling erroneous information). The archival record, moreover, is meager. Harrison's publishers did not preserve materials pertaining to her book, and even the comprehensive Sedgwick papers yield no traces, an archival vacuum for which racial views might account. Sources about her book and life are confined to promotional materials, public records, and a small cache of papers donated by an African American family that befriended her in Pasadena, California. Recovering the epistolary origins of *My Great, Wide, Beautiful World* reveals Harrison's textual practice to be both a strategic, intersubjective enterprise and of a more complex racial and class composition than the *Atlantic* would have it. This chapter attends closely to the discrepancies between the stories that Sedgwick and other envoys of mainstream print culture circulated about Harrison and those presented by the historical record and by Harrison herself.

The epilogue returns to Gertrude Stein and *The Autobiography of Alice B. Toklas*, gathering up arguments made across the course of the book even as it moves it in a new direction. Wresting this modernist exemplar off its high-literary pedestal, I suggest for it a different origin story: Sedgwick's history with faraway women paved the way for his

accepting the memoir, and Stein's familiarity with this *Atlantic* movement influenced her actual construction of it. Conceiving the text thus
provides another way to read it, as one *Atlantic* life narrative among
others. Reciprocally, the incorporation of Stein's text within this group
draws our attention to the fictional, performative qualities they all share,
as well as how relationships among differently situated women serve as
theme and medium alike. The hybrid genres they worked within situate
faraway women at a literary borderland akin to the borderland places
they write from, placement that closes their distance from the modernist
practitioners with whom they share the *Atlantic* page.

The major influence of women on the *Atlantic* remains largely unseen,
to the extent that some scholarship replicates the magazine's masculine
bias.[15] In respect to both genders, moreover, attention is usually confined to prominent contributors. Yet investigating only writers of the
stature of a Sarah Orne Jewett or Henry James—or an Amy Lowell or
Charles Chesnutt—makes for a skewed portrait. While each issue of the
Atlantic includes luminaries, today even scholars scarcely recognize the
names of most of its contributors. I like Ellery Sedgwick III's staging
of the emotions of the *Atlantic* researcher, "surveying with mixed melancholy and relief the legions of forgotten authors, manuscripts, and
passions that have passed into near oblivion in the volumes gathering
dust in library stacks." Those who work with periodicals routinely
decry the excision of advertisements from bound volumes, that "hole
in the archive," but much of the printed material that actually is present
is passed over.[16]

This study complicates the *Atlantic*'s elite status, as the only substantial investigation of the role played by popular writing in so-called
quality magazines—identified by Nancy Glazener as the defining vehi-
cle of high realism—and it joins the work of scholars such as June Howard, Charles Johanningsmeier, and Mark J. Noonan, who investigate
relationships among periodical participants, especially as exhibited
in archival documents. To apply only the techniques of literary close
reading to these *Atlantic* texts is to miss how they unsettle the elite and
the popular, to miss the interplay of regional writers' agency and their
submission to editorial demands. Mapping the interactions among
editor, writers, readers, and patrons proves the value of print culture
methodologies for western women's literature, contributing to critical
conversations that show regional writing was far from locally defined.

The study also identifies an updated model of regionalism. The dominant nineteenth-century version features a middle-class intermediary, an outsider with privileged access to the community who elicits, receives, and broadcasts a local tale told by a local person. (Jewett and Chesnutt's *Atlantic* stories about rural Maine and North Carolina, respectively, are exemplary.) In my set of texts, however, the resident is herself the author. Consequently, the intermediary is displaced to the text's margins or frame, still the recipient but no longer the transmitter. She brokers rather than reproduces the tale, sells it rather than tells it. If regions are understood to be relationally produced, an outcome of differences between sets of places, then what better site of regional investigation than narratives written by women residing in one place for the benefit—and often at the behest—of women residing in another? One reason I am so attached to the category of the "faraway" is that it has the notion of different subjects' perspectives on places built into it.

For Stewart, Whiteley, Rose, and Harrison, *Atlantic* publication had measurable social, economic, and psychological impact. Their circles expanded to include increasingly influential women and men, their finances became a shade less precarious, and their self-images were transformed. The *Atlantic,* stressing the anomaly of their presence between its covers, may have represented them as anything but authors, but they viewed their inclusion as conferring this status, for life. The magazine was deeply meaningful to them as both a cultural institution that established professional standing and a far-flung community that fostered social ties and emotional bonds. They reveled in new identities as published authors and, if not literary insiders, then at least as bearers of an informed vantage point. Fifteen years after the publication of her only book, Harrison still identified her profession as that of "author."

That said, in some lights this book is composed of records of failure. These writers all had dramatic debuts, devoted readers, and significant royalty income, but subsequently published very little in the *Atlantic* or anywhere else. As literary novices, they had won the "fearful lottery" of *Atlantic* submission, to borrow Elizabeth Stuart Phelps's metaphor, without even knowing they had a ticket.[17] Flush with confidence and driven by their perpetual need for cash, with the exception of Harrison they tried to sustain that level of achievement with new hastily wrought compositions, including short fiction, poetry, memoirs, travel writing, and novels. They were reluctant, moreover, to consider the mass-market venues that might have welcomed them, unwilling to settle for anything less than the *Atlantic.*

The effects of such naïveté were compounded by Sedgwick's gate-keeping. From faraway women, he wanted only life stories. Given that he never fully conceived of them as *authors*—as opposed to *writers*—he was not invested in helping them produce and place other kinds of texts. For these working women, the generosity for which he was known was more likely to take the form of material aid than professional mentoring—rescuing Harrison in Buenos Aires by pulling strings at her bank, encouraging *Atlantic* readers to bestow a "Christmas remembrance" on Rose. His intent but exclusive interest in auto-biography helped establish memoir as the leading form of western women's writing today.

Yet in the end, much of it comes down to neither these writers' nor their editor's choices and acts, but rather, more systemically, the limitations of the genre that launched them. Writing about their experiences in places perceived as remote was their sole and narrow path to authorship. This path was particularly accessible to the unschooled, to writers whose familiarity with "a way of life apart from the culturally dominant" constituted their primary literary capital.[18] But just as important, the composite nature of their texts—assembled from journal entries and letters—made them highly amenable to editorial shaping and intervention. Sedgwick and the others who handled them could cull out the most vivid portions, to be organized into their most dramatic arrangements.

This mode of literary production had its own dissolution built in. They were published as representative of their place and position—the typical homesteader, or child, or maid. Yet their texts argue otherwise, as performances of fundamental difference from the people around them. Indeed, the very act of writing distinguished them. In their daily lives, they strove for experiences and subject positions atypical for their locations, and in their texts, they sought to present themselves accordingly. Public authorship confirmed the difference for which they argued, intensifying the subjective strain. The more ambitious they became, the less representative they seemed, and thus the less able and inclined to produce the texts expected of them. The same class and regional structures that occasioned their authorship constricted its development.

But as compensation, as we will see, they were able to convert their early meteoric success into enduring forms of social capital and to profit in numerous ways from their continued commitment to writing. *Atlantic Monthly* achievement took these faraway women unawares. At their debut, the magazine was at the periphery of their cultural purview, if visible at all, and its impact was evident only in the useful checks that followed, converted into grain binders, canvas tents, and silver spoons. Soon, however, they came to recognize *Atlantic* authorship as an event of great magnitude. Their lives went on very much as they had before, yet were utterly changed.

CHAPTER ONE

ELLERY SEDGWICK

AND THE

DISTAFF

The Women's Atlantic

Many years ago, I had it in my mind that it would be a great thing to be published by the *Atlantic Monthly*. . . . If I'd given it a moment's rational thought, I would have realized that the last thing on earth a Boston-based, male-dominated, utterly dignified magazine would want or need would be the semi-hysterical, heartbroken howlings of a West Coast divorcee. I didn't realize it, though.

—Carolyn See, *Making a Literary Life: Advice for Writers and Other Dreamers*

None of the texts I discuss could be conceived as "heartbroken howlings." Nevertheless, Carolyn See's comments about the discrepancy between the staidly prestigious, eastern, masculinist *Atlantic* and the dispatches she submitted about her "raffish life" in a 1960s bohemian enclave outside Los Angeles well express the disjuncture, decades earlier, of the hearing that Ellery Sedgwick extended his faraway women.[1] Pertinent, too, is See's indication that she profited from her sheer ignorance of *Atlantic* protocol; she goes on to recount how she submitted her work to the magazine for so long and so doggedly as to form a long-distance relationship with its editor.

Suspending a discussion of the writers themselves, this chapter limns Sedgwick's editorial practice and career, identifying the personal and institutional factors that contributed to his profiling of faraway women. Partly, this history is meant to show how his policies constituted both *Atlantic* continuity and change and how he participated in larger periodical movements. Yet it is also to indicate the kind of beliefs that faraway women contested, in the very act of infiltrating the nation's most elite literary organ. The views Sedgwick expressed about working-class women and the West are not identical to those of his class, magazine, or readership, but they do roughly align, indicating more widely shared cultural assumptions. I then discuss his actual dealings with faraway women, to the extent that one can generalize about them, to frame the case studies that follow. His practice often reads as contradictory, not least because he relied on stereotypes and cliché to conceptualize the same writers to whom he granted an unprecedented platform for self-expression. His conservatism was at odds with their daring and innovation, both textually and in lived experience, generating numerous points of friction.

"Everyone knows that you are the creator of the re-created Atlantic," pronounced an admiring friend to Sedgwick as early as 1919.[2] In his capacity as new owner and editor of the *Atlantic Monthly*, he had conjoined the magazine's high-literary traditions and an emerging commitment to "human interest," sustaining a measure of its belles lettres practice while adopting a more journalistic mode. The *Atlantic* was once the nation's premier literary magazine, featuring the most illustrious writers of the day. By the turn of the twentieth century, however, to borrow the assessments of his contemporaries, it was viewed as a "wheelchair for valetudinary literary men," a "last flower of the waning culture of discreet New England."[3] Factors contributing to the decline include the explosion of mass-market magazines, the advent of "little magazines," and the redistribution of literary authority from magazines to universities.[4] When Sedgwick took over in 1908, the *Atlantic* was barely meeting operating expenses, with a monthly subscription rate of 17,000. Under his direction, by 1930 it had hit a new peak of over 135,000.[5]

The *Atlantic*'s transformation corresponded with the era's proliferation of mass-market magazines. However, as an august institution adapting to changing markets, its trajectory was distinct; even as its standards shifted and subscription rate rose, it preserved its identity as an elite publication oriented to the discerning. Consequently, while its change in scale may look insignificant compared to the astounding figures commanded by popular magazines like the *Ladies' Home Journal* (the first of many to reach a circulation of 1 million), its revival had an outsize impact on American periodicals. According to *Harper's* editor Frederick Lewis Allen, Sedgwick's "convincing demonstration" that "erudite writing need not be dull, that human interest need not be vulgar"—and that a paying readership existed for both—helped "resuscitate" other prestige magazines like *Harper's* and hewed a path for new enterprises such as *American Mercury* and the *New Yorker*.[6]

A dinner celebrating Sedgwick's ten-year anniversary was capped with the reading of "An Atlantic Port," which expressed his achievement thus:

> Yet sales were growing obsolete, far lands lay unexplored,
> Fresh voyages beckoned when a new young captain stepped on board. . . .
> Signed year by year a growing crew—mates, seamen, yeomen, brave—
> Yeowomen, too![7]

This metaphor of journeying to "far lands" recurs some thirty years later in Sedgwick's memoir, which repeatedly deploys images of distance: "faraway women," "outlying territories of Literature," "an original *Atlantic* claim," "satellites of literature," writers "poised on the very threshold of your friendship" (*HP* 197–98) (the sentiment about "yeowomen" is also prescient). And in a quite literal way, he positions Boston as the site from which such distance is measured, the nation's cultural and intellectual center.

So invested was Sedgwick in Boston's identity as "the Hub," he maintained that his upbringing in western Massachusetts indelibly marked him as an outsider. Such a claim was, of course, disingenuous. By 1872, the year of his birth, the Sedgwick family had long been a signal presence in New England law, politics, and arts. As one of his contemporaries put it, "The Sedgwicks have been the squire family of the Berkshires ever since Judge Sedgwick built the family manse in Stockbridge in 1785, and have maintained their position not by wealth but by intellectual alertness, wide contacts with the world, a persistent sense of *noblesse oblige*, and an equally persistent and charming gift for unselfconscious eccentricity."[8] Theodore Sedgwick has a place in history for successfully pleading the manumission of Elizabeth Freeman in 1781. Illustrious family members in literature include novelist Catharine Maria Sedgwick and poet William Ellery Channing. (From the other generational side, Edie Sedgwick was his great-niece.) Sedgwick recollected Matthew Arnold's visit to his boyhood home (*AH* xvii). Following family tradition, he was educated at Groton School and Harvard University, and his marriage to Mabel Cabot, scion of one of the city's most influential families, consolidated his position within Boston's close-knit social and cultural elite.

During the early years of his career, Sedgwick was tutored in new business models at *Youth's Companion,* as assistant editor from 1896 to 1900, and *Frank Leslie's Popular Monthly,* as editor and shareholder from 1900 to 1905; he was also briefly affiliated with *McClure's Magazine.* However, fellow editor Mark Antony De Wolfe Howe's characterization of this period in Sedgwick's life as "rigorous training in the editing and publishing of periodicals" little reflects its chaotic nature, as he moved from job to job in an industry that was reinventing itself.[9] Magazine publishing had undergone a seismic shift in 1893, the year *Munsey's* made advertising its primary revenue and slashed prices to just fifteen cents a copy—and then ten—a lead that most other popular magazines quickly followed.

Youth's Companion did much to shape the new periodical landscape. Founded in 1827 in Boston to instill religious values in children, by century's end it had reinvented itself as a purveyor of wholesome family entertainment. In 1885 it commanded the nation's largest magazine readership with a circulation of 385,000, and ten years later that number had risen to 600,000.[10] Leading women fiction writers contributed to its success, including Louisa May Alcott, Kate Chopin, Mary Wilkins Freeman, Sarah Orne Jewett, Harriet Beecher Stowe, and Edith Wharton.[11] (Intriguingly, "For Marse Chouchoute," the first of its eleven juvenile stories by Chopin, ran in 1891, just after Sedgwick's departure.)[12] *Youth's Companion*'s move from pious instruction to leisure reading anticipated the analogous change Sedgwick made at the *Atlantic,* redirecting it from "literature with a big 'L'" to tales of "human interest." Reflecting Sedgwick's past association, the Atlantic Monthly Company acquired it in 1925.

Sedgwick's experiences in New York at *Frank Leslie's,* an illustrated news and literary magazine founded by its namesake in 1855, further prepared him for the *Atlantic* editorship. New York was soon to succeed Boston as the nation's publishing center, and Sedgwick's peers perceived him as fusing the periodical cultures of both cities, "domesticat[ing] on the Hub the passion for a 'story' that in his salad days, was flaming up in New York journalism." During his tenure, *Leslie's* ran Yone Noguchi's *The American Diary of a Japanese Girl.* Published anonymously in 1901, the California memoir was perhaps Sedgwick's original "faraway woman" life narrative, never mind that it was fiction and that Noguchi was a man. Noguchi breathlessly reported of his manuscript, "I don't admire much that magazine [*Leslie's*], but the editor [Sedgwick] was kind enough asking something from my pen. . . . I was conceited when the editor said that my Ms. was the best one he ever came across." The diary was a sensation, as readers tried to guess the identity of its author: "Who is the American man who poses as Miss Morning Glory?" Sedgwick gave equally decisive encouragement to Dorothy Canfield at the inception of her career, who at age twenty-six confided to her parents, "Did I tell you I had a long letter from Mr. Sedgwick (Leslie's Editor you know) very warm and friendly and unexpectedly serious. He says that my 'talent, heaven be praised, lies outside the ordinary channels of magazine literature.'"[13]

But *Leslie's* struggled to survive, as the many names it cycled through indicate: *Frank Leslie's Popular Monthly, Leslie's Monthly Magazine, Leslie's Magazine,* the *American Illustrated Magazine,* and finally *American Magazine.* Sedgwick had borrowed money to buy *Leslie's;* several years later, he sold it, with much relief, to the mutinying staff of *McClure's,* who could no longer tolerate the erratic behavior of founder Samuel McClure.[14] He then joined the McClure enterprise himself, working for the newspaper fiction syndicate that shared offices with its magazine. At the time, *McClure's* was winning renown for its scrupulous investigative reporting, among others Ida M. Tarbell's *The History of the Standard Oil Company* and Lincoln Steffens's *The Shame of the Cities.*

We can view McClure—whom Steffens called "the wild editor"—as a more personally adventurous prototype for Sedgwick. McClure actively sought to keep his magazine fresh, formulating the venture thus: "Oh! the magazine, the magazine! it means seven years of travail, study, thought, and energy. I must read the current newspapers to find out who can best write for me. Then I must read all current magazines and reviews and weeklies." At the *Atlantic,* Sedgwick would combine McClure's zest for novelty with more sober business methods and financial acumen. His time at *McClure's,* he maintained, came to an end when he was fired.[15]

In 1908 he bought out Houghton Mifflin as the *Atlantic's* majority shareholder and installed himself as editor; he subsequently established Atlantic Monthly Books, a press that competed with Houghton Mifflin.[16] He thereby became the first *Atlantic* editor to be president of its publishing company and indeed the first since James Fields to be directly involved in its business operations.[17] His garrulous, crotchety reminiscences make for a refreshingly irreverent *Atlantic* history: "I never was very nice to Mr. Mifflin. He was very nice to me. He was such a jackass. I look back on that with least satisfaction. I was tired out. I finally bought the Atlantic for 50,000, borrowed, and from my investments. Waldo Forbes gave me 10,000 and Mabel 10,000. Uncle Henry Cabot was very dubious. I said I knew how to run it and the most frugal way, that I didn't mean to make a failure."[18] He soon purchased Mifflin's remaining shares.

Sedgwick's policies extended the work of several predecessors who had adapted the *Atlantic* for changing markets and readerships, including Fields, William Dean Howells, and Walter Hines Page. Evaluating the development, Howells recalled, "We were growing, whether we liked it or not, more and more American. Without ceasing to be New England, without ceasing to be Bostonian at heart, we had become southern, mid-western, and far-western in our sympathies." In *A History of the "Atlantic Monthly," 1862–1909,* Ellery Sedgwick III (Sedgwick's grandson) explains that the *Atlantic* "had been increasingly altered, both for better and for worse, by the pressures of the marketplace, democratic ideology, democratic journalism, and the new values of each generation that succeeded to the editorship." Sedgwick III's study tracks this "more American" turn, a movement that was not one-way. Thomas Bailey Aldrich restricted content to create an especially highbrow profile. Horace Scudder, more inclusive but retrospectively inclined, lionized prominent early contributors. During his influential short tenure, Page redirected the *Atlantic* to progressive journalism, leading Sedgwick to identify him as "the first person to make it an interesting magazine." Page was succeeded by the erudite Bliss Perry, who restored a quotient of the literary criticism and reviews he had kiboshed. When Sedgwick took over, these features were phased out once more, to Perry's dismay.[19]

To use Sedgwick III's phrase, the new editor's business instincts were "positively serendipitous."[20] Of his early *Atlantic* days, he recalled, "I had every kind of article and gradually got to know an assortment of strange but very prominent people. It then began to be known that the Atlantic was influential."[21] He continued, "Nobody lost anything and then it began to make money. I bought the House Beautiful—250,000 a year profit after that—Very good, frugal organization—working like Thunder!" The political causes he espoused further contributed to his success. Edward Weeks, his *Atlantic* successor, maintained, "He was at his brilliant best during World War I; he early swung the full force of the magazine to the side of the Allies, and the response to his editing was immediate: the circulation tripled."[22] That he gave a hearing to Alfred E. Smith, the first Roman Catholic nominee for president, and published Felix Frankfurter's defense of Sacco and Vanzetti earned him further accolades. After 1930 circulation started to taper off again,[23] but when Sedgwick sold his majority shares in 1939, it was for a "cash transaction" that was "reputed to be the largest in recent periodical history."[24]

Sedgwick's endorsement of General Francisco Franco made for an ignominious end to his editorship. Following a tour of Spain as Franco's guest, he voiced his support for him in two *New York Times* articles, and he vehemently defended his position on attack. The outrage expressed by this *Atlantic* reader was widely shared: "That anyone with an interest in the humanities, literary or actual, could describe a country writhing in civil war so blithely, is beyond belief." "May the bodies of Howells and Holmes and Lowell turn in their graves, and may their curses forever resound in your ears," another swore. The controversy contributed to Sedgwick's June 12, 1938, resignation as editor and his selling of the *Atlantic* the following year.[25]

However, his continued high regard is evident in the largely positive and even fawning reception of the two career retrospectives he published in the mid-1940s, *Atlantic Harvest: Memoirs of the "Atlantic,"* an anthology with extensive personal commentary, and *The Happy Profession*, the memoir that grew out of an overly long introduction to the other book.[26] Both were reviewed in most major American newspapers and spent months on nonfiction best-seller lists. After retirement, Sedgwick continued to work on *Atlantic* projects in which he took a personal interest, "those of old friends."[27]

The prevailing view of the *Atlantic* as simply washed up by Sedgwick's advent surely contributes to the dearth of scholarship about this stage in its history. Yet even the *Atlantic*'s heyday is understudied. Widely acknowledged as the nation's leading literary magazine, its identity and conditions are often taken as a given. "Hagiographic" portraits are "legion," as Nancy Glazener puts it;[28] critical analyses are scant. Along with Sedgwick III's survey of its editorial policies, Glazener's *Reading for Realism: The History of a U.S. Literary Institution, 1850–1910* and Richard Brodhead's *Cultures of Letters: Scenes of Reading and Writing in Nineteenth-Century America* remain the most influential critical discussions. Glazener analyzes nineteenth-century ideologies of reading and authorship through the lens of the "quality magazines" she dubs the "*Atlantic* group," while Brodhead uses case studies of writers like Charles Chesnutt and Sarah Orne Jewett to examine the "cultures of letters" the *Atlantic* helped create. Susan Goodman's *Republic of Words: The "Atlantic Monthly" and Its Writers, 1857–1925* surveys prominent topics, editors, and contributors; an incisive essay by Anne E. Boyd maps women's declining *Atlantic* influence.

Goodman's aside, none of these studies looks past the point that Sedgwick's term commenced. "The famed editor Ellery Sedgwick," as Werner Sollors has called him,[29] often crops up in the biographies of well-known authors, but he has attracted less critical attention than not only influential predecessors like Fields and Howells but also more peripheral ones like Aldrich and Scudder. The sole article devoted to him concerns not literature but politics, his startling support of Franco. Even Sedgwick III, who wrote his Ph.D. thesis on his grandfather's career, omits his tenure from his monograph. The front matter of his book goes so far as to identify Sedgwick's *Atlantic* purchase as terminating its reign as "the most respected literary periodical in the United States," and Glazener similarly chooses 1910 as the year that "might conveniently mark the end of the *Atlantic* group's special influence."[30] We thus have no accounts of the mechanics of Sedgwick's revival, nor of how the *Atlantic* charted the course of attracting a broader readership while still promising an exclusive cultural experience. We also lack discussions of how it influenced other magazines facing like challenges. Studies of early-twentieth-century periodicals typically focus on either their contributions to modernism or the role of mass-market magazines in shaping a new consumer age. The *Atlantic* is commonly viewed as uninvolved in and even antipathetic to these projects. Yet the *Atlantic*, too, was changing—not simply eroding from the cultural landscape—in ways that were connected to both developments even as it preserved an earlier, quite different, kind of legacy.

On the *Atlantic*'s founding, Henry Wadsworth Longfellow averred, "I would write for it if I would write for any magazine," and over the next eight decades writers and readers of all ilk continued to make equally vehement statements. To some adherents, the *Atlantic* offered an assurance of enduring cultural standards. Mary Ellen Chase, Maine novelist and professor of English at Smith College, confided, "I sometimes wonder what the few of us people who believe in the purely useless and aesthetic sort of writing are going to do if the Atlantic, the only great rock in a weary land, joins hands with the belligerent and the provocative magazines. After all there are people in this world who like to read useless things." From Canfield, we hear, "In my family, as in so many other New England families praise from the Atlantic means more than any other success." Robert Frost stated in 1916, "I don't want any of my poetry left out of The Atlantic that can be possibly got in," and close to twenty years later he commented on "the pleasure I feel in being back in the Atlantic, my home-states [*sic*] magazine." Frost's wife, Elinor, wrote Sedgwick a poignant letter asking that he publish a sonnet their daughter Marjorie Fraser had written shortly before she died. (He didn't, but three of her poems were published later that year in *Poetry*.) In a letter printed in a 1936 issue, author Nora Waln stated, "The *Atlantic* belongs to my childhood. Dear and familiar, it has followed me into far places, always a sure and steady friend."[31]

Yet Sedgwick's *Atlantic* was meaningful not only to those looking backward. Even as she took him to task for outdated notions, Amy Lowell allowed that "poems in 'The Atlantic' are more widely quoted than poems in any other magazine," having once rather plaintively confided, "You see I cannot bear to feel that I can no longer contribute to 'The Atlantic,' and as you shut the door on my poetry I should like to keep my footing there with prose if you will let me." In proposing an essay about meeting Gustave Flaubert's niece in France, Willa Cather casually commented it would mean more to an *Atlantic* readership than any other. Willfully ignoring the discrepancy between her experimental prose and the *Atlantic*'s more usual fare, Gertrude Stein sent Sedgwick poems, essays, and stories for more than a decade before he finally accepted "Autobiography of Alice B. Toklas." As late as the mid-1940s, Jean Stafford was disappointed at having to give up on the Atlantic Monthly Press and settle for the *New Yorker*, which she viewed as distressingly middlebrow by contrast.[32]

From the other side of the page, readers like Gertrude K. Bogart suggest the forceful impact of Sedgwick's changes coupled with the *Atlantic's* enduring prestige:

> Since 1917 we have read the Atlantic Monthly. We were young then, and we didn't have the diploma which is ordinarily thought of as introducing one to the higher realm of understanding, but there was that about the Atlantic which, once it was read always invited another reading. We were held by the story of Opal, we enjoyed A. Edward Newton, Agnes Repplier, Nora Waln, Hilda and her stump farm, all of them. . . . We have always been thankful that we had the courage to open that high-brow cover the first time and help ourselves to one of the greatest enjoyments of our life.[33]

Note that the Bogarts' *Atlantic* relationship *began* in 1917, well after the date identified as the magazine's putative end, to endure for three decades. This testament puts a face on the circulation statistics, showing how Sedgwick sustained the impression of offering exclusive cultural access even as he recruited a broader readership. The daughter of a carriage painter, raised in Maine and residing with her milkman husband in New York,[34] Gertrude Bogart well fits Amy Blair's characterization of the aspirational "literary novice." The "high-brow cover" she opened in 1917 little differed from the *Atlantic* covers that predated Sedgwick, devoid of illustrations, intimidatingly austere. But the magazine's interior, her letter suggests, now verged on the homey—"enjoyable" and "inviting." Several years after the Bogarts became converts, Sedgwick solicited the greater involvement of such readers by introducing the "Contributors' Column," a substantial feature composed of letters from subscribers and the editor himself that weighed in on *Atlantic* texts, authors, and developments. The "Column" manifests the *Atlantic's* "tendency toward self-mythologizing," as Goodman puts it, metacommentary on its practice. Yet at the same time, launching this conversational forum recast a practice entrenched in women's magazines, traced by Margaret Beetham back to the 1850s, of including "a letters column or a space in which the community of readers was invited to share the journalistic space"—still another way in which Sedgwick gave the *Atlantic* a more "feminine" texture.[35]

"Interest is the nub of it," Sedgwick pronounces in *The Happy Profession*, summing up his editorial credo. "Pick up a book. If, after a reasonable interval, you stir in your chair, fumble with your watch, grow conscious of gentle intrusions, the sense of errands undone, letters neglected, then your book is imperfectly interesting. But if children cease to distract and the dinner bell to interrupt, and you two, the Book and you, are alone in a timeless world, then the interest is real" (187). "Real books," he insists, "buy oblivion of all else." Much can be said about the class and gender implications of this statement, but it suffices here to comment that it reflects long-standing debates about what makes a book good. Was finding "oblivion" in a book to its credit or discredit?[36] The regret Sedgwick voices in *Atlantic Harvest* for the demise of an organic writing process complements his endorsement of oblivious reading: "In the old days contributions to a magazine in large measure wrote themselves. Intense experience cried aloud for expression. But as time went on an urbanity slipped into the place of conviction, men wrote because they had the will to write" (xi). His nostalgia for bygone ways notwithstanding, by virtue of privileging pleasure and escape he actually signals more contemporary allegiances: his participation in a turn-of-the-twentieth-century shift from a didactic to a human interest aesthetic distinguished him from *Atlantic* forebears who stressed moral and cultural instruction.

Sedgwick had four children and a long marriage with Mabel, and after he was widowed he wed Marjorie Russell. Described by one of its members as "extraordinarily devoted," the Sedgwick family had both a city residence and a 114-acre summer estate in nearby Beverly, and they participated in the many social and civic activities one would expect of a leading Boston family. Nevertheless, Sedgwick found the time and energy to cultivate an extensive personal and professional network with countless women—friends, coworkers, and, most especially, *Atlantic* writers. *Atlantic Harvest* is dedicated to "the Daughters of my House and Heart," giving literal expression to the paternal stance he took toward his female contributors as well as his actual offspring. He advised Hetty Hemenway to eschew children for the good of her career (she didn't). He urged the unnamed "Moonshiner's Wife" to return with her husband to his Appalachia home. He supported Canfield's efforts to work as a novelist from her Vermont family farm. Most remarkably, he moved Opal Whiteley into his mother-in-law's household. "By odd chance," he reported of Whiteley, "I have found myself acting more or less in the capacity of guardian."[37]

Sedgwick's *Atlantic* papers of course include many letters to and from men. However, his correspondence with women is of a special tenor. Over years—decades—he solicited, accepted, rejected, and edited their manuscripts; offered them jobs; visited and hosted them; passed on their greetings; wrote letters of introduction for their relatives and friends. The tone of the letters they wrote in return is consistently warm, confiding, admiring, and, above all, grateful. Having commented, "Everyone knows that you are the creator of the re-created Atlantic," Annie Winslow Allen continues, "but not everyone knows that you are frequently the creator of its writers. Who would guess that it was you who made Mary Antin appear to be a literary genius, and Vernon Kellogg appear to be almost uncannily a gentleman, and George a clear thinker and me a limpid writer?" Canfield divulges, "I feel moved about once in so often to testify to what gets greater as the years go by, my immense satisfaction that you exist . . . and that you edit the Atlantic!" Allowing for a due measure of shrewd flattery, some gave him credit for their very texts. "I am writing you an essay just now," Chase declares. "Here is hope that you like it, but if you do not, I shall write one that you will."[38]

Avid for their stories, he inspired many confidences. Whiteley commented—rather darkly—"I think you have a very understanding soul to have gotten me to tell you what I have." L. Adams Beck (Elizabeth L. Moresby) announced, "You ask about my life—your sympathy and insight are so extraordinary that I no longer hesitate to tell you what I have told no other of my Editors. I am a woman." (Beck was one of the faraway women that *The Happy Profession* names as such, having lived in China, India, Egypt, and Japan before settling in Victoria, B.C.) Her confidence less than justified, she also stated, "Your own broad mind may make it difficult for you to credit that even today it is easier for people to believe in a man's scholarship and research than in a woman's." Betty Smith tendered a detailed reckoning that concludes, "This is the history of my life in Chapel Hill. Forgive the lengthy letter but your interest led me on." Sedgwick continued to write to many contributors long after their official dealings with the magazine had ceased.[39]

One of Chase's letters includes the postscript, "Your niece, Susan Cabot, is in my Nineteenth Century Prose class [at Smith College]. It is nice to watch her face."[40] His correspondence summons an insular social world, and many of the women fiction writers he favored during his early editorship, conservative in tastes and values, moved in circles close to his own.[41] This insider texture makes for an unlikely ground for the magazine's faraway women, a subject to which the next chapter returns. Sedgwick's *Atlantic* reflects his close identification with an American upper class, even as he was intrigued by those he viewed as outliers.

His commitment to women's life narratives was steadfast throughout his career, from its inception with Yone Noguchi and *The American Diary of a Japanese Girl*, to Mary Antin and *The Promised Land* at the onset of his *Atlantic* editorship, to the host of faraway women I discuss, to Gertrude Stein and *The Autobiography of Alice B. Toklas*, and to Betty Smith, the playwright whom he advised from retirement on what became *A Tree Grows in Brooklyn*. (Weeks continued the trajectory by serializing *The Egg and I*, Betty MacDonald's comic record of her experiences as a chicken farmer in rural Washington; one of the top sellers of 1945, its influence endures, as the genesis of Universal Studios' Ma and Pa Kettle film series.) Sedgwick's promotion of faraway women was part of a deliberate strategy to broaden the *Atlantic*'s appeal, and his interest in the life stories of ordinary, uncelebrated women fed into and sharpened a keen national appetite for such texts. Yet at the same time, his was a personal, idiosyncratic investment. Even as there was a market demand for them that other magazines also looked to satisfy, his backing of women's life narrative was conspicuous.

Texts by faraway women constitute only a fraction of the work he published—outnumbered, by far, by those authored by more traditional contributors. Nevertheless, they loom large in both his and others' assessments of his editorship, singled out as a distinguishing feature. Sedgwick devotes two chapters of *The Happy Profession* to faraway women, and he recruits them in *Atlantic Harvest* to dramatize an editor's bliss: "Think of being paid for fishing in the morning's mail: a letter from a missionary's wife in the Solomon Islands stranded among cannibal neighbors . . . another from the Woman Homesteader in the bleak Northwest whose courage was tonic to the soul; still another giving a shrewd report of political breezes in Kansas" (xv). Reviewers of his books followed his lead, with supporters and detractors alike underscoring his "delight in discovering some pioneer woman in

Nebraska with a story to tell" or "the tender elegance with which he writes about his women friends."[42] Reviewer Beulah Rector remarked, "He delighted to hear from all kinds of people of their struggle against handicaps . . . which brought Opal Whiteley to the attention of magazine readers, the woman who ran the stump farm, Lester Monks, and Juanita Harrison, the engaging colored girl who worked her way around the world and wrote so jauntily of her travels."[43] (If only she had mentioned Stewart instead of Monks.) According to Weeks's *Atlantic* retrospective, "He had a remarkable attraction for stories of personal adventure, such as 'Black Sheep' by Jean Kenyon Mackenzie, or 'The Stump Farm' by Hilda Rose. When he was reading what he believed to be a discovery, the office would echo with his shouts of 'Oh, oh, oh!' or his laughter. He made many discoveries, and because he was a believer and an enthusiast, he was occasionally susceptible. 'The Lincoln Letters,' a forgery, and, some would add, 'The Diary of Opal Whiteley' were instances of his misplaced confidence."[44] All the texts referenced in this passage are by faraway women, and in the piece as a whole, Alfred E. Smith's "Catholic and Patriot" is the only other that Weeks identifies by name. His *My Green Age: A Memoir* offers a more informal assessment: "The girls came from everywhere, from the Kentucky mountains and the Ozarks. Jean Kenyon Mackenzie on her African farm was sturdily authentic; so too was Hilda Rose. . . . Serials such as these built circulation."[45] And as we have seen, from among the hundreds of writers Sedgwick published, faraway women dominate reader Bogart's overview of her favorites: "We were held by the story of Opal, we enjoyed A. Edward Newton, Agnes Repplier, Nora Waln, Hilda and her stump farm, all of them."[46]

Sedgwick's penchant for the literary production of women, genteel insiders and lonely outsiders alike, jostled against his commitment to preserving the *Atlantic*'s "scholarly and gentlemanlike" character, to use the adjectives of one of its founders.[47] Sedgwick himself calls attention to the seeming paradox in *The Happy Profession:* "Thus it happened that while it was to women I was forever writing letters of affectionate solicitude, my familiar company has been with men." He insists, "It has never occurred to me to change the colophon of the Atlantic to a distaff, and I have taken conscious pains that a preponderance of its contributors should be masculine." To limit the number of women was to reject the counsel of his friend Edward W. Bok, editor of the booming

Ladies' Home Journal, but gain the sanction of men like fellow Harvardian William Roscoe Thayer, who regularly noted, "I see the men are still
ahead in this month's *Atlantic*" (216). Even as he acknowledged bonds
of friendship with women, Sedgwick disavowed them professionally.

Emphatic statements such as "I have never surrendered my personal
loyalty to the sex I was born to represent" (ibid.) betray Sedgwick's
anxiety that his known enthusiasm for women writers impugned
his editorship. His perception of the problem they posed to both his
own reputation and that of the *Atlantic*—as well as the real discrim-
inatory practice that attended his affable condescension—positions
him squarely within the ranks of his predecessors. From its inception,
women's status at the *Atlantic* was vexed. The *Atlantic* resembled other
elite magazines in struggling to strike a balance between upholding a
select image and expanding its readership, crudely conceived as the
by-product, respectively, of male and female contributors. Its direc-
tors believed that featuring women's writing would swell profits but
threaten the magazine's literary character. "It is amusing to think what
the Atlantic would be like had it been turned into a salon," Sedgwick
remarked, "but I prefer the idea of a club" (ibid.).

The *Atlantic,* of course, was a critical launching ground for many
women writers, especially those working in the genre of regionalism,
a legacy that Sedgwick's faraway women extended. Mid- to late-
nineteenth-century writers such as Louisa May Alcott, Rose Terry
Cooke, Rebecca Harding Davis, Sarah Orne Jewett, Mary Noailles Murfree, Harriet Prescott Spofford, Harriet Beecher Stowe, Celia Thaxter,
and Constance Fenimore Woolson all published there. The succeeding
generation continued the tradition, with contributors such as Mary
Austin, Mary Hallock Foote, and Zitkala-Ša, whose presence also attests
to the *Atlantic*'s increasing commitment to western writing. Elizabeth
Ammons, Josephine Donovan, Judith Fetterley, Stephanie C. Palmer,
Marjorie Pryse, and others have explored the conditions that fostered
women's success in the genre, which often found periodic expression.[48]

The prevalence of regional texts is one example of how the explosion
of periodical markets created new opportunities for women writers,
especially those crafting collaborative, hybrid work. Yet the *Atlantic* had
distinct conditions, and women were consistently subordinated. Shirley
Marchalonis's quantitative study shows that during the *Atlantic*'s first
five decades, close to two-thirds of its content was composed of nonfiction

essays, and three-quarters of these essays were male-authored.[49] Boyd argues, moreover, that while women contributed roughly as much fiction as men, they were relegated to less prestigious genres. She traces trajectories of declining influence among contributors such as Alcott, Davis, and Spofford, and she documents their erasure from official histories. Publishing in a magazine required much less economic and cultural capital than creating a bound book,[50] and like countless other late-nineteenth-century and early-twentieth-century periodicals—whether "popular," "mass," "quality," or "little"—the *Atlantic* afforded women unprecedented ways to enter into print. Nevertheless, as an institution looking to maintain its masculine high-literary identity, it still curtailed their participation.

Atlantic histories by *Atlantic* insiders—prototypes for *The Happy Profession*—highlight the discomfort, surprise, and amusement that women's presence provoked. "It is a genial circumstance that most of the decisions regarding the early courses of the Atlantic were made at dinner tables," Howe reports, affairs that were exclusively male. The tacit rule was broken for a dinner for Harriet Beecher Stowe, whose "potent" influence, as an *Atlantic* founder, persuaded the magazine's first publisher to take it on. Stowe agreed to attend once promised that no alcohol would be served, but as the evening wore on, one by one the men had their water glasses refreshed, "suffused with a rosy hue." Their complicity in drinking behind her back enforced male solidarity, not only during the actual event but also in retellings like Howe's. Boyd and Joan D. Hedrick both reference Stowe's experience as illustrative of women's peripheral position in *Atlantic* rooms, pages, and records. Hedrick states that her role as "a prime mover" in the *Atlantic* should have ensured her routine inclusion in its business meetings, but "Boston society was organized around a structure of overlapping men's clubs, and the *Atlantic* was grafted onto this structure." No women were invited to the gala dinner the *Atlantic* held to celebrate John Greenleaf Whittier's seventieth birthday, inciting public protest.[51]

Other *Atlantic* stories similarly register women as disruptive. Mary Noailles Murfree, a Tennessean who first published under the pseudonym "Charles Craddock," was one of the magazine's most important fiction writers. In stories and serialized novels such as her hugely popular *In the Clouds*, she chronicled unfamiliar Appalachian ways. But instead of the impact her fiction had on the *Atlantic* and its readers, the emphasis is on how Craddock confounded Thomas Bailey Aldrich when "he" first walked into the *Atlantic* office. Harriet Spofford wrote under her own name, but such was the pungency of her first *Atlantic* submission, "In a Cellar," that she was suspected of being "some first-class Frenchman" rather than a "demure little Yankee girl."[52] Thomas Wentworth Higginson (at the time an informal editorial assistant) had to vouch for her. In respect to the *Atlantic,* Higginson is best known, of course, for the 1862 "Letter to a Young Contributor" that prompted an enduring correspondence with Emily Dickinson. His letter notes in passing that many *Atlantic* submissions were "superscribe[d] . . . with very masculine names in very feminine handwriting," a resort to pseudonyms that reveals a keen awareness of gender handicap.[53] Essayist Mary Abigail Dodge caused an uproar when she campaigned to receive money due her from James Fields, who routinely paid women contributors less than men. As Susan Coultrap-McQuin discusses, Dodge exposed the fiction of a business masquerading as a social club.[54] Perhaps the most revealing story—albeit one not relayed by *Atlantic* leaders—is that of perennial editorial assistant Susan Francis. Francis started work during Fields's tenure; it was she who called his attention to Bret Harte, whose $10,000 advance for a series of California stories would soon set a new record. Yet a half century later, just before Sedgwick's entry, she was still dealing with the slush pile of unsolicited manuscripts.[55]

We can see, then, what a crucial service Annie Adams Fields offered the women of the *Atlantic.* James Fields's affluent and well-connected young wife gave the magazine the financial support and social contacts it needed to survive, even as her weekly gatherings at her Boston home were "the one place where women writers, excluded from the network of male clubs, could meet on an equal footing with male writers and publishers."[56] Willa Cather's 1922 essay, "The House on Charles Street," commemorates her advocacy.[57]

Early in his editorship, Sedgwick enjoyed cordial relations with the now elderly Fields, receiving notes from her along the lines of "Your magazine is so truly successful that it must be an old tale now to say so."[58] However, in his express repudiation of the "salon" in favor of the "club," we can detect a rejection of her influence and, more generally, of a feminized *Atlantic.* His preface to *Atlantic Harvest* justifies the book's low number of women writers with an affable four-page treatise about their inferiority in every genre, along the way roundly disparaging women's suffrage. "Women do have emotions and can express them," he concedes. "One would suppose the lyric certain to give them the ripest opportunity, but there the record stands" (xxxii–xxxiii). They are improving in fiction, but "the nicety of their observation" does not match the "masterful hand" of male counterparts (xxxiii). Yet this was the man who ushered so many women into print and whom so many credited with inspiring their best efforts. The reams of letters congratulating him on *Atlantic Harvest* register no protest to this misogynistic sally.

But if Sedgwick sometimes escapes accountability, at other times he is unjustly accused, as we see in respect to his negotiations with Mary Antin about *The Promised Land*. As Antin began work on her autobiography, he advised her to excise extraneous incidents and Russian and Hebrew phrases, and to an extent she heeded his advice. Responding to his suggestions for her first *Atlantic* story, Antin wrote, "Your letter of the 6th received, and contents taken to heart. I shall return 'Malinke' very soon, trimmed, I hope, to your liking. Perhaps in my first letter I sounded as if I meant to be obstinate. The truth is that I value your advice, and I think I have the strength of mind to give in where it is a question of my notions against your convictions."[59] For urging that she "trim" her work Sedgwick has been taken to task, deemed a coercive editor intent on disciplining transgressive voices, even as Antin is praised for resisting him. Editors of his class are especially vulnerable to such charges; Sedgwick III has shown how reflexively Fields, Higginson, and even Howells are portrayed as conservative gatekeepers.[60] Sedgwick himself viewed his treatment as gingerly, allowing, "I might lead you far astray if you were foolish enough to follow my notions," and he and Antin soon reached a compromise over the edits.[61] (Keren R. McGinity uses the word "banter" to describe their correspondence.)[62] The counsel he gave her can be read as not overbearing but simply practical. Readers do, after all, prefer a smattering of foreign phrases to a raft of them. Moreover, he did permit the smattering—he was not intent on a whitewash. *The Promised Land* went on to garner accolades that echo his own well-known evaluation of the book as "at once more interesting and more significant than any description I know of Americans in the making."[63]

He took a quite similar approach to Betty Smith's *A Tree Grows in Brooklyn*, a good thirty years later. Reminiscent of *The Promised Land*,

Smith's novel about growing up Irish and poor in New York recounts how its autobiographical protagonist overcame a dire urban environment to thrive. Sedgwick, by then retired, was its first reader. Smith's response suggests the nature of his evaluation: "Thank you for your kindness in giving me instructions about my novel. I am beginning to see it now—how to rework it. . . . I'll eliminate the life of Aunt Maimie and her desertions and delete the chapter about the Chinese laundry man and Sis's getting her baby."[64] Like Antin, she proffered a resounding American success story, and she found an even larger readership. Frank Luther Mott classifies *A Tree Grows in Brooklyn* with *Uncle Tom's Cabin* and *Gone With the Wind* as among those books "which occupy a kind of best-seller heaven of their own."[65] Without Sedgwick's intervention, the narratives he backed might have been more evidently multicultural, more graphic, more complex. Indisputably, however, they would have been less successful in their day.

After his death, May Sarton, poet and novelist, reminisced, "Two Chinese peonies speak to me always of Ellery Sedgwick, being wheeled out in his last years to sit and contemplate one after another of these beauties, an old man whose exuberant delight flew out from him as if it were a flotilla of butterflies, to rest on this flower or that—a winged *attention* he gave also to those he loved, to poetry, to creation itself."[66] Sarton's memory of an aesthete delighting in flowers and poems departs from most public assessments. Sedgwick is typically figured as either the Brahmin of Mount Vernon Street dedicated to upholding a faded legacy or the New York–trained businessman bent on a scoop—as reclining in "velvet-jacketed ease" or decked out in "garishly checked suits," to use his contemporaries' phrases.[67] Neither position, insular gentleman or grasping merchant, allows for original, thoughtful, estimable literary tastes.

When he did publish important writers, the story goes, it was only when his convictions were overcome by sheer talent. His succinct initial rejection of Robert Frost is oft told: "We are sorry that we have no place in *The Atlantic Monthly* for your vigorous verse." Later, he grew keen to accept some of this verse after all, including "Birches" and "The Road Not Taken," no less. According to Frost, he met with Sedgwick at his office and teasingly held a manuscript just beyond his reach; the editor who once rebuffed him now literally had to snatch for his poems. In "Arriere-Garde," a review of *Atlantic Harvest*, Newton Arvin objected, "One looks in vain for the writers of short fiction who, during the thirty years of Mr. Sedgwick's editorship, were at work on the frontiers of literary expansion and discovery—Sherwood Anderson, say, or Virginia Woolf, or Katherine Anne Porter, or William Faulkner— and what one does find is Katherine Fullerton Gerould, Mary Webb, Hetty Hemenway, and Walter D. Edmonds." Although Arvin's choice of writers speaks as much to changing literary fashions as intrinsic merit (Gerould, for example, was once likened to Edith Wharton, while Webb's novels about the Welsh borderlands were pronounced works of genius), their declining reputations helped him portray Sedgwick as mired in the static center that gives meaning to modernist "frontiers."[68]

Sedgwick's intractability precipitated trenchant credos. In 1912 Willa Cather consoled Elizabeth Shepley Sergeant after he rejected a submission: "The real truth is this, my friend—you probably know it—you are not flat enough for Ellery. He doesn't know but your laugh may be dangerous; he doesn't know just where you stand; you won't give him the one solid paragraph that would make him feel safe about you. He's afraid that if he follows your giddy pen about he may suddenly find himself laughing at something he shouldn't laugh at." (Her assessment stemmed in part from personal acquaintance during her and Sedgwick's overlapping employment in the *McClure's* offices.) He and Amy Lowell (Mabel Cabot's childhood friend) had a long-running critical feud. Lowell craved inclusion in his magazine, never mind that she privately referred to him as a "silly ass." "Oh! Ellery," she apostrophized, "You are a dear, kind, non-understanding thing! What difference does it make to me whether the 'thing' is poetry or not? I have no particular desire to write poetry any more than anything else. I want to write something which shall be vivid and compelling; I want my work to have force. Sometimes I want my voice to have charm, and I do not care whether it comes under any of the recognized headings or not." In the midst of her quest for *Atlantic* publication, Gertrude Stein, famously, declared, "I am sorry you have not taken the poems for really you ought to. I may say without exaggeration that my stuff has genuine literary quality, frankly let us say the only important literature that has come out of America since Henry James. After all Henry James was a picture puzzle but the Atlantic did not hesitate." In resisting Sedgwick and his certitudes, this group of writers—women all—articulated alternative aesthetic precepts. "Ellery" was a useful foil to highlight their criteria for good writing. This was due to more than just Sedgwick's position as *Atlantic* gatekeeper. He displayed an irritated, ambivalent interest in modernist expression: both through occasional publications and in the "rather argumentative answer[s]" (*AABT* 202), to use Stein's phrase, that were just enough qualified to encourage counterarguments. Sarton thus presented him with a pamphlet of poems she had hand-copied, "A posy of Modern Poems (???!!!)," featuring writers such as Frost, T. S. Eliot, and W. B. Yeats. Her note about the gift indicates the pleasure both parties found in their debates: "I have been amusing myself mightily by choosing twelve modern poems on which Ellery can sharpen his foil."[69]

Joining other magazines that likewise pursued "large, diverse and mobile readerships" through featuring multiple voices and perspectives,[70] Sedgwick's *Atlantic* juxtaposed what we might call modernist lite, texts by authors including Lowell, Frost, Stein, and Ernest Hemingway, with the stories of faraway women. Even as Sedgwick desired more conventional work from the iconoclastic, he detected promise in narratives that on first inspection might appear uncrafted. The same sensibility that inclined him to resist the most deliberately literary led him to promote texts of everyday provenance. And startlingly enough, these genres start to approach each other. The life narratives of his faraway women can feel very modern indeed, with their immediate, intersubjective, self-reflexive, colloquial, generically fluid features. Juanita Harrison sometimes sounds just like Gertrude Stein.

Not, however, that Sedgwick recognized such affinity—quite the contrary. Part of his attraction to faraway women stemmed from his conviction of their artlessness. This belief led to certain silences in his accounts of them. For one, it precluded him from representing his own labor, the considerable editorial work their narratives required. He was wont to liken himself, as *Atlantic* editor, to a host presiding over a genial dinner party, an emphasis on authorial personalities over editorial procedures that led *Harper's* Allen to complain that he obscured "the necessary housekeeping arrangements for such a dinner party—the daily grind of manuscript-reading and schedule-making, and advance planning and negotiating with authors."[71] But more important, praising these writers as artless left him no discursive space to endorse their literary agency, any "will to write."

Atlantic Harvest includes a characteristic anecdote about a meeting with Jean Kenyon Mackenzie, the Presbyterian missionary:

> I had heard of her talent for letter writing and called upon her. Obviously she was startled by an editor's visit, and told me she was no writer. "You have written letters home," said I, "and my guess is that your father and mother have kept them." "Yes," she replied, "isn't it absurd, there is a whole trunkful upstairs." I had what I wanted. The trunkful went back to Boston with me and out of that faithful record came a clearer picture of the hearts of black men and women than I have ever known. (523)

Here we see Sedgwick in the role he so savored, the editor-pioneer who unearths a trove of raw material, toted back to the city to process. Even with no outside knowledge, it is hard not to suspect a more complex history. To whom had Mackenzie written, how had she constructed her letters, and what else had she done such that her "talent" came to his attention? Indeed, she had already written a guidebook for new missionaries, and she went on to publish a memoir, short fiction, a novel, a biography, and a volume of poems.[72]

Sedgwick represented Stewart, Whiteley, Rose, and Harrison in similar ways. Extolling talent but downplaying artistry, his highest words of praise for them included "ingenuous," "genuine," and "authentic." His account of first learning about Whiteley's diary shares much with the Mackenzie story:

> One close question followed another regarding the surroundings of her girlhood. The answers were so detailed, so sharply remembered, that the next question was natural.
>
> "If you remember like that, you must have kept a diary."
>
> Her eyes opened wide, "Yes, always. I do still."
>
> "Then it is not the book I want, but the diary."[73]

As appealing as it may be, the archive proves the tale false. Sedgwick had previously received a letter of introduction from Whiteley, written in her distinctive rounded handwriting, that informed him, "Last winter I published my first book. . . . In it are part of the journal of my childhood (I am twenty-one now). I will bring this book with me when I come to see you."[74] Sedgwick depicted his faraway women as unaware of both the potency and the commercial potential of their work. This recognition is the province only of middle-class supporters and the editor himself. Such denial is linked to his promotion of these individualistic and even eccentric women as representative of their place, age, class, race, or occupation. *The Story of Opal* offers "a tiny golden key" to "children's hearts" (*HP* 261). Stewart is a "woman homesteader." Rose speaks for "every pioneer."[75] Perniciously enough, *The Happy Profession* lauds Harrison as a "Black Pearl among the servants of this earth" (211).

Two incidents connected to Sedgwick's domestic and international travels demonstrate how he processed otherness—people, places, cultures, and events outside his customary purview. The first arose from a visit he made to Appalachia, as recounted in his *Atlantic Harvest* introduction to the anonymously published "Our Unsuitable Marriage." The author, identified only as the "Moonshiner's Wife," is still another of the faraway women profiled in *The Happy Profession*. A Harvard legacy and archbishop's granddaughter, on graduating from college she had moved to West Virginia to do social work at a settlement house for veterans, and she also taught school part-time. Sedgwick opens his long, confusing introduction by describing his response to first hearing about her:

> I had ridden through the moonshiners' country and had sat on hickory logs passing the time of day with squirrel shooters over a pipe of rough-cut. I had followed trails past signboards warning "REVENOORS Keep Out" and had gasped what I thought my last breath as I washed down corn pone and bacon fat with a sip of liquid lightning. So it was a lively picture that rose in my mind when I heard the story of a young lady, educated and accomplished, leaving a New York home where every proper convention was observed to unite herself in marriage with an illiterate Kentucky mountaineer. A friend of hers told me the tale in barest outline, and at first I suspected exaggeration. Here was King Cophetua and the beggar maid reversed. (404)

He goes on to proffer the false "tale" he was so ready to receive, a complement to the "lively picture": courtship by an older student who, having faithfully tended the schoolroom fire and water bucket, at last proposed with the prelude, "Teacher, may I see you for a spell after school?" (405). Sedgwick's "at first I suspected exaggeration" (as opposed to "from the first") encourages the misconception that the story was not exaggerated after all. He reminds us only in passing of his narrative frame, through comments like "such was the tale as I heard it" and the literally parenthetical "(such was the story)" (404). Like the western pioneer bettering herself or the jolly black maid, the young teacher in her one-room schoolhouse was such an iconic American character that he could not resist, marshaling a tortured apophasis to tell the kind of story he enjoyed. "Finally came the true story which is printed below," he at last concedes. "At this point let the moonshiner's wife take up the story" (405). It is almost as if he dramatizes his dependence on cliché, juxtaposing for the reader's inspection his version of a woman's life with her own.[76] He always leaves open the question of whether he circulated notions like these because they reflected his actual beliefs or simply because he relished their formulation.

His foray into art collecting supplies the second example. While touring Nara, Japan, he bought a thirteenth-century wooden statue of the revered Buddhist regent Prince Shoutoku. "The Sedgwick Statue of the Infant Shōtoku Taishi" was later loaned to the Museum of Fine Arts in Boston, where experts discovered what its new owner, understandably enough, had not: a hidden compartment housing rare dedicatory objects. Extracted from a hole in its feet, they included a twelfth-century Lotus Sutra from South China, esoteric Japanese documents, and eight wooden figurines.[77] Sedgwick's shrewd business instincts, along with his penchant for the exotic, had led him to a rare find. By his own account, so too did the down-to-earth tastes that inclined him to a piece "not . . . of the noblest order": surfeited with abstract "masterpieces," on happening across the small statue he was moved by "a sense of humanity, a directness, an utter simplicity."[78] He was able to recognize value even when operating entirely outside his professional field. Upper-class habits as a well-traveled, well-connected, well-heeled man afforded ample opportunity to exercise this skill, and his civic dedication made the results available to scholars and the public at large. Yet he was unable to detect the presence of his treasure's hidden texts, its quite literally deeper meanings. It would take others to bring them to light.

Redirecting our gaze from the religious artifacts of ancient Japan to the literary marketplace of twentieth-century Boston, we can see the likeness to his dealings with faraway women. In his capacity as *Atlantic* editor, Sedgwick produced a set of texts that were at once simple and extraordinary, whose full worth he sometimes seemed unable to see. He depicted the "interesting person[s]" he published as less interesting than they actually were, the irregular edges of their personalities and circumstances honed to banality. In promoting them as generic types—child, pioneer, maid—he wrote himself into a corner, with no narrative space to acknowledge their purposeful shaping of their texts and authorship.

Yet we can also see that while Sedgwick certainly influenced how these writers were perceived, he was only the most vocal spokesperson for a broader cultural consensus. Readers viewed Whiteley as a representative child, the precocious moments that score her book notwithstanding. Harrison's reviewers characterized her as an untutored "colored domestic," unable to recognize her cosmopolitanism.[79] In portraits of Stewart as a humble working woman, we see nothing of her confident engagement with a mainstream American literary tradition. Rose insisted that she fled to the wilderness to escape the masses, but *The Stump Farm* was received as populist inspiration. To note these kinds of discrepancies is not merely a matter of setting the historical record straight. It is also a reckoning of the assumptions to which these writers responded in their texts. The succeeding chapters gather an array of narratives about faraway women, both their own and those others transmitted, to investigate their connections, tensions, and contradictions along with the multifarious interpretive possibilities they yield.

CHAPTER TWO

ELINORE PRUITT STEWART

AND

HER SILENT PARTNERS

Letters of a Woman Homesteader

What is it that makes your letters to Mary labored and artificial, while your eager pen—when addressing Margaret— ... scrawls the spontaneous and fluent phrases which only you could write, and which you could write only to Margaret?

—"The Incomplete Letter-Writer," *Atlantic Monthly,* 1912

llery Sedgwick's memoir, *The Happy Profession,* offers a brief account of how Elinore Pruitt Stewart's *Letters of a Woman Homesteader* came to be: "Never a week without its adventure. Every settler had his own story to tell Mrs. Rupert, the tale to be relayed to Mrs. Coney and thence to the *Atlantic*" (199). This statement is aggravating. For one, it is untrue. Rather than feeding Stewart's letters to Sedgwick week by week, Coney submitted a stockpile—having first edited and typed them. But more important, Stewart's authorial agency goes unacknowledged, with the writer made to look like a mere conduit for "the tale" in its journey from Wyoming to Boston.

Nevertheless, the following discussion underscores just this "relay" between Stewart and the two people I identify as *Letters of a Woman*

Homesteader's "silent partners," Juliet Coney and Sedgwick himself. A primary goal is to uncover Coney's history and amplify her voice. Given that her side of the correspondence was not published, Coney can be heard only through the filter of Stewart's words, and the editorial work that she contributed has been effaced. Conversely, Sedgwick was far from silent, but his very loquaciousness can obscure his professional and personal agendas, and he was committed to keeping his interventions behind the scenes. I approach *Letters of a Woman Homesteader* as a form of "sentimental collaboration," to use Mary Louise Kete's paradigm (on which more later), evaluating the personal relationships and collaborative enterprise that formed—and sometimes constricted—Stewart's literary production and career, as she strove to circulate her frontier writing within both a gift economy and the commercial marketplace. Brimming with contradictions, her interactions with her mentors expose the fundamental paradox of faraway women, as both connected to and removed from social worlds and structures of power.

The following discussion focuses on the relational qualities of *Letters of a Woman Homesteader*. It also includes a biographical account of Coney, as some recompense for the loss of the texts she herself produced, the series of letters that prompted and shaped Stewart's. It concludes with a reckoning of Stewart's post-*Atlantic* career and the role Sedgwick played in it. Publishing in the *Atlantic* catalyzed her correspondence and deepened her print-culture immersion, even as her literary ambitions largely went unfulfilled.

A scant three years into his *Atlantic* editorship, Sedgwick initiated four letter serials within the space of twelve months, November 1912 to October 1913. Each of the first two commemorates a prominent, recently deceased Harvard man of letters, Charles Eliot Norton and William Vaughn Moody, distinguished scholars almost absurdly typical of the *Atlantic*. Their publication extends the prevalent nineteenth-century practice of producing volumes of "Life and Letters" (or "Life in Letters"), biographies composed of selected correspondence. Extracts from such books, and reviews of the same, were an *Atlantic* staple in the years leading into Sedgwick's advent. However, the two that followed, the anonymously authored "Letters of a Down-and-Out" and, six months later, "Letters of a Woman Homesteader," were something new, Sedgwick's first venture into publishing letters by unknown people. An *Atlantic* advertisement claimed that the former, which recounts the economic and spiritual renewal of a New York businessman in northwestern logging camps, inspired the submission of Stewart's work.[1]

Sedgwick's epistolary enthusiasm was still running high in 1915, which saw a cluster of letter serials by American women: Stewart's sequel, "Letters on an Elk Hunt" (perhaps displaced from the coveted January issue to February by Martha Bianchi Dickinson's selection of her Aunt Emily's letters); Mildred Aldrich's "A Little House on the Marne," the writer's observations of the First Battle of the Marne from her country home outside Paris; and Jean Kenyon Mackenzie's "Black Sheep," a record of her missionary work in Cameroon. First-person narratives of ordinary Americans were already ubiquitous in popular magazines, whose proliferation created innumerable opportunities for emerging authors. (Indeed, during the same period as the "Woman Homesteader" serial, *Ladies' World,* a magazine with a largely working-class readership, featured a column by Caroline Henderson in her capacity as the "Homestead Lady" of Oklahoma.)[2] Sedgwick's innovation lay in incorporating such texts into the fabric of the illustrious *Atlantic.*

"The Incomplete Letter-Writer" from which I take this chapter's epigraph, an anonymously authored item in the January 1912 "Contributors' Column," registers the *Atlantic*'s move from the correspondence of famous men to that of obscure women, and it also offers a timely evaluation of the role played by the epistolary interlocutor. The short essay begins by referencing the most famed literary correspondences of the past century, those conducted by Emerson and Carlyle and by Browning and Barrett, and relies on the "universal" "he" to make its arguments. However, the agenda then seems to shift, as the writer discloses her own gender, uses the names Mary and Margaret to represent hypothetical readers, and identifies everyday correspondence as female practice, a writer's attempt to "successfully reveal her own *ego.*" The thrust of the argument is that readers influence the kind of letters they are sent. "It would be delightful to be able to write good letters, but I think it would be more delightful to be able to receive them. We hear a great deal nowadays of the lost art of good letter-writing, but we hear nothing at all of the equally rare art of good letter-receiving." The writer concludes, "We, as silent partners, play an important part in English letters."[3]

These musings on personal alchemy well speak to the place of Juliet Coney in Stewart's writing project, the employer turned friend to whom Stewart addressed her published letters. "How glad I am to have you to tell little things to," she once exclaimed (*LEH* 1). Yet *Letters of a Woman Homesteader*, like the other texts in this study, reflects social processes more complex than mere compatibility. While the author of "The Incomplete Letter-Writer" assumes that writer and reader inhabit the same cultural milieu, Sedgwick's faraway women show that not only resonating personalities but also complementary class and geographical positions result in inspired texts.

Elinore Pruitt Stewart and *Letters of a Woman Homesteader*

Born in 1876, Elinore Pruitt grew up on Chickasaw Indian Territory in what is now the state of Oklahoma. Her mother and father were from Arkansas and Virginia, respectively, and she identified as a southerner.[4] Elinore was the oldest of nine children, and her education was meager. She had lost her parents by the age of eighteen, following which she struggled to support herself and several siblings as they moved around Oklahoma. Her earliest training as a writer began in the ubiquitous nineteenth-century practice of using letters to maintain ties among far-flung families, enabled by the expansion of the U.S. Post Office Department. However, she subsequently strove to convert her writing into income. She had short pieces, including advice columns about child care, published in the *Kansas City Star*, made plans (unrealized) to write about the cliff dwellings at Mesa Verde, and submitted fiction to magazine contests.

Elinore Pruitt married Harry Cramer Rupert in 1902, and she briefly homesteaded with him in Grand, Oklahoma. Yet she was single by the time their daughter, Jerrine, was born in 1906, and she settled in Denver with her shortly afterward. Stewart claimed that Rupert had been killed while inspecting a bridge in his capacity as engineer; her biographer Susanne George Bloomfield surmises that she invented the accident to dodge the stigma of divorce.[5] Regardless, once single, she took various service positions to support herself and Jerrine, including that of nurse and maid to Juliet Coney, a widow from Massachusetts whose own move to Denver preceded hers by about twenty years. In 1909 she departed for southwestern Wyoming to take a job as housekeeper for Clyde Stewart, a rancher. Within seven weeks of her arrival, she filed on land adjoining Clyde's, and she married him a week later.

Stewart wrote Coney regularly, keeping her abreast of her homesteader progress. Her letters express her desire to do new kinds of labor and redefine herself accordingly, as one absorbed in the productive work of ranching rather than the maintenance work of her service past and homemaking present. Yet they also register her attraction to an entirely different form of labor, writing. Especially in light of her past efforts in other genres, the length, craft, and polish of her letters suggest that she wrote to Coney with the intent of ultimately publishing—if not the letters themselves, then at least like accounts of the local incidents they portray.

Moving to Wyoming flooded Stewart with new subject matter. Events in her neighbors' lives and her own yielded abundant stories and themes. However, it was not her environment alone that accelerated her development as a writer. Rather, it was the coupling of this environment with her ongoing association with Coney, the Denver transplant whose eastern, high-culture affiliations were enduring enough that she continued to subscribe to her hometown magazine, the *Atlantic*. Even as Stewart responded viscerally to the open spaces and frontier dynamics of Wyoming, she responded literally to her older friend. Coney helped Stewart rehearse her life for the *Atlantic* readership to whom she eventually directed her texts, but she was also a real woman—and, not incidentally, another westerner—to whom she wrote for personal ends. She sought both to invigorate and to impress Coney. Although both women, as we shall see, shared a working-class background, and although not so many miles separate Burntfork and Denver, Stewart regarded Coney as her entrée to the cultural and class positions she desired, a paragon of urban, middle-class, eastern propriety.

Stewart's letters ran across six *Atlantic* issues, October 1913 to April 1914, and *Letters of a Woman Homesteader* was published as a bound volume shortly afterward.[6] The text introduces a frontier mix of peoples, French, Irish, English, Scottish, German, Mexican, Mormon, and southern, as they advance toward a sense of community, in part through Stewart's acts. She comes off as a rather bumbling character who nonetheless performs remarkable feats, like tackling the mowing or coping in the mountains with a sudden storm, and she also felicitously engineers her neighbors' relationships, as when she serves as matchmaker or reunites a displaced Tennessean with his family. Much of the text is composed

FIGURE 2. Elinore Pruitt Stewart on the hay mower. *From the Elinore Pruitt Stewart family collection, Sweetwater County Historical Museum.*

of extended stories that could stand on their own, their subjects indicated by chapter titles such as "The Adventure of the Christmas Tree" or "Among the Mormons." Stewart's renditions of local happenings are thickly embroidered, and the men and women they feature, while inspired by the district's residents, are her own creations—"the kinds of characters most novelists only dream of," as the *Christian Science Monitor* put it.[7] (Tellingly, Doubleday, Page & Company solicited her for "a novel picturing life as you have done in these letters.")[8] In one instance, she atypically reports on the welfare of her children and then concludes, "I must say good-night; it is twelve o'clock, and I am so sleepy" (*LWH* 228). In all the book, it is here that it reads most like a letter as commonly conceived. Yet she evaluates it as just the opposite: "Now this is really not a letter; it is just a reply." For Stewart, simply to "reply" to another text was lazy evasion; a real letter reflected a deeper level of intention and craft. Bloomfield supplies a useful term for the hybrid genre she devised, "story-letters" (*AWH* 133).

The *Atlantic* introduced the serial as "genuine letters, written without thought of publication, simply to tell a friendly story," and characterized it similarly at its close, as "completely ingenuous letters." To preserve this quality, during its course Sedgwick took pains to conceal his "true objective" from Stewart—his intention to collect the letters into a book—lest she be smitten with an attack of "self-consciousness." Reviewers of her books looked to second the *Atlantic*'s assertion of artlessness. *Letters of a Woman Homesteader* was praised, for example, for its "manifest guiltlessness of ulterior design" and "racy, idiomatic, unstudied style," and its sequel, *Letters on an Elk Hunt,* for evincing "no assumption of finished style, no attempt at fine language, no unified plot development, simply the natural recital of incident to the friend at home."[9]

Such responses, introducing the possibility of artifice only to deny it, may protest too much. The *Outlook*'s conflicted assessment suggested that while Stewart's "brilliant talents" seem incommensurate with "occasional letters," her choice of genre actually safeguards them: "Her extraordinary freedom, her delicious humor, her unrivaled naturalness of impression and expression, could hardly escape the deadening influence of formal writing for print" (quoted in *AWH* 69). In the *Mississippi Valley Historical Review,* V. Poovey stressed that the text belies epistolary expectations: "It is true that the book is a series of letters. . . . But if one expects to find only the prosaic chronicle of the everyday life of a homesteader he will be pleasantly surprised for the author has the happy faculty of arraying even the most commonplace events in clothing which makes them extremely attractive." This historian recognized Stewart as an artist whose "happy faculty" transforms the "commonplace" conditions depicted. Even an *Atlantic* advertisement suggested the inadequacy of the usual generic categories in stating, "These letters fall naturally into a series of complete stories" and "The *Atlantic* will print them like a serial novel."[10]

At first glance, Stewart's published letters do not look much like letters. While they retain salutations and valedictions, most personal exchanges have been removed. They include no inquiry into Coney's life and no response to the news she must have relayed. Many commence with an ellipsis, indicating that Stewart's habit was to preface her tales with some personal comments, later excised.[11] Sedgwick could have recast Stewart's material as a diary, a memoir, or even a collection of short stories. Why keep the letter frame at all?

One answer is that the choice supports the impression of "ingenuousness" readers crave from western writing. As Nathaniel Lewis has demonstrated in *Unsettling the Literary West: Authenticity and Authorship,* the successful text about the West must above all seem realistic. Presenting Stewart's narrative as letters buttresses its identity as a true report of western life. Yet we can also, I believe, argue something more specific: that by preserving an epistolary frame, the *Atlantic* showed its commitment to the conversation as much as to the record. Sedgwick was drawn to the letters for their depiction of frontier exploits as filtered through a class-structured relationship. The subject of *Letters of a Woman Homesteader* is not homesteading alone, but also the enduring friendship forged by an Oklahoma transplant in Wyoming with the Massachusetts native in Denver whose household she once shared. Presenting the letters as such calls attention to the *Atlantic's* extended project of having "faraway" writers portray their lives for the gratification of those "nearby." And in turn, Stewart's actual position in the *Atlantic* suggests the magazine's internal dialogue, between its faraway women and its more traditional contributors, women whose outlook and apparent class position resembled Coney's.

The earliest discussions of Stewart evaluated her work as historical source material, as when Helen Winter Stauffer and Susan J. Rosowski's *Women and Western American Literature* introduced her as an "articulate spokeswoman of an almost forgotten group, single women homesteaders."[12] Scholarship then evolved to argue for how purposely she created a narrative persona and adapted American literary traditions. Working against reductive notions of her textual production as unstudied correspondence, the prevailing impulse now is to demonstrate its fictional and self-consciously literary qualities.

One consequence, however, has been a naturalizing of *Letters of a Woman Homesteader* as "always already" a book, unmoored from its epistolary origins. Stewart's portrait of a developing community, comic narration of her escapades, and, most especially, confident assumption of a western identity distract attention from the text's less sexy epistolary premise and its author's relationship with her elderly interlocutor. Passages like the following, in which Stewart describes a madcap journey with a doughty companion, are much on display in critical discussions of the book (including my own): "Tam O'Shanter and Paul Revere were snails compared to us. We didn't follow any road either, but went sweeping along across country. No one else in the world could have done it unless they were drunk" (*LWH* 70). What we do not see, though, are readings of statements like this: "I really don't know how to write you . . . and now that my last letter made you sick I almost wish so many things didn't happen to me, because I always want to tell you" (*LWH* 45). What does it mean to say, "I really don't know how to write you"? What had she told Coney to make her sick? And what do we make of her signing off as "Your ex-washlady" (*LWH* 44)? Although seemingly pedestrian, these rhetorical gestures are not separate from, but rather help constitute, Stewart's revisionary portrait of the West.

The powerful elements of western romance in Stewart's personal story can make the text's intersubjective history seem insignificant or even incongruous. Linda Karell argues that "narratives deemed western are doubly pressured to uphold the dominating mythology" of "individual creativity" and, consequently, their collaborative aspects are overlooked or suppressed.[13] That Stewart responds to another woman—from Massachusetts, no less—amplifies the discordance, as the principal actors of these narratives are understood to be male. If only men shape the West, then western women writers can respond only to them. Stewart's allusions to writers like Twain and Cooper attract frequent comment, even as Coney's role is disregarded.

More broadly, the privileging of American individualism contributes to the paucity of scholarship about the inherently intersubjective genre of American letters. The nation's epistolary *fiction* long attracted the most notice, with the odd consequence that theories developed in respect to fictional letters dominated analyses of actual ones. Although the twentieth century remains understudied, *The Edinburgh Companion to Nineteenth-Century American Letters and Letter-Writing* has recently remedied this dearth. Elizabeth Hewitt observes that the volume's collected essays signal a shift from focusing on what letters reveal about individual personalities to examining how their authors construct and negotiate multiple "social attachments" within a "network of correspondence," a critical approach I share.[14]

To adapt a phrase from William Merrill Decker's *Epistolary Practices: Letter Writing in America before Telecommunications,* my aim in the following discussion is to return *Letters of a Woman Homesteader* to its original "rhetorical life"—to illuminate its persistent identity as a collection of "occasional letters." I attend to the specific social conditions and outcomes of Stewart's correspondence, and I assess it in respect to the constitutive features of epistolarity, a series of reciprocal texts addressed to a particular reader or readers operating within shared social contexts,

exchanged for concrete ends across space and over time. "A true letter," Decker argues, "is one that figures successfully in an interpersonal
relationship." Decker shows that even the most flowery letter has real-
world effects, and the same holds true for the most simple. Anne Bower,
introducing her *Epistolary Responses: The Letter in Twentieth-Century
American Fiction,* recalls her first intimations of their power: plaintive
dispatches from camp elicited "cookies, money, the wished-for phone
call"; a description of her appearance to a pen pal "created the body she
saw." Even as much of their content is fictional, Stewart's letters were
actual physical objects sent from writer to reader through the U.S. Post.
"Here I am boring you to death with things that cannot interest you!"
(*LWH* 216), she exclaims to Coney following an emphatic endorsement
of women's homesteading. "You'd think I wanted you to homestead,
wouldn't you?" The comment could be viewed as a clumsy attempt to
accommodate the letter premise to her "real" text, a treatise about frontier opportunity for women. Yet we can also see it as a telling epistolary
moment, in which Stewart abruptly recollects that while Coney is a
potential member of the group she would recruit, her age and position
make her an unlikely candidate.[15]

Stewart and Coney

An early *Atlantic* advertisement for Stewart's letters maintains:

> Most Atlantic features are born of much thinking and correspondence.
> These letters were a gift of Providence. A lady who lives in Denver had read
> the "Letters of a Down-and-Out" in our pages last year, and so sent us a
> bundle of the correspondence she had received from a woman homesteader
> who once, through a singular twist of fate, had been a washwoman in her
> employ. More delightful letters we never read in manuscript. They tell a
> connected story of pioneer life, full of buoyancy and pluck and the spirit
> of adventure. The contrast they present between the freedom of glorious
> opportunity and days of sweated labor in Denver give the reader an exhila-
> rated sense of holiday.[16]

My usual inclination would be to look at the disservice this statement
does Stewart: labeling her a "washwoman," denying her authorial
agency, lauding the "exhilarated sense of holiday" her strenuous life
offered a middle-class readership. If Coney really did associate her with

the "down-and-out," then no wonder Stewart was anxious to exhibit her accomplishments. Yet we might question the *Atlantic*'s representation of Coney, too, this "lady" who presumed to handle the affairs of a woman from whom she had once—the advertisement implies—extracted "sweated labor."

From the considerable body of research on Stewart, we have learned not to view her as a representative homesteader. Coney, though, remains a cypher. When not overlooked altogether, she appears as a stock figure, either a standard-bearer of Victorian values—Stewart's genteel foil—or a stand-in for a homogenously conceived *Atlantic* readership. In other words, scholars have followed the *Atlantic*'s lead in insisting on a class gulf between her and Stewart. Yet the gap is less wide than first appearances suggest. While Coney is inevitably characterized, to use Bloomfield's words, as a "widowed and wealthy former schoolteacher originally from Boston" (*AWH* 220), public records reveal she was never a schoolteacher, she was closer to poor than wealthy, and she was not even from Boston.

Discussions of Coney typically begin and end with Stewart's uneasy "confession" that she and Clyde had married. Victoria Lamont's "Li(v)es of a Woman Homesteader" is an exception, investigating the "particular social relation" within which Stewart writes, and I build on this work. On the other end of the spectrum, in *Writing the Pioneer Woman* Janet Floyd literally edits out Coney's presence, Stewart's "you," to flattening effect. Sherry L. Smith's important account of the discrepancies between Stewart's text and the historical record incorrectly identifies Coney as "a well-to-do and widowed schoolteacher from Boston," while Natalie Dykstra's insightful discussion of the "curative space" of the West does not examine Stewart's patient. Even Bloomfield's pathbreaking biography overlooks her.[17]

The following thumbnail biography is a move to recover Juliet Coney from obscurity and cliché, tracing not only the life events that led to her and Stewart's association in Denver but also the personal circumstances that nurtured their correspondence. My choice to make Coney a leading presence in this chapter could be viewed as rather perverse. I redirect the critical gaze from aspirational working-class sensibility to seemingly entrenched gentility, from the West to the New England that has always been the baseline for American literary studies, from cattle ranches to shoe factories. Above all, I steal time from the writer for the reader.

However, the reciprocal, intersubjective nature of Stewart's literary production entreats us to consider both parties. As Hewitt argues, since a letter is "a document that articulates the junction between reader and writer," as outside readers, "our own interpretation is inevitably sundered by the question of whether to identify with the epistolary author or with the recipient."[18] A fuller record illuminates the material conditions of Stewart's authorship, but, more important, coupling her life story with Coney's better conveys the nature of their exchange itself. A more even treatment of this epistolary pair fills the conversational void created by the evacuation of Coney's letters from the published text, and it mirrors their actual writing project, in which two perspectives, histories, and lives intertwined.

I have culled Coney's life history from censuses, a family genealogy, and birth, marriage, pension, and death records. Her place of origins is reflected in the sheer wealth of material at hand, a consequence of Massachusetts's comprehensive record keeping and the intergenerational family stability the state long afforded. What we lack, though, are autobiographical statements. Stewart's life and views are on record due to her frontier endeavor, which, as Lamont comments, "frames her experience as exemplary and therefore worthy to be represented."[19] Coney's are not, neither published nor preserved in any known collections. While Coney may well have had no desire to disseminate her life story, neither was it an option. The literary marketplace within which she descried Stewart's opportunity held no room for *this* kind of ordinary woman, this widow in her Denver apartment.

"By happy chance," Sedgwick recalled, "Mrs. Coney was a devotee of the *Atlantic*" (*HP* 197). But more than chance accounts for her devotion, given that she came of age just outside Boston during the *Atlantic*'s halcyon years. In a 1914 letter to Stewart, Coney referred to the magazine as "our first love" (quoted in *AWH* 34), and it may have mapped a route to greater cultural literacy and higher class standing for not only her protégée but also herself: during years of poverty and uncertain prospects in her home state, and again while navigating the economic and social changes wrought by her late-life move to Colorado. (In a 1985 interview with Bloomfield, Clyde Stewart Jr. refreshingly inverted the usual scenario in stating, "Mother read the *Atlantic,* and no doubt Mrs. Coney did, too.")[20] Coney has her own history of dependency, struggle, and aspiration—and of western relocation and renewal—that shares qualities with Stewart's. Indeed, by some measures, she took the longer journey. While to Stewart she appeared as the embodiment of an eastern bourgeois—which she succinctly expressed in deeming her "so very 'Bostony'" (quoted in *AWH* 38)—Coney was no Brahmin. As a widow with two young daughters, she had once supported her family with factory outwork as a shoe stitcher, a trade she had learned from her cordwainer husband.

"Mrs. Coney" was born Sarah Juliet Graves to Ebenezer and Hannah Moor Campbell Graves on March 9, 1837. She passed her first fifty years within twenty miles of her birthplace: on the family farm in North Reading, Massachusetts, and with her husband, Edwin Sanborn Coney, in the same town; once widowed, with Edwin's relatives in Wakefield (formerly South Reading); and then in Boston with her married daughter's young family, the Allens. The Graveses, Coneys, and Allens had lived in Reading and nearby Lynnfield for generations, a network of kin that for density and rootedness rivaled that of the Sedgwicks to the west of them. As farmers, artisans, and merchants, however, they did not have the Sedgwicks' elite status—no "family manse" for them.[21]

Coney signed her 1914 letter to Stewart "J. S. Coney." In public records, her name is variously rendered S. J., Sarah J., Sarah Juliet, Sarah Juliette, Juliette S., Juliett S., Juliet S., and Juliet. I would like to think this inconsistency reflects not only the caprice of census takers but also a spirit of active self-fashioning. A darker source may be the fate of the first Sarah Juliet Graves, the older half-sister who had died at age three, perhaps inhibiting strong feelings of attachment to the name.[22] Graves's first wife, Abigail Flint, predeceased their child. One of the district's more prosperous farmers, Graves married Campbell in 1836.[23] J. S. was the eldest of their six children to survive infancy, all girls except for Ebenezer Francis (he who later sent Stewart's young daughter a necklace [*LWH* 132]). Two of J. S.'s sisters became teachers and another, Mary Hannah, was a preacher.[24]

J. S. was an outlier among her sisters, in that she left her natal household at twenty-one to marry Edwin. Their daughters, Florence Edna and Clara Juliet, were born the two succeeding years. Edwin Coney had worked as a shoemaker with his father, Jeremiah, in Lynnfield,[25] long the nation's shoe capital, just as the industry was making the transition to specialized labor that anticipated the move from home shops to factories. While Edwin's family had fewer assets than J. S.'s, his ability to establish a household at the age of twenty-four indicates relative means. On his wedding day, he identified himself as a "shoe manufacturer" as opposed to the more usual "shoemaker," intimating at least the aspiration of business on a larger scale.[26]

The enterprise ceased when he enlisted in the Massachusetts Heavy Artillery in 1862. He was on duty at Fort Warren, Boston Harbor, until his discharge for tuberculosis in April 1865, and he died of the disease the following year.[27] His widow and children then joined the household of his younger sister Frances Octavia and her grocer husband, John H. Perkins. It is likely that the trio lived there for more than a decade, up until Florence's marriage in 1879. The extended household also included Frances and Edwin's orphaned cousin, Pamelia Coney, and two boarders. One of the boarders was a carpenter, and the other was "In the Rattan Works," the wicker furniture company so vital to South Reading that the town was renamed for its founder, Cyrus Wakefield. In 1870 Florence and Clara were in school, Pamelia was a "Domestic Servant," and Coney was a "Shoe Stitcher."[28]

Herself a farm girl, J. S. would have learned the skill of shoe stitching, always done by women, through working with her husband in the family business. Men cut the leather in the shop, and women stitched the uppers at home.[29] However, after Edwin died she did not contribute to a family enterprise. Instead, she did outwork for one or more of the city's many factories, supplementing the federal pension she received as a soldier's widow.[30] "Outwork was synonymous with women's work," Christine Stansell comments in her study of the era's working women, and Coney's income was likely sporadic and low.[31] Most of the workers in her neighborhood were employed in the industry, with trades that included "Shoemaker," "Shoe dealer," "Shoe Cutter," and "Overseer in Shoe Shop."[32]

Unlike many young women in Wakefield, Florence and Clara did not go into the factories. Instead, they got teaching degrees from the Salem Normal School, class of 1878.[33] (Although J. S. herself is widely reported to have been a schoolteacher, there is no evidence of her having any teacher training or employment.)[34] The degrees mark a turning point in this small family's class status. There is a telling difference between the fate of cousin Pamelia, who also lost her father in the war and also entered the Perkins household, and that of the sisters. Pamelia experienced a downward class trajectory. Her father, too, had been a shoemaker, but at eighteen she was working as a servant, and ten years later sees her living with her uncle Jeremiah Coney in the capacity of housekeeper.[35] Florence and Clara, in contrast, embarked on lifelong careers. Their teaching jobs were likely a key factor in Stewart's perception of the Coney family as belonging to a different social order than her own. While it is not clear how much she knew about J. S.'s past, what we do know is that she viewed her as the personification of genteel womanhood.

By 1880 Coney's situation looked more comfortable, although no less dependent. She and Clara lived in Boston with Florence and her husband, Frank H. Allen, a shoemaker turned grocer.[36] The couple had two children, Ethelind Florence and Maynard Coney. And at last, we reach Arapahoe County, Colorado, where the Allens moved after Maynard's birth and where Stewart and J. S. eventually met. Colorado had been granted statehood in 1876, with Denver the new capital, and its population and economy were booming thanks to new rail connections and a silver strike.

Allen became a "ranchman," making for a trajectory from shoemaking to shopkeeping to farming.[37] However, he died in 1889, widowing Florence at the exact same age as her mother, twenty-nine.[38] Although we do not know just when (especially since the pertinent 1890 records in both Massachusetts and Colorado were lost to fire), we can surmise that J. S. and Clara moved to Denver to join Florence soon afterward, freeing her to begin work in the city's school district. In 1900 J. S. is head of household in Denver, living with her daughters and grandchildren.[39] Later Clara, too, established herself as a teacher in Denver, although sometime prior to 1902 she returned to her natal Reading and Wakefield and worked in their public schools.[40] It may have been Clara who developed the connections to approach Sedgwick, not, as usually reported, her mother: even overlooking their disparate social status, J. S. had left Massachusetts when Sedgwick was scarcely out of short pants.

Stewart made a series of moves over the course of fifteen years, from her Oklahoma birthplace to different locations within the territory, to Colorado, and finally to Wyoming, and thereafter she moved seasonally between Burntfork and Boulder. Coney, in contrast, went from Boston to Denver in one go. The transition must have been wrenching. This woman who had lived her entire life in one district, surrounded by siblings, uncles, aunts, and cousins in the midst of other equally rooted families, came two thousand miles to a new state where she knew no more than three people—two of them, children. The continuity of her *Atlantic* subscription surely helped ease her passage.

Stewart began work in Coney's home in 1907, receiving two dollars for a seven-day week.[41] These conditions are often cited as proof of exploitation. I wonder, though, whether the relationship was more informal and less contractual than these numbers make it appear, with Coney giving Stewart financial assistance in exchange for a contribution of labor. Although his stories about *Atlantic* contributors, as we know, are not wholly trustworthy, Sedgwick intimates that theirs was not a typical arrangement: "In instant need of support, she had turned laundress to a kind mistress, one Mrs. Coney of Denver. This helped her over the blank wall right ahead" (*HP* 198). We can go further to dislodge the conceptual frame of mistress-servant altogether to view Coney and Stewart as two marginal single women eking out frugal lives in the city, who for a time, to their mutual benefit, shared a household—and it was Stewart who did the laundry, as she jokingly reminded her friend in later letters. If Coney was not the schoolteacher she is always said to be, then perhaps Stewart was no servant, either.[42]

Regardless of the nature of their association, there is no evidence to support the usual claims about Coney's affluence. She did factory piecework in Wakefield, following which she has no record of paid employment. She was unlikely to have had much of an inheritance, given that at his death decades earlier, her father's potential heirs included his much younger widow, five unmarried daughters, and a son. Her war-widow benefits were meager, as they were calculated at a percentage of the wages that an unskilled laborer could earn.[43] (Edwin Coney's younger brother, Charles W. H. Coney, was likewise a Union solider; he survived the war but lost an arm. During the same period in which Coney employed Stewart, his widow received a $12 monthly pension.)[44] Another likely marker of economic instability, Coney's household shifted form and location more than once in the years just before and after her time with Stewart.[45] She lived in a boardinghouse by the time she prepared the letters for publication, and Stewart's insistence that she share in her first $500 *Atlantic* payment may have been motivated as much by an awareness of her financial need as by a conception of her as partner to the enterprise. According to Jerrine Rupert Wire (her married name), after first demurring Coney accepted the money from her mother.[46] Such a choice obliterates the favored scenario of a "wealthy lady" looking to aid her former maid by boosting her into print. Blurring the lines between friendship, patronage, and collaboration, the relationships that faraway women formed in the course of authorship show that power and influence flowed both ways.

The sole extant letter we have from Coney to Stewart was written just prior to the close of the first *Atlantic* serial, March 10, 1914. Coney addresses her as "Dear, dear Mrs. Stewart," thanks her for passing on her *Atlantic* fan mail, and continues, "I am proud of my acquaintance with you inasmuch as I know what a level head you have and good sense so that you wont let whatever any body and every body may say turn it a bit from your husband children or home—or *me*. Dont [sic] you think I am conceited?" The statement opens on a rather stuffy and prescriptive note, urging Stewart to keep her priorities straight, home and family first. However, it then turns affectionately playful, as Coney stages her own "conceit," the same vice against which she cautions Stewart. Moreover, while she may not appear to rank her continued literary efforts high, in fact she does: urging her not to "turn . . . from . . . *me*" constitutes urging her to write to her, which is not only the primary means by which Stewart focuses on her friend but also her primary authorial mode. Stewart's comments in *Letters of a Woman Homesteader* can lead one to view Coney as at once exacting and forlorn, poised to pounce on infelicities in the very letters that served as her lifeline. Yet in her own letter, Coney appears as neither, positing a state of exact requital: "I am hoping for a letter from you soon for I am sure I look for yours as eagerly as you do for mine" (quoted in *AWH* 34).

While Stewart references several well-known authors, Coney too was a literary influence, in that her succession of letters helped determine how Stewart shaped her own. Her relationship with Coney was as much that of reader as writer. "Every time I get a new letter from you I get a new inspiration" (*LWH* 184), she declares. Without her side of the correspondence, we must listen for echoes of Coney in Stewart's text. We know at least that she asked many questions, praised and rebuked, and wrote more frequently than Stewart could. And we know, of course, that she valued Stewart's letters enough to save them, having a "bundle" on hand for Sedgwick's inspection.[47]

As others have noted, *Letters of a Woman Homesteader* both participates in frontier mythologies with its version of the self-made American and revises them by spotlighting women's experience and community. The epistolary mode reinforces this emphasis, attesting to not solitary heroic pursuit but women's mutual support. Stewart's feelings for Coney are a complex brew of affection, gratitude, deference, and defensive pride. The letters include many fond avowals, as when she imagines receiving Coney in her home: "I feel just like visiting to-night, so I am going to 'play like' you have come. It is so good to have you to chat with. Please be seated in this low rocker" (*LWH* 137). Yet they also reveal her view of Coney as a judge, in a position to evaluate both her venture and her character. Stewart looked to show Coney that she was no longer a wageworker but rather an independent landowner, even as she continued to see in her a model for the feminine conduct to which she aspired—kind, meticulous, righteous, and modest—mapping a route to a more desirable class location. Further complicating the relationship, she was the grateful recipient of many gifts from Denver, including household items, used clothing, and reading material. Maintaining her correspondence with Coney was crucial to her family's comfort, if not their survival. (Suggesting by way of contrast her own social tactics, Stewart once wrote despairingly of Jerrine that her friendships were so disinterested she would never advance in life.)[48] And not least, Coney connected her to a public readership.

In reminiscing about Coney, Stewart disclosed both the intensity of the relationship and its perceived conditions: "I don't think it was possible for any one to know her and not long for her friendship and wish to be worthy of it. I feel her influence after all these years. Many times I do something a little better because I know she would have done it better, a little better work at darning or mending, a little more careful in cleaning, a little more kind—a little less hasty in criticism" (*AWH* 152). "She meant more to me than any one else" (*AWH* 162), she stated a full fifteen years after her death. It is easy to read *Letters of a Woman Homesteader* for the tensions that permeated an asymmetrically structured friendship and as a reckoning of its costs and benefits. But disrupting any facile conclusions are Stewart's avowals of the powerful love she felt for the woman she called "My Beloved." Their emotional bond was more profound than any pragmatic calculations, even though these calculations were certainly present.

Mary Louise Kete's *Sentimental Collaborations: Mourning and Middle-Class Identity in Nineteenth-Century America* identifies writing, reading, and, most especially, exchanging sentimental texts as "generated by the need to counteract—to nullify—the effect of loss." The study's cornerstone is its analysis of "Harriet Gould's Book," a handmade album of elegies for lost children authored by Gould and her relatives in their rural Vermont community. Kete's argument about the function of such memorial projects accords with Decker's observation that absence is the abiding subject of nineteenth-century American epistolarity, scored by expressions "of separation, loneliness, and apprehension that death will intervene before the parties can reunite."[49]

It is certainly accurate to identify Stewart and Coney's correspondence as an epistolary version of "sentimental collaboration": a joint literary project, threaded with declarations of love, that worked to assuage painful separation. Yet when they first began writing each other, they had yet to have formed a close relationship for the letters to preserve. Rather, over the years the letters themselves created it. Stewart and Coney's original social connection little resembles that of Harriet Gould's intimate group, those Vermont villagers with their shared local knowledge and kin networks. Stewart was only in Denver for about two years, and she held other jobs in the city before and possibly after her time with Coney. Had she not moved away, their respective positions may well have precluded their eventual attachment. While it may be amusing to write, "I am going to make you a cup of tea and wonder if you will see anything familiar about the teapot. You should, I think, for it is another of your many gifts to me" (*LWH* 141–42), such a display was perhaps awkward in the event.

Conjecture about tea parties aside, more revealing is the lack of intimacy evident in Stewart's decision not to invite Coney into her mourning for her infant son. Somewhat more than a year into their correspondence, Stewart alludes to the death of a child without identifying it as her own, in a letter that with fuller knowledge reads as a text bursting at its seams as her careful management of her epistolary project starts to unravel. The letter begins with an extended, comically pathetic account of her young neighbor Cora Belle and the girl's trials with her hapless grandparents, culminating with a party at Stewart's home. The "hee-haw, hee-haw" of Cora Belle's donkey as she drives away, the rags on her cart "playfully fluttering," is immediately followed by, "I have been a very busy woman since I began this letter to you several days ago. A dear little child has joined the angels. I dressed him and helped to make his casket" (*LWH* 98). Stewart had written herself into a corner. She was unable to tell Coney she had lost a child, much as she might have wished to, because she had disclosed only two months earlier that she had married Clyde, and she had yet to tell her about their son.

Shortly after moving to Wyoming, she gave Coney a detailed account of filing on land adjacent to Clyde's but did not reveal their new relationship until months later. In an advance letter, she had warned Coney she had something important to tell her and asked her to promise beforehand to forgive a "deceitful" omission: "I know that is unfair, but it is the only way I can see out of a difficulty that my foolish reticence has led me into" (*LWH* 79). Coney did not reply, which Stewart surely must have found discomfiting. Instead, she only sent a card—two months later—that made no reference to her request. Impelled by the mute card, Stewart finally wrote, "I reckon I had better confess and get it done with. The thing I have done is to marry Mr. Stewart. It was such an inconsistent thing to do that I was ashamed to tell you" (*LWH* 79–80).

Her concern about appearing "inconsistent" references her known investment in women's independence, and in a much later letter, she explained she had feared Coney would judge her to be "a Becky Sharp of a person" (*LWH* 184). This statement has been much quoted. However, in the course of the revelation itself, she identifies another, less predictable, concern: "And, too, I was afraid you would think I didn't need your friendship and might desert me. Another of my friends thinks that way" (*LWH* 80). Experience has taught her that marriage can trigger abandonment, due to a prevailing belief that husbands are to displace women friends. Her marriage, moreover, took place at that crisis point in a correspondence, just after separation when it is unclear if and how relations can be maintained from afar. She closes the letter, "Your old friend with a new name." Her deferral of the important news, Lamont argues, is an attempt to "locate a space for agency within marriage,"[50] and the correspondence as a whole can be understood likewise. Privileging a relationship with another woman through dedicated correspondence keeps her marital status from becoming the defining fact of her identity.

In *Letters of a Woman Homesteader*, Stewart follows through on this impulse to dislodge marriage's primacy, by both recording small acts of rebellion against Clyde and, more important, curtailing the narrative attention she accords him. Nevertheless, the text is internally conflicted about the status of marriage, in that even as the author's marriage is pushed to its margins, those of other people are made a central concern. The subject of matrimony crops up at every turn, whether in respect to polygamous Mormon marriages, comic partnerships, thwarted unions, or Stewart's matchmaking success.

Having none other than Coney as her first reader, I would submit, helped contain this conservative impulse and stimulate other stories. While Stewart's efforts to appease her made for some notable silences, Coney was as much muse as censor. Herself exemplifying female self-reliance, she was receptive to Stewart's profiling of women's achievement, and perhaps especially sympathetic toward tales of their relocation, transformation, and class advancement. Due to her emphasis on female autonomy, Stewart has been viewed as an honorary single woman. Yet the real single woman was, of course, her older friend. Coney had long operated outside of the world of heterosexual relations in which Stewart was immersed. She was widowed at the age of twenty-nine. She lived with her daughter Florence, a teacher, who was also widowed at twenty-nine. Her other daughter, Clara, also a teacher, never married. Three of her four sisters remained single, too.[51]

The predominance of single women among the Graveses and Coneys reflects regional patterns along with individual circumstance and choice. New England had always had the nation's highest percentage of unmarried women, due to the greater educational and employment opportunities women enjoyed. Moreover, war and western migration subsequently evacuated the region of young men, creating a drastic gender imbalance.[52] The New England "spinster"—who eventually developed into the American "New Woman"—was both a demographic actuality and a pronounced cultural presence. She had distinct private and public roles, a measure of social acceptance, and, most important, a range of ways to support herself.

The gender ratio was the inverse in the frontier West. Consequently, women could marry and remarry at younger ages and in higher percentages, even as their limited employment options made them more dependent on the institution.[53] Just as the marital choices of Coney's family manifest the East, so do those of Stewart's family manifest the West. Elinore's widowed mother married her first husband's brother. Her own second marriage followed closely on her first, and Clyde may have used his need for a housekeeper as a pretext to search for a wife (*AWH* 11).

Coney and her daughters exported westward a northeastern equanimity about life without men. From 1889 onward, J. S., Florence, and Clara were all single in Denver. Despite the cultural expectations and favorable demographics that encouraged marriage in the West, none of them found it imperative. Yet their lives also reflect the potential costs of this choice, reminding us why Stewart made a different one. As a widow, Coney experienced dependency and a narrowed sphere, living in the Massachusetts homes of her brother-in-law and son-in-law. She was head of her three-generation household in Denver, but in the last years of her life occupied a single room in a boardinghouse. Five years after her death, Florence and Clara, too, were boarding in Denver—the former in a large establishment that lodged twenty-five men and women from all over the country.[54] Apparently, neither was in a position to establish a home of her own, even though Clara was by then a school principal and Florence taught in the same city.[55]

I propose that we refine the usual regional story that is told about *Letters of a Woman Homesteader*. Indisputably, Stewart's frontier location fostered her championing of intrepid, independent women. However, so too did Coney's New England origins, which are evinced as much by her marital status as by any code of manners. Wyoming and Massachusetts share credit for the "Woman Homesteader."

Stewart's deferred revelation of her marriage and the apology that ensued, as we have seen, is the interpretive crux of her text, in respect to both the construction of her homesteader identity and the management of her relationship with Coney. This is flanked by a host of other, more minor, apologies, many so perfunctory as to seem mere epistolary convention, but occurring at such frequency as to take on critical weight. Decker notes that an extended correspondence is characterized by "a seeking of assurances that the two correspondents agree on the matter of what constitutes mutually perpetuating discourse," and Stewart beseeches such assurance at every turn.[56] While she appears remarkably confident as an American regionalist, inserting herself within a western literary tradition through using James Fenimore Cooper's, Mark Twain's, and Jack London's accounts of frontier experiences as touchstones for her own, she is far less so as a private correspondent. Her protestations of deficient skill and judgment are relentless.

That her letters are so long makes her fear she is tedious, demanding, and tactless. At the same time, she is concerned that not writing Coney often enough signals indifference and neglect. She represents her missives as at once daunting and craved, burden and boon: "I don't want you to think for one moment that you are bothering me when I write you. It is a real pleasure to do so. You're always so good to let me tell you everything. I am only afraid of trying your patience too far" (*LWH* 192). "Please don't entirely forget me," she implores. "Your letters mean so much to me and I will try to answer more promptly" (*LWH* 22). Writing is a fulfilling but taxing affair that is further impeded by her chronic eye troubles, ranch work and housework, and uncertain health. "At last I can write you as I want to" (*LWH* 180) is a persistent refrain. "I am really ashamed of the way I have treated you, but I know you will forgive me. I am not strong yet, and my eyes are still bothering me, but I hope to be all right soon now, and I promise you a better letter next time" (*LWH* 132). Her emphasis on the ephemerality of viable writing conditions underscores the labor that her dexterous letters demanded. The domestic work she once did for Coney is succeeded by a different kind of work—gladly undertaken, but work nonetheless.

Coney's influence permeated her domestic practice, social interactions, and, not least, self-expression. The first ready conclusion, as noted, is that she is responsible for certain silences in *Letters of a Woman Homesteader*, especially in respect to Stewart's marriage. Suggesting how she had internalized Coney as a censor, Stewart confided, "Often when a thoughtless remark almost escapes me I think, 'I wouldn't say that in *her* presence,' many many times that happens" (*AWH* 152). A letter to a Massachusetts acquaintance of Clara's, a Mr. Zaiss, gives an actual example of the material she took care to keep from her friend. Noting "the rough way Western women talk," she remarks, "I have often wondered what my beloved Mrs. Coney would have thought if she could have heard" (quoted in *AWH* 171). While she "wondered" about her response, the risk was too great to find out.

Despite the greater liberties she took with Zaiss, she was anxious about his sensibilities, too. She once informed him, "Well, after I wrote you about the horse hunt and received no reply I thought I must have outraged your sense of decency. When the lovely card came I thought a letter would come telling me how terribly my escapade seemed to civilized persons." She continued, "If I have offended I am sincerely sorry and beg your pardon, if I ever offend it will be unintentional. Please take my crudities that way" (quoted in *AWH* 162). As a writer, Stewart inhabited an uneasy middle ground. She distinguished herself both from "Western women" with their "rough way" of expression and from

"civilized persons" offended by "crudities"—the very group most dis-
posed to read about frontier life. The source of her discursive struggle
was her conviction that to protect readerly sensibility and writerly cred-
ibility alike, harsh conditions must not be fully disclosed. In discussing a
later project, a memoir, she maintained that her "white childhood in the
Indian Territory" defied representation: "I very much doubt that I can
do it. For such a recital should be the truth and no one would believe the
actual truth of my own childhood fifty years ago." "I wonder what I *can*
write of that won't be shocking" (quoted in *AWH* 193).

Yet elsewhere, Stewart presents "shocking" as exactly her aim, and she
implies, moreover, that the fount of her narrative vitality is her difference from the "cultured people" who read her letters—her possession of
"absolutely no manners" (quoted in *AWH* 119). In recounting the genesis
of *Letters of a Woman Homesteader,* she explained that Coney was "so very
'Bostony' that I used to try to shock her mildly and at the same time give
her as nearly as I could a true picture of the West. She was so very conventional that some one who was not so had the best chance of being
enteresting [*sic*] and entertaining" (quoted in *AWH* 38–39). Her challenge
is to bring about that contradiction in terms, to "shock mildly." As her
reader, Coney posed distinct narrative opportunities and narrative problems. While she was so innocent as to be easily impressed, Stewart must
discern how to convey a "true picture" of her life without upsetting her.
The following expresses a real crisis of representation: "I was dreadfully
afraid that my last letter was too much for you and now I feel plumb
guilty. I really don't know how to write you, for I have to write so much
to say so little, and now that my last letter made you sick I almost wish
so many things didn't happen to me, for I always want to tell you. Many
things have happened since I last wrote" (*LWH* 45). To enlighten her is
potentially "too much for her." If the woman she sought to cheer was
refined and fastidious, then how could she represent frontier life, which
was otherwise? And if Coney modeled womanly decorum, then how
could she tell stories starring herself? "From something you wrote I think
I must have written boastingly to you at some time. I have certainly not
intended to, and you must please forgive me and remember how ignorant I am and how hard it is for me to express myself properly," Stewart insists. "If you only knew how far short I fall of my own hopes you
would know I could *never* boast." This defense is followed by a closing
she occasionally employs, "Your ex-washlady" (*LWH* 63). The sign-off

serves as a reminder of her former lower status, wryly reinforcing her plea to "remember how ignorant I am." But it also emphasizes that their relationship has changed, perhaps hinting, too, that Coney no longer has the same right to criticize her.

"If you only knew" is a phrase Stewart repeats, suggesting the gulf she perceives between Coney's experience and her own. For her part, Coney worked to more closely align their home life and cultural outlook by means of regular gifts. The accoutrements of middle-class domesticity, the largely secondhand items she sent her included books, magazines, pictures, Christmas ornaments, a tablecloth, a hassock, and the aforementioned teapot. In describing her sitting room, Stewart remarks, "I am sure this room must look familiar to you, for there is so much in it that was once yours" (*LWH* 137). The comfort the gifts provide is tempered by the anxiety they induce, a reminder at every turn of their unequal positions. Coney once gave Stewart housekeeping directives; now she more indirectly shapes her domestic practice through the objects she sends, a custom that, moreover, drives home the disparity of their means. "I wish I could do nice things for you, but all I can do is to love you" (*LWH* 142), Stewart states in thanking her for one of them, allaying her unease about the lack of reciprocity with one of her characteristic declarations of affection. And throughout the book, she does the same by underscoring her own benevolence, her ability to give as well as receive charitably as she dispenses succor and aid to struggling neighbors. Her account of a holiday party she arranged for two destitute Mormon families shows her literally passing on one of her friend's presents: "Your largest bell, dear Mrs. Coney, dangled from the topmost branch" (*LWH* 208).

Yet the primary restitution is, of course, the letters themselves, by means of which Stewart transmits the "big, clean, beautiful outdoors" (*LWH* 220) to her urban friend. Of a higher order altogether than teapots, they require thought, labor, creativity, and time—as she so frequently points out. The role that she asks Coney, her reader, to play is that of one psychically and even physically in dire need of what she can offer, a near-formulaic expression of the purported function of regional literature. For all her self-deprecation and deference, she profoundly questions Coney's choices and lifestyle, her "so very conventional" ways. Her own desire to travel and explore, to work outdoors, to meet strangers (including men), to range socially and literally beyond home and family—all are at odds with the conventionally gendered behavior Coney modeled.

The driving conviction of Stewart's writing project is that dwelling in the open spaces of the West amid the "free, ready sympathy and hospitality of these frontier people" (*LWH* 221) is superior to city life. A rather aggressive joke contrasts the invigorating hardship of camping out with her past duties "down in Denver . . . at Mrs. Coney's, digging with a skewer into the corners seeking dirt which might be there, yea, even eating codfish" (*LWH* 11). Stewart died of a stroke at fifty-seven, while the frailer woman she sought to brace lived into her seventies. Yet despite the toll her strenuous life exacted, she always presented it as therapeutic. "I am so afraid that you will get an overdose of culture from your visit to the Hub," she wrote Coney prior to a trip she took to Boston, "and am sending you an antidote of our sage, sand, and sunshine" (*LWH* 157). Like the magazine that published her, Stewart proposes counterbalancing the cultural bounty of New England with offerings from other, more rugged, U.S. regions.

Through such references, *Letters of a Woman Homesteader* keeps in play not only its partners' different places of residence—the frontier and the urban West—but also their different places of origin, the South and New England. Foregrounding her identity as a southerner also creates opportunities for Stewart to express racial views. Her grandmother had owned slaves, who allegedly followed her to Oklahoma after emancipation, and she told fond stories about the older woman's paternalism, of the order of indulging routine pilfering from her smokehouse.[57] Knowing this family lore helps us descry textual signs that Stewart viewed her personal trajectory through a racial lens. Her recourse to the "ex-washlady" valediction, for example, points to the figurative role of African American women's wage labor in her formulation of white women's homesteading. Its first showing comes right after she relays the tribute, predicated on a racial evaluation, she received from a homesick southerner: "'Why, I would jist as soon talk to you as to a nigger. Yes'm, I would. It has been almost as good as talking to old Aunt Dilsey.'" "If a Yankee had said the same to me," Stewart continues, "I would have demanded instant apology, but I know how the Southern heart longs for the dear, kindly old 'niggers,' so I came on homeward, thankful for the first time that I can't talk correctly" (*LWH* 44). Laundry was an occupation closely associated with African American women, especially in the South, and Stewart presents it as the debased alternative to homesteading, insisting, "It really requires less strength and labor to raise plenty to satisfy a large family than it does to go out to wash" (*LWH* 215). Confirming as racially inspired her choice of laundry to represent unrewarding work in *Letters of a Woman Homesteader,* one of her earliest stories featured an African American protagonist, "Aunty Smith," whose circumstances resembled Stewart's own at the time: a poor southerner who works as a laundress, lives in a Denver apartment, and craves an outing (*AWH* 8–9).

In the book, Stewart registers actual black presence with the comment, "I even enjoyed looking at the Negro porter, although I suspect he expected to be called Mister" (*LWH* 268), and she recounts comforting a homesick Alabaman—recovering from childbirth and ruing her marriage to a Mormon—with homemade chocolates shaped as dark "babies." The grotesque gift, which delights its recipient, symbolically reincorporates the young wife within a community of southern women. At such moments, Stewart recruits the whiteness she shared with Coney to strengthen a social bond across a geographical and class divide. For all her anxiety about offending, she did not think to suppress her racial epithets. Coney, for her part, rather than excise them from the letter transcriptions, passed them on to Sedgwick, who in turn saw fit to purvey them to a national readership. The nature of Coney's racial outlook is unknown, but private and public statements reveal Sedgwick's to be virulent. That the *Atlantic* had a reputation for championing abolition and other liberal causes does not mean that none of its editors, contributors, and readers were invested in racial hierarchies.

Less contentious is Stewart's use of her daughter to argue for frontier opportunity. Jerrine appears in the book not only as budding homesteader—working by her mother's side—but also as apprentice writer, sharing in her literary labors. Stewart promises Coney that they will both write soon, signs a letter "Jerrine and her Mama," and in another juxtaposes their efforts: "Jerrine writes a little every day to you. I have been preparing a set of indoor outings for invalids" (*LWH* 192, 132, 228). Sedgwick endorsed this emphasis by including one of Jerrine's letters to Coney in the *Atlantic* serial, and then again in *Letters of a Woman Homesteader,* anticipating his publication of Opal Whiteley's child diary six years later. The three-paragraph letter is studded with orthographic errors en route to its valediction, "very speakfully, Jerrine" (*LWH* 219).

The choice to feature Jerrine in her serial can be read as denying Stewart literary accomplishment, proof that the sheer fact of Wyoming residence can usher anyone into authorship. (Imagine a like appearance by Edith Wharton's daughter or Henry James's son, had either child existed.) Yet while placing Jerrine's work alongside that of her mother may implicate the latter as equally untutored and naive, it supports the *Atlantic*'s proposal that the relational premise of Stewart's text matters as much as the events it recounts.

Jerrine begins by thanking Coney for her gift of *Black Beauty*. A fictional autobiography written by an invalid with her mother's aid, this powerful lesson in empathy well served Coney's schooling of mother and daughter in a text-based culture of sentiment. After using the book to assess her neighbor's cruelty to his horse, Jerrine narrates the week's main event: "Our Clyde is still away. We were going to visit Stella. Mama was driving, the horses raned away. We goed very fast as the wind. I almost fall out Mama hanged on to the lines. if she let go we may all be kill. At last she raned them into a fence. they stop and a man ran to help so we are well but mama hands and arms are still so sore she cant write you yet." Here we see Stewart's formula in miniature: a gender- and class-loaded textual exchange, a tale about western adventure that exacts a toll from one's ability to write, and finally an adroit expression of affection: "I thank you for my good little book, and I love you for it too" (*LWH* 219). We might note that Stewart's three sons do not partake of Coney's bounty. While they were too young to write, it is arresting that Stewart does not mention—not once—Coney sending them anything. Her offerings were confined to mother and daughter, complementing the narrative focus of Stewart's letters, in which the boys scarcely figure. N. C. Wyeth's cover illustration for the original edition of *Letters of a Woman Homesteader* captures this condition by simply leaving all the male Stewarts out.

But of course: not everyone can be included in every exchange, portrait, or history. Thus, in the previous pages I found no place to represent Georgia Waggoner and her contributions to Stewart's book. Waggoner lived across the hall from Coney in the same boardinghouse in Denver, and it was she who typed Stewart's letters at Coney's behest. Houghton Mifflin believed Coney edited out personal references from the letters before submitting them to the *Atlantic*, and perhaps Waggoner assisted her.[58] That she was living alone in the city and could type points to a modern young woman who may have had an office job, but all that is definitively known about her is that she walked with difficulty and lost her mother shortly after Stewart left Denver, prompting an effusive letter of condolence from Burntfork. If Coney is overlooked in Stewart scholarship, then Waggoner has yet to be sighted. As much as I have endeavored to piece together the full story of this text, there is always more to tell, more participants to acknowledge.

Atlantic Legacy

The final chapter of *Letters of a Woman Homesteader*, "Success," is composed of a single letter that did not have a previous *Atlantic* showing. Its absence from the serial along with its retrospective outlook indicate it did not originate as an actual letter to Coney, or at the least was written after Stewart began working with Sedgwick. The possibility that Sedgwick commissioned the text lends new meaning to its opening, "I must write to you." It also inflects the statement that follows: "Now, this is the letter I have been wanting to write you for a long time, but could not because until now I had not actually proven all I wanted to prove" (279). We can posit an alternative explanation: Stewart had long wanted to enumerate her successes, but it is only now that she can, when the actual recipient of her letter is not the older friend wont to reprimand her for boasting.

Rather than "Success," the *Atlantic* serial ends with a January 1914 letter addressed to Sedgwick himself. Its inclusion displays a remarkable *Atlantic* willingness—all the assurances of "completely ingenuous" letters notwithstanding—to represent its contributor as engaged in contractual writing. Addressed to "Dear Mr. Editor" and closing with "Hoping I may not disappoint you," the letter responds to Sedgwick's request for new material. Stewart had been very sick, she explains. "That is why you have not heard from me, and as I could not send you the letters in time for continuation I thought you would not care for any more and I was mighty blue. I felt so unworthy and negligent to have let *such* an opportunity slip by." She goes on to describe the fan mail Sedgwick had taken special care to forward her:

> Indeed you are right about my getting letters and cards from many people on account of my Atlantic articles. It makes me wish I *could* deserve all the good things they say. One dear old lady eight-four years old wrote me that

she had always wanted to live the life I am living, but could not, and that the Letters satisfied her every wish. She said she had only to shut her eyes to see it all, to smell the pines and the sage. . . . I had a letter from a little crippled boy whose mother also wrote, both saying how the Letters had cheered them and eased the pain of the poor young flickering life. The mother said she wanted to thank one who had brought so much of the clean, bright outdoors into her helpless little son's life. I wrote her it was you who ought to be thanked and not I.[59]

By publishing this letter, Sedgwick foregrounded the difficulties that "faraway" authorship posed. Yet the letter also demonstrates how it fostered a socially and geographically expansive *Atlantic* community, one that included people very unlike the privileged readers usually associated with the magazine.

Modesty did not compel him to edit out Stewart's "it was you who ought to be thanked," and the following year he mused over his new role. "Many thanks for all your letters," he wrote her. "I seem to have become a silent partner in this pleasant correspondence" (quoted in *AWH* 32). The statement indicates that the scope of the letters Stewart wrote him was wider than just business, and his expression of satisfaction seems sincere, as he steps within her and Coney's affective circle amid its flow of texts, objects, and sentiment. Stewart sent him the resonantly local offering of a set of elk teeth, and he and Jerrine exchanged letters, cards, books, and gifts. For years he closed letters with "Give my love to Jerrine."[60]

In *The Happy Profession*, Sedgwick exclaims over the "delightful and persistent comradeship" he enjoyed with Stewart: "How warm is the friendship engendered by correspondence!" He goes on, however, to qualify its nature: "Distance . . . blunts the prickles of human contacts. Angularities lose their rough edges when writers are at a safe distance, and how refreshing to office existence are the fresh breezes blowing from brave and far-away acquaintances who seem poised on the very threshold of your friendship" (197). The classist implication is that friendship with such a woman is possible only from the "safe distance" that softens "rough edges." But we can look past this to recognize his fascination with how remote textual exchanges constructed relationships between social unequals. His comment could apply as much to Coney's interactions with Stewart as to his own, and it also, as we will see, speaks to those of Hilda Rose and Juanita Harrison with their sometime patrons, sometime friends.

Letters of a Woman Homesteader was quickly followed by *Letters on an Elk Hunt.* Sedgwick had commissioned the text, and Stewart joined the hunt with the express plan of using it as source material.[61] That she was newly writing to order prompted him to reassure her, "You need not try to write regularly, for I have an idea that you are one of the geniuses who write best when the spirit moves them; so when the blind madness of writing (as my old Latin book used to say) comes over you, give way to it whether an elk is sighted or not." While it is easy to read this statement as denying Stewart craft, in the context of the task at hand we can also recognize it as an attempt to allay new pressures. He continues, "I am announcing a new series by you just to show my confidence" (quoted in *AWH* 30). Stewart's success also encouraged him to feature Mildred Aldrich's letters from France (taken up in this book's epilogue), the correspondence of another kind of faraway woman. The serial prototype of Aldrich's *A Hilltop on the Marne* appeared in the *Atlantic* just after that of *Elk Hunt,* and Houghton Mifflin promoted the two books in the same advertisement.[62]

One of Stewart's *Elk Hunt* letters—addressed to Coney—begins, "It seems so odd to be writing you and getting no answers. . . . One of the main reasons I came on this hunt was to take the trip for *you*" (95). Another of the "main reasons" was her *Atlantic* contract. (Another, mayhap, was meat.) While ostensibly she gets no replies from Coney because she is on the road, the real cause is that she sends her dispatches directly to Sedgwick. The letters effect no interpersonal business with Coney, and they are not written in response to her own. The disquiet this pretense engendered must have been intensified by the knowledge that Coney was in a critical decline. She died just two months after the serial concluded, in September 1915. "Good-night, dear friend," Stewart closes another letter, repeating, "I am glad I can take this trip *for* you" (*LEH* 129).

Compared to *Woman Homesteader, Elk Hunt* reads quite bland. Far from making a case for the abilities of single women, it is saturated with tales of thwarted courtship, noble sacrifice, and glad reunion, and its controlling theme is that of making, losing, and longing for homes. Its history as a hastily written bespoke text, as opposed to a compilation of actual letters penned over months and years, undoubtedly contributes to the thinness and sentiment. But we can sharpen this to posit that absent the checking influence of Stewart's long-standing epistolary partner—a woman who exemplified female self-reliance—stories of idealized heterosexual relations ran rampant. The disparity between the two books confirms *Letters of a Woman Homesteader*'s dedication to women's agency as fostered not only by its frontier setting but also by its first reader. Indicating the crucial role Coney played in both her personal life and her literary expression, Stewart identified her loss as incapacitating: "I seem unable to write without an objective point and since my beloved has gone there seems no one to have good times for or to tell them to" (quoted in *AWH* 44). To use the formulation of the *Atlantic* contributor with which I opened this chapter, Coney had mastered the "rare art of good letter-receiving."

Stewart continued to correspond with Coney's elder daughter, Florence E. Allen, until her own death in 1933. Their relationship was rather formal, but deep. She annually marked Coney's birthday, the ninth of March, by sending Allen a "memorial letter" that included a freshly wrought Wyoming story; during a hard summer, a loan from Allen was so pivotal that she informed her, "Thanks to you, we now think that we will not go under" (quoted in *AWH* 149, 128). Kete characterizes "sentimental collaboration" as a "system of exchange in which evidence of one's affection is given in such a way as to elicit not only a return donation of affection but also a continued circulation of affection among an increasing circle of association," and Stewart's correspondence with Coney's family shows that her epistolary activity underwent just this manner of organic expansion.[63] The difference, however, is that the process was abruptly accelerated by the nation's premier literary organ. Stewart's relationship with Coney modeled for *Atlantic* readers the interaction they too might have with her, and she was inundated with fan mail.

Unimpressed by its caliber, she confided to Maria Wood, a new and favored correspondent from Missouri, "I get a great many letters from people who just write it seems, to be writing, so when there is a real chance to make a friend I am mighty glad to find the good grain among so much chaf [*sic*]" (quoted in *AWH* 22). Another sign of the interest he took in Stewart's social connections, Sedgwick had forwarded the card Wood sent him about her serial, having assured Wood, "Your postal . . . exactly expresses our feeling." Several years later, Stewart reminded her, "Mr. Sedgwick . . . said 'I think you will be glad to have this card,'" reminiscing as late as 1929, "Mr. Sedgwick . . . was as proud of that message as I am." In an interview with Bloomfield, Jerrine Wire succinctly formulated this social process, with Wood and many others: "They met through the book." Stewart's network swelled, as she corresponded with educated, affluent, and in some cases quite influential men and women, interacting with them on increasingly assured and familiar terms. A number of them traveled to Wyoming to stay at the ranch, like the two "high brows" from Pennsylvania (one a Wellesley and Johns Hopkins graduate) and another party who startled her with their modern habit of nude sunbathing. The most illustrious was Mary Antin, whose *Atlantic* serial just preceded Stewart's. Looking forward to a vacation in the West, Antin warned her that she and her daughter would arrive with their own saddles and "a mountain of hand luggage" and inquired whether she had riding horses. Stewart was anxious about the visit, not in respect to her equestrian resources but because she had found *The Promised Land* "dry as the dictionary."[64]

Closer to home, she also wrote to Grace Raymond Hebard, the prominent trustee, librarian, and historian at the University of Wyoming in Laramie who claimed her as the state's own.[65] Another important correspondent was Margaret G. Emerson in New York (remembered by Jerrine Wire as "a big shot"), who became a kind of epistolary surrogate for Coney, likewise sparking her frontier narrative. The services she rendered her, including reviewing a manuscript "to see if it merits publication," in Stewart's words, prefigure her later role as Rose's agent. Jerrine continued to facilitate such exchanges, receiving a silk Japanese scarf and a copy of *The Story of Opal* from Emerson and like sundry gifts from others. According to her mother, she made a "'remembry' quilt" out of scraps of material donated by Coney, Wood, and herself, literally patching their textile remnants into a sentimental artifact. "People used to beg me for letters," Jerrine recalled.[66]

Stewart passed on some of the gifts she received to those in greater need, and she sought to funnel aid directly to her community, as when she instructed a friend on how to buy a Christmas tree for the local school. She also became a confident purveyor of print culture in her own right. Even as her friends kept her in reading material, she herself copied poems, donated magazines, recommended books, and forwarded letters. "Have you ever read 'Death Comes for the Archbishop,' by Willa Cather?" she asked Zaiss. "Please let me know."[67] She even submitted some of their letters for the consideration of the *Atlantic*.[68] Despite her remote location and manual labor, the published author, after all, was she.

Stewart's emerging relations with women like Emerson and Wood both increased her proximity to the social and cultural milieus that attracted her and extended her writing career. She continued to route through distant friends that "provisional mode of self-inscription" she specialized in, to use Lamont's formulation, "located somewhere on the continuum between private experience and its public circulation."[69] "I wanted to send these letters on to you a month ago, but just monkeyed around and didn't," she explains to Wood in introducing one dispatch: "These letters are addressed to Mrs. Coney's sister. That was done to lend enterest [*sic*] if ever we should decide to send the letters to the publishers but that is a remote possibility so if my beloved friends can get any enjoyment out of them they shall as fast as I can find time and energy to get them in readable shape. It is little enough to do for you and all the rest who are so good to me" (quoted in *AWH* 69–70). Her comments suggest the blend of affection and pragmatism in which her ongoing correspondence was steeped. She presents the letters as redress to her generous friends, even as she calls attention to the "time and energy" they consume. She goes on to give some instructions: "If you think they are worth while will you, after you have read them, send them on to Miss Ida Howorth, 17 Grove St. West Point Miss. That is, send the last two letters. She has had the first one, keep *that* until some time when you write me and tuck it in if you will." (Howorth was an elementary school teacher and principal.) While letters are usually understood as a binary exchange between sender and recipient, Stewart's practice demonstrates how diffuse and multiply located the epistolary process can be. A wide-cast community of women helped her generate, circulate, and occasionally place her writing. *Atlantic* publication expanded her epistolary circle, which replenished her national profile in turn.

Her recourse to "Mrs. Coney's sister" is also revealing. As we know, Coney had not just one sister but four: Mary Hannah, Caroline Wellington, Hellen M., and Elizabeth J. While the odds are low that Stewart met any of them, her choice of fictional addressee points to the generational premise of her project. She had long written volubly to her grandmother, and from a biographical perspective, we can see this as having prepared her to correspond with Coney and other older women. More significant, it reflects her immersion in an older mode of textual production, which Coney redirected to a modern commercial forum. The letters both celebrate agrarian self-sufficiency in an age in which the nation was moving the opposite way and speak to an affective women's culture of a kind that flourished just as Coney—and her sisters—was coming of age in mid-nineteenth-century New England. Canvasing Coney for the names of "old persons . . . who would like letters such as I write," Stewart craved such readers not only because she believed they most needed her rejuvenating frontier tales but also because they were versed in the kind of literary exchanges she desired. "You will be doing me a favor to let me know," she insisted (*LWH* 78).[70]

Nine months after its Missouri debut, the set of letters to "Mrs. Coney's sister" was published in the *Atlantic* as "Snow: An Adventure of the Woman Homesteader." Stewart gleefully reported, "*Now* my Dear Miss Wood, See what you and my dear Mrs. Tidball have perpetrated upon the American Public" (quoted in *AWH* 77). Yet overall the title yield was slender, as her wondering comment about the missive that became "The Return of the Woman Homesteader" underscores: "And our letter was a success wasn't it? I don't see how it happens."[71] (And note the attribution of shared authorship.) While routing prospective publications through epistolary networks preserved her fresh style, the method was haphazard. Moreover, as Wire later observed, writing so prolifically to "hundreds" absorbed time she could have spent on more focused writing projects.[72] Aside from these two *Atlantic* pieces, Stewart's further publications were confined to several stories in *Youth's Companion* and another in a B. A. Botkin *Folk-Say* volume.

In 1926, with rather desperate humor she avowed, "If I knew of a single publisher who would accept a single thing from my pen I would seat myself and take my pen in my hand and drop him a few lines real quick!"[73] Nothing in the archive, however, indicates attempts to range outside of the narrow *Atlantic*-affiliated circle of Houghton Mifflin, *Youth's Companion, House Beautiful,* and the *Atlantic* itself. This despite the capaciousness of her periodical intake. "I have much to read," she once commented. "National Geographic, Atlantic, American, Women's Home Companion, Colliers, Author and Journals. A couple of newspapers, the Women's Journal."[74] Yet she locates their value in the escapism they offer as opposed to the professional opportunities they afford: "While I can think of the Mongolian method of capturing and breaking wild horses I can darn contentedly—mend heavy, sheepskin coats while I ponder catching tigers in Bengal." She positions herself as a reader of these magazines, not a prospective contributor to them.

Her attempts to continue publishing were "degrading and tearful and frustrating,"[75] to use Wire's adjectives, trials that Sedgwick references in a 1922 letter offering genial but vague encouragement:

> I am ever so glad to have your letter, for even though the news is not particularly cheerful, it shows that nothing particularly disastrous has happened, and that you are still in the land of the living.
>
> I have heard nothing of the manuscript of your novel since it was returned from Boston. If you have any luck with it in New York, be sure to let me know.
>
> Overland in a wagon across the Rockies sounds like a cheerful subject, and I should think there was a very good chance of such an article finding its way into the Atlantic.
>
> I had no idea that you were sending material to the House Beautiful, but I could have told you that there would be but little chance for it. You see, the House Beautiful is almost a technical magazine. It covers or is supposed to cover, the interests of a person building, improving or renovating a house. (Quoted in *AWH* 68)[76]

Given her ignorance, why not suggest some apt venues? The absence of the invaluable advice Sedgwick was so well placed to give makes his cheery "be sure to let me know"—lodged amid encouragement of a future project and solicitous inquiries—read as near cruel. (Contrast his reserve to Samuel McClure's practice of bankrolling young writers, including Frank Norris and Jack London, to free them to work on new projects.)[77] Typical of his involvement with faraway women, Sedgwick can appear more concerned with creating social contacts for Stewart than professional ones. Publishing her narrative in epistolary form, he showcased relationships across class and regional lines, but did little to support her efforts to enter U.S. literary networks.

Stewart's loyalty to the *Atlantic* hindered the development of her career. With scant knowledge of literary markets and her class insecurity driving a fear of a misstep, she believed that to publish anywhere less prestigious was in questionable taste. She even regretted placing the story with Botkin, whose important *Folk-Say* volumes feature writers of the stature of Sterling Brown, Langston Hughes, Louise Pound, Carl Sandburg, and Mari Sandoz. In an uncharacteristically sharp comment that was perhaps racially motivated, she stated, "When my copy reached me I regretted contributing, for to me 'Folk Says' [*sic*] is trash" (quoted in *AWH* 192).[78] In what would be her last *Atlantic* publication, "Snow," she rather ingratiatingly suggests that even the rats at an abandoned cabin "preferred the *Atlantic Monthly*."[79] The same class dynamics that made her defer to Coney made her exalt the *Atlantic*. Yet her preference was rooted in sentiment, too. Her association with the magazine had begun with writing acts she conceived as conferring personal affection, and the *Atlantic* seemed to offer a way to continue in that vein even as she marketed her work.[80]

In this she was abetted by Coney. In reassuring her it was acceptable to submit fiction to *Youth's Companion* (praising the "honorable way" it contacted her, "through the Atlantic"), she formulated Stewart's connection as emotional rather than professional: "But I don't believe you will ever give up our first love the Atlantic" (quoted in *AWH* 34). Asserting the primacy of affect, Coney ascribed her own position to her friend, not aspiring author but fond reader. Such devotion was ubiquitous among *Atlantic* subscribers. Yet while loyalty only enhanced the experience of readers, it could be detrimental to authors. Those who could struck a balance between the *Atlantic*'s prestige and the monetary incentives of less select forums. Charles Johanningsmeier has shown that even a writer as closely associated with the *Atlantic* as Sarah Orne Jewett published many stories in mass-market magazines, and she sold countless more to newspaper syndicates. Leading authors including Edith Wharton, Willa Cather, and Virginia Woolf bargained with Sedgwick for fees closer to those offered by "the popular magazines," as Cather put it in making a pitch, and when denied they went elsewhere.[81]

Like Coney, Sedgwick, too, endorsed Stewart's disinclination to assay a wider playing field. At the close of the first serial, he informed her, "You will unquestionably get invitations to write elsewhere, but it is my honest opinion that, for the present, it will be best for you not to scatter your seed, and, above all, not to cheapen your material by writing too much" (quoted in *AWH* 207). That he found it necessary to stress it was his "honest opinion" invites the opposite interpretation. Although his urge to keep her exclusive to the *Atlantic* is understandable, his counsel

about the "cheapening" effects of "writing too much" both is class
laden and reflects his view of her work as the product of sensibility, not
artistry. The most concrete professional advice he ever gave her was
to "lie fallow" until "all your vital forces reassert themselves."[82] Her
partners encouraged Stewart's inclination to spurn standard authorial
practice. Coney was a relic, and Sedgwick, sometimes, a doof.

Yet as always, backing off from too judgmental an evaluation of
Sedgwick affords a more illuminating view of faraway women and
their work. At its onset, he introduced Stewart's serial as a tale of class
uplift: "The writer of the following letters is a young woman who lost
her husband in a railroad accident and went to Denver to seek support
for herself and her two-year-old daughter, Jerrine. Turning her hand to
the nearest work, she went out by the day as housecleaner and laundress. Later, seeking to better herself, she accepted employment as a
housekeeper for a well-to-do Scotch Cattleman."[83] Here he seems to
reduce her experience to cliché. But Stewart's actual text, I would argue,
encouraged statements like this. Thus, we can read his words another
way: as those of a man inveigled by the "fiction of selfhood" Stewart
extended. Taking at face value her humorous references to her past
position as Coney's "washlady," he dubs her a "laundress." She plots
her advance toward the middle class, and so he describes her indebted
husband as "well-to-do." She seeks to cheer her friend by highlighting
her rare outdoor excursions, and consequently her letters are lauded
for their "exhilarated sense of holiday." In discussing *Letters of a Woman
Homesteader*, Sedgwick reproduces its primary colors—which compose
a romantic portrait of a valiant life—while missing the secondary hues
over which its author had less control: the defensive posturing and wry
asides, the allusions to financial anxiety and grinding labor, the sub-
text of exhaustion and sickness. Considered in this light, Sedgwick's
condescending remarks become a tribute to her skill. She strives to
make her artful letters look natural, to showcase the liberating aspects
of her life, to appear plucky and bold—and with all the weight of his
cultural authority, he corroborates her story. The problem was that he
became so invested in the iconic figure of "the Woman Homesteader
in the bleak Northwest" (*AH* xv) that he could not recognize her as a
struggling author, too.

Stewart's death at fifty-seven denied her further opportunities to redirect and develop her writing career. Her "story-letters," however, have

endured. *Letters of a Woman Homesteader* has undergone a remarkable revival, with reprints by major presses, the film adaptation, Bloomfield's biography, and incisive historical and literary studies.

The obscure fate of a contemporaneous frontier memoir, Margaret Lynn's *A Stepdaughter of the Prairie*, is an instructive counterpoint to Stewart's critical currency. Between 1911 and 1914, Sedgwick published a number of Lynn's meditative essays about her sheltered childhood in northwestern Missouri, subsequently expanded into a bound volume. Only sixteen pages separate Lynn and Stewart in the April 1914 *Atlantic*, and their books were published the same year. Like Stewart, Lynn stages the acquisition of a new regional identity. Avid girlhood reading had led her to internalize a cultural frame of reference that made her actual physical environment feel alien. "If Lowell and Whittier and Tennyson—most of all, Tennyson—had written of slough-grass and ground squirrels and barbed-wire fences," she states, "those despised elements would have taken on new aspects."[84] Akin to Cather's belated embrace of Nebraska, Lynn underwent a series of intense outdoor experiences that made her recognize that the prairie could be the stuff of literature.

Echoing Lynn's nostalgic lament about the passing of the frontier, by then an established discursive mode, Sedgwick praised *A Stepdaughter of the Prairie* for its depiction of its protagonist's life as "springing from the prairie, colored by it, belonging to it, although that prairie disappears beneath the plough and exists no more forever on the face of earth."[85] Lynn, who became an English professor at the University of Kansas, is also the author of novels about Kansas's abolitionist past, short stories (some anthologized), and essays on poetry, language, and culture. She was familiarly coupled with Hamlin Garland as a writer who set the standard for "do[ing] . . . handsomely by the flowering meadows of the Middle West," and Sedgwick continued to publish her fiction and essays through the 1920s.[86] Yet she is absent from the "Faraway Women" chapter in *The Happy Profession*, a chapter Stewart launches. The omission suggests not that Lynn was an atypical Sedgwick writer but, on the contrary, a too familiar one. While her geographical location was indisputably "faraway," her professional and class identity situated her squarely in *Atlantic* home territory. The tenor of her work is akin to that of the contributors prominent during the early years of his editorship, women such as Cornelia Comer, Katherine

Gerould, Agnes Repplier, and Margaret Sherwood who extended the magazine's "American genteel tradition" into the twentieth century.[87]

Of greater significance than her absence from this single editor's reminiscences, Lynn has dropped out of scholarly memory altogether. Her book is decades out of print, and it has attracted almost no study.[88] Stewart's and Lynn's relative standing suggests the kind of western stories that are most privileged. Foregrounding her ties to distant places and distant cultural forms, Lynn receded from view, even as western literary production was structured by just these kinds of affiliations.

And this brings us back to Juliet Coney. From the perspective of the aspiring writer who had cared for her home in Denver, this former farm girl, shoe stitcher, and struggling widow from Massachusetts appeared as the epitome of upper-class gentility, due both to her own deeds and demeanor and to Stewart's impressionability. Stewart went on to disseminate her impressions to an American public at large, and the way she positions herself in respect to Coney is mirrored in her position in the *Atlantic* itself, a "faraway" woman among other women contributors who by contrast appear so "nearby."

CHAPTER THREE

COLLABORATIVE ALCHEMY

AND

ACRIMONY

Opal Whiteley and The Story of Opal

In the end, it all boils down to ink and paper, doesn't it?

—Lee Child, *Killing Field*

n her engagingly titled essay "Historians Who Love Too Much," Jill
Lepore identifies the microhistorian's task as the pursuit of "small
mysteries" as she tracks "elusive subjects through slender records."
Ava Chamberlain characterizes her research about Puritan Elizabeth
Tuttle as an attempt "to open a quiet space in which to listen for [her]
voice." With a similar emphasis on scarcity, other biographers, especially of women, note their quest for the odd detail or singular act that
illuminates their subjects' lives and amplifies their voices. Yet both the
history of Opal Whiteley and that of her book *The Story of Opal: The Journal of an Understanding Heart* are crammed with such mysteries, details,
and acts, and Whiteley spoke very loudly, indeed. Right up until her
death in 1992, she insisted she was actually Françoise d'Orléans, daughter of French naturalist, geographer, and explorer Henri d'Orléans and
thus a direct descendent of Louis-Philippe d'Orléans, France's last king.
She always claimed, moreover, that *The Story of Opal* was a faithful

reconstruction of the diary she kept as a child of six and seven, recounting the trials of a princess adopted by rough woodland folk. As a result of her notorious authorship and conviction of royal blood, she came to associate with notable personages around the world.[1]

Sedgwick labored to chronicle Whiteley's astonishing activities, but he also conceded the impossibility of "tell[ing] the full story of Opal Whiteley." Such a project, he maintained, "would require a documented volume, illustrated by photographs, of the masses of material still in the *Atlantic*'s possession, and to complete it, strange adventures of my own should be added, tales of espionage, flights, and pilgrimages, still difficult to understand" (*HP* 263). More modest than this "full story," I seek to shed light on the making of *The Story of Opal* and to show how such knowledge affords the text a new interpretative context. The crux of this chapter is Whiteley's adversarial, generative relationship with Sedgwick, as it played out both within and outside the text. However, I also limn the contours of her remarkable life, which as Sedgwick learned—to his rue—are inextricable from any discussion of the diary. While much of the work for this book's other writers entails uncovering obscure histories and restoring the voices of "silent partners," for Whiteley it consists of sifting through a glut of archival and published materials. The Massachusetts Historical Society, the University of Oregon, and the University of London house reams of papers by and about her, and she is the subject of much commentary.

The Story of Opal has attracted a fair number of critical readings, including studies by Blake Allmendinger, Juliet McMaster, Roni Natov, Deborah Garfield, and myself that variously emphasize its western identity, revelations about child psychology, linguistic codes, and domestic arguments. This chapter offers a new way of thinking about the book, as a "realization of relationships," to use Holly Laird's paradigm in *Women Co-authors*. I follow the path Laird has cleared in her study of collaboratively authored texts, which shows how such texts inscribe the social processes that produced them. Laird proposes, "To redirect attention as far as possible from the 'true' lives lived (as if lives themselves were not multiple, concocted in part by the people inside them and the social structures circumscribing them) to the stories they have written, I suggest that a reader think of collaboration as itself reproduced and thematized in writing." Melissa Homestead has proved the wider value of her theories in applying them to Edith Lewis and Willa Cather's writing projects, resulting in a stunning reading of *The Professor's House* as not merely informed by Lewis's contributions but as actually commenting on the couple's shared work.[2]

An easily overlooked statement in *The Story of Opal* captures the social and material conditions of Whiteley's textual efforts. "I sit here on the doorstep," the child diarist confides, "printing this on the wrapping-paper Sadie McKibben gave me. The baby is in bed, asleep. The mamma and the rest of the folks is gone" (13). In a narrowly textual context, this scene of Whitely writing on donated paper—alone—at the threshold of her home indicates how *The Story of Opal* both represents and is produced by the writer's distance from her family and the outside support it prompted. But more broadly, it anticipates Whiteley's separation from her small Oregon community and her lifelong history of mentorship. Authorship was only one of the many outcomes of her intensive social networking, as she moved from Star, Oregon, to Eugene; Los Angeles; Boston; New York; Washington, D.C.; Rome; Vienna; London; and Udaipur, India.

As a child in rural Oregon, she was assisted by neighbors, teachers, and librarians who recognized her ambition and, often, her troubles at home. The aid continued in adjacent cities at the hand of professors, journalists, and ministers keen to help a girl they believed might "become one of the greatest minds Oregon ever has produced." Her circle widened in Los Angeles to include not only transplanted middle-class Oregonians but also a department store heiress, members of exclusive women's clubs, regional boosters, New Age enthusiasts, and minor celebrities. Once she entered the *Atlantic*'s orbit, Sedgwick introduced her to altruistic associates in Boston, and later she came under the influence of theosophists in New York City and diplomats in Washington, D.C. Thereafter, some of her unlikely backers included Roman nuns, the British civil service, and an Indian maharana. As one of Whiteley's acquaintances observed, "While she asks for nothing it seems as if that very quality caused every one, who is fortunate enough to come in touch with her to vie with each other in smoothing her pathway." With more asperity, Maud Harwood Bales, a former landlady in Los Angeles, complained, "I'll swear I know of no one individual who has ever received so much unusual kindness from so many people. Opal is lucky to be so small and she has traded on it very cleverly."[3]

As this last remark suggests, while *The Story of Opal* records only felicitous exchanges between a little girl and affectionate friends, Whiteley left a trail of hurt, resentful champions in her wake. Her most recent biographer, Kathrine Beck, supplies a telling anecdote about her association with Cornelia Marvin, Oregon's high-powered state librarian. Having afforded Whiteley a steady diet of interlibrary loans throughout her girlhood, Marvin pressed her, to no avail, to return a long-overdue book. Whiteley's library card is inscribed in her hand, "Dead Beat!!! No more books ever."[4] Her friend Ruth Gentle expressed her dismay in more modulated tones after Whiteley abruptly decamped from Los Angeles for Boston: "It was nice to know a genius but awfully hard to live with one. . . . Opal did things one had been taught always not to do and got away with it."[5] It fell to Gentle to put into storage the belongings she left behind. More publicly, Oregon journalist Elbert Bede wrote a caustic biography some forty years after giving Whiteley her first taste of celebrity, having likened her to "the child Savior, reared in lowly surroundings, [who] stood in the temple and imparted knowledge to the wise men."[6]

And of course there is Ellery Sedgwick, who often referred to Whiteley as "the child." At the onset of the diary project, he enthused, "I like your little papers so much—oh, so much! If all the rest of your story, hidden away in that great pile of torn scraps, is as good as this, we shall not only print the articles in The Atlantic, but will make a book of them, which will, I think, help you in all your future work very much indeed. . . . Isn't it nice that everything goes so well?" He installed her in his mother-in-law's household and viewed himself as her de facto guardian. Following six months of work together, "The Story of Opal" commenced its six-issue *Atlantic* run, March to August 1920, and the book was released at the serial's close. But by September, his fond notes to his charge had given way to affronted reprimands like "the kindness which you have had—I say it quite simply and without wishing to have you more than fair in regard to me—has been such as does not often come to young and comparatively helpless people."[7]

Whiteley's readers can experience kindred, if less personal, disillusionment. Initial enchantment with *The Story of Opal* and its author gives way to frustration when both prove intractable, resisting conclusive readings. It is impossible to know whether the events the book describes actually took place. More important for many, it is indeterminable how much, if any, of the text was written when Whiteley was a child. She proffered not just inconsistent but outright delusional accounts of her past, and the question of when she wrote the diary is still unanswered: whether as a child in Star, as a young adult in Los Angeles, or as a fledgling *Atlantic* contributor in Boston, directed if not tutored by Sedgwick.

Whiteley's defenders point to the book's production history to argue for child authorship. If the manuscript was a hoax, then why rip it up and why leave it behind in a hatbox in Los Angeles? Detractors point to factual inaccuracies and a display of knowledge outside a child's ken. Both sides cite eyewitnesses, such as her father testifying that as a child she "was always writing,"[8] or Bales recalling her perusing a French grammar. Some make confident judgments about the authenticity of the diary based on its conforming to their conception of how children think and write, while others point to a blend of child and adult insights. Another group links the text's creative processes to the mental illnesses that have been attributed to Whiteley.

Yet with the evidence available, we simply cannot determine when she first wrote the sentences that compose *The Story of Opal* or to what degree she was assisted. No other texts on record—whether written by the young Whiteley, the adult Whiteley, or Sedgwick—resemble the published text. What we can definitively say is that it was the extraordinary outcome of her and Sedgwick's joint enterprise. She pieced together, and in the process rewrote, fragments of what might have been childhood writing, which Sedgwick then shaped into a single, if fissured, text. The alchemy was astounding. The usual writing style of both Sedgwick and Whiteley can well be described as banal, yet together they produced an enchanting book. I like this contemporary reader's affirmation: "I do not want to reason about it, any more than I want to reason about the beauty of a rose."[9]

As an alternative to this reader's choice to "not . . . reason," in this chapter I subordinate unanswerable questions of authenticity, provenance, and motive to focus on the relational aspects of Whiteley's text. Given that *The Story of Opal* originated not as letters (inherently intersubjective) but as diary (usually a private venture), its relational qualities are less readily apparent than those of the other texts I discuss. These qualities, however, are pervasive, at several levels. For one, *The Story of Opal* was literally produced for, and implicitly addressed to, Whiteley's mother. Hovering between private and public expression, it reads as the writer's indictment of her family's behavior and defense of her own. Equally important, her epistolary practice persistently features in the text itself, along with the social transactions that fostered it. The diary records the first stage of the patronage that supported its creation, as Whiteley withdrew from her family and sought to enter the lofty circles she believed to be her literal birthright.

Sedgwick was the pivotal agent in this process. Beyond affording *The Story of Opal* a national platform, he was deeply involved in its actual construction, to the extent that he can be viewed as a coauthor. Even as his public accounts of the book highlight *discovering* a text, he clearly relished *creating* one. He worked closely with Whiteley in reconstructing the diary from the many text fragments. Moreover, the choice of which portions of the manuscript to publish was his alone, and he strove to suppress material that might mar a portrait of an innocent child communing with nature. *The Story of Opal* intimates the contest of author and editor over its identity, whether it was to tell the tale of a displaced French aristocrat—as Whiteley would have it—or that of the universal child, as Sedgwick desired.

In the end, the balance tipped in Whiteley's favor. While Sedgwick insisted—"Quite frankly"—that Whiteley's entries were "simply expressions of a child's naivete," *The Story of Opal* is an uncanny tale, its picturesque scenes steeped in the author's compulsions and fantasies. The text, I argue, got away from him, becoming a very different book than the one he envisioned. He tried to excise Whiteley's "romantic theory" about her true family, but found it was "closely interwoven in the texture of the diary." More materially, after publication Whiteley removed *The Story of Opal* from his jurisdiction by threatening to sue the *Atlantic* and by accusing him personally of mistreatment. He responded by swiftly selling the book rights to G. P. Putnam's in London.[10]

However, for decades after his contractual dealings with Whiteley ceased, he sought discursive control of her story. Employing the same metaphor, "piecing," that he always used in describing the text's restoration, he accurately commented that he was "tireless" in his efforts "to piece together the complete mosaic of her past." He conducted extensive investigations into her activities in western Oregon and Los Angeles and in both private letters and published statements expounded on her text, person, and life. Two decades later, *The Happy Profession* has an entire chapter on her. In this Sedgwick went against the advice of his Little, Brown editor, Alfred McIntyre, who urged him to cut all the Whiteley material as recollecting a controversial *Atlantic* incident. But he could not resist the opportunity to direct readers on how to understand her, and to have the last word.[11]

Before the *Atlantic*

In her introduction to *The Story of Opal*, Whiteley claims that working with the diary manuscript led to the recovery of some early memories: "As piece by piece the journal comes together, some things come back" (1). She describes traveling "a long, long way" with "strange people that I had never seen before" until finally reaching her destination. "Then it was they put me with Mrs. Whiteley. . . . She called me Opal Whiteley, the same name as that of another little girl who was the same size as I was when her mother lost her" (3). Her scant family legacy consisted of two homemade "Angel Books" (taken from her), embroidered garments fit for a princess (which also disappeared), eclectic knowledge about ancient and European history, and occasional recourse to French.

The verified events in her life include the following. Born in Colton, Washington, on December 11, 1897, Opal was the oldest of Mary Elizabeth and Charles Edward Whiteley's five children, all girls except for the Benjamin: Opal Irene, Pearl, Gail Faye, Bertha Chloe, and Edwin. The Whiteleys were perched on a very low rung of the middle-class ladder, moving around Washington and Oregon as different jobs became available for Edward (both he and his wife went by their middle names). Although he identified his training as that of an engineer, Edward worked as a farmer, ranch hand, logger, and, eventually, lumber camp manager.[12] Elizabeth occasionally took positions as a laundress and a ranch cook, labor that likewise did not align with her education, which included some teacher training. Opal cleaned rooms and picked berries to pay for school supplies and as she grew older did washing and housework to fund special occasions.

Known locally as the "Little Nature Study Girl,"[13] all of her activities were outsize. At church, she was said to reel off scores of Bible verses by heart. Her high school principal recalled, "She would practically exhaust every phase in study—she would use the Dictionary, the Encyclopedia, the entire Library." She amassed an enormous collection of nature specimens—rocks, plants, insects, and shells—which were displayed in a school exhibit visited by "1200 people young and old."[14] At thirteen she joined her local chapter of Junior Christian Endeavor, an ecumenical youth group. Membership soared after she became the organization's state president, and in connection with the position she lectured around the state with offerings like "Nearer to the Heart of Nature" and "Music and Musicians Out of Doors." The talk she gave at Gladstone Chautauqua was said to have drawn thousands.[15]

Her 1915 debut lecture in Eugene is an oft-reported event in Whiteley profiles. The "tiny seventeen-year-old mountain girl," according to the *Eugene Register-Guard,* had university faculty "gasping for breath." "In three days, she became the talk of the faculty of three educational institutions. Entrance rules have been cast aside; scholarships are proposed; a home was found for her in Eugene—everything has been done to keep her here."[16] Perhaps due to this statement, the usual story is that sponsors stepped forward so she could attend the University of Oregon. But according to Sedgwick's record, financial assistance, at least, was minimal. The following year Edward Whiteley lost his job, which led Opal to work, unhappily, as a domestic in an affluent Eugene home. She subsequently took a summer job in the small town of Heppner, teaching children's nature classes. Finally, she matriculated in the fall of 1916, renting a small house in Eugene. Aid from the university was confined to a $12.50 loan per term.[17]

Her quirky behavior and ambitious plans of the order of establishing a children's nature museum soon made her a well-known campus personality. The *Oregonian,* Portland's daily newspaper, reported on her eclectic study program: "natural sciences, eugenics, biography, the Bible, art, and homemaking."[18] (Her interest in eugenics was surely linked to her emerging conviction of noble pedigree.) She sought out publicity opportunities and had a penchant for having herself photographed. However, her mother died in May 1917, and she failed to complete many of her courses, events that contributed to her decision the following winter to move to Los Angeles. At this juncture she largely severed contact with her family, although she did maintain an enduring correspondence with her old friend Nellie Hemenway of Cottage Grove (who lived to be 101, predeceasing her by just one year). For money to leave home on, she took out a $200 loan from a local bank, cosigned by Nellie's father.[19]

Once in Los Angeles, she boarded, in turn, with a Mrs. Stephens,[20]

Bales, and the Gentle family. All were western Oregon transplants attracted by the city's economic and cultural opportunities; Whiteley's first major move was facilitated by the more modest ambitions of women and men who had likewise relocated from the rural Northwest to this burgeoning metropolis. However, while she initially relied on the goodwill of home acquaintances, her circle swiftly expanded. Bales informed Sedgwick, "When she came to us she had only 30.00 which she transferred from a City Bank to the First National Hollywood. Can you see yourself landing in a new place miles from anyone you knew with only 30.00? Opal was not sure that we were in Los Angeles either." Later, she found a more worldly host in Pasadena, leading the resentful Bales to complain that "[only] Opal . . . would have had the nerve to go over to that rich lady in Pasadena—an absolute stranger and ask for money."[21] She also boarded for a time with Charles Lummis and his family at his northeastern Los Angeles estate, El Alisal, a rustic haven frequented by artists, writers, musicians, and civic leaders. Over the years Lummis hosted close to seven thousand guests at his eclectic house parties, and the many signatures in his "House Book" include that of "Opal Stanley Whiteley."[22] By then she had jettisoned her given middle name, Irene, in favor of one that linked her to the Earl of Derby.

Whiteley's 1918–19 sojourn in Los Angeles was the crucible of her authorship. She wrote and self-published her first book, *The Fairyland around Us;* attracted the sponsors who would facilitate the production of her second book, *The Story of Opal;* and possibly, as some critics charge, wrote portions of the putative diary itself. Authorship, however, was not her original California goal. Before leaving Eugene, in anticipation of searching out work in film, she assembled a portfolio of photographs of herself in romantic poses, the likes of holding a violin, in classical Greek drapery, and "in big armchair with books and holding curls at throat," as she formulated it.[23] She also announced grand plans for conducting nature research throughout the length of California, touring state and national parks. In fact, she paused only in Oakland to visit friends before continuing to Los Angeles. Six weeks of cold-calling Hollywood followed. These efforts failed, but she did attract notice: John Steven McGroarty, a prominent regional booster (and future California poet laureate), likened her in a *Los Angeles Times* column to Mary Pickford.[24]

In Los Angeles, Whiteley joined several exclusive women's clubs, including the Friday Morning Club and the Southern California Woman's Press Club, and eventually taught nature classes to members' children. The Friday Morning Club, the oldest and largest of its kind in California, had power, influence, and money, to the extent that in 1923 it built a new six-story clubhouse and a theater that sat three thousand. The Southern California Woman's Press Club was of similar prominence, with a membership that included many journalists as well as dedicated fiction writers. In reference to its "Short Story Section," a club historian noted the group's "technical study of short story construction and constant study of markets" along with their ambition to found "a literary magazine on the Pacific Coast which shall approximate the 'big four' of the Atlantic Coast."[25] Perhaps Whiteley's desire to publish a nature book had its source in this organization, with its self-consciously regional literary ambition, and it may have served as her introduction to Lummis.

Although far fewer than she had planned, Whiteley printed a number of copies of *The Fairyland around Us,* with forewords by both Lummis and David Starr Jordan, eugenics proponent and founding president of Stanford University. *Fairyland* has yet to attract study outside the context of source material for *The Story of Opal,* but it is richer and more complex than usually credited. Through an assembly of short stories and encyclopedia-style entries about plants, birds, and animals, it schools children on the natural world. One chapter, for example, features the wanderings of a "tiny girl, not quite two inches tall," who visits a number of birds of different species "in search of the homes of Fairyland that other Girls and other Boys might know how other folks around them lived." The lessons are interspersed with inspirational statements and verse by writers including Milton, Longfellow, Gene Stratton-Porter, and Shakespeare along with photographs from other publications, pasted in with blithe disregard to copyright. Deborah Garfield aptly describes *Fairyland* as the work "of an educated adult who had created a biological fantasy suspended between scientific classification and the memories of a girlishly mystified Oregon nature."[26]

Lummis's foreword concludes by stating, "This tireless young woman has financed the book by her own efforts, has been her own publisher and circulator." Yet Whiteley did receive considerable aid. Her method was to solicit, by mail, eminent men and women for endorsements and advance orders, ranging from Gene Stratton-Porter to Douglas Fairbanks and Queen Victoria Eugenia of Spain. Closer to home, W. M. Gentle, father of Ruth, lent her a room complete with "private telephone" within his suite in the storied San Fernando Building, at the time one of the most elegant office buildings in Los Angeles. "Personally my confidence in the integrity and veracity of this delightful child-lady is unbounded," he later assured Sedgwick. Willard C. James, a lawyer in the same building, recollected, "Seeing and believing her to be one of the brightest minds that it has ever been my lot to meet; considering her youth, I came to her rescue financially."[27]

Most important, Whiteley's fellow clubwomen funded her search for a commercial publisher in the East after she reached an impasse with *Fairyland*. As one of them told Sedgwick, "Some of the ladies in Los Angeles had been more than kind to Opal, and between us all had got Opal fitted out to go to Boston. Mrs. Forbes has been so very good to her, and it is through her that Opal has had the great good fortune to come in touch with you."[28] The group included Marie Rose Mullen, who put the family department store, Mullen & Bluett Clothing Company, at Whiteley's disposal to store her belongings, including boxes of diary fragments. Some of these women would send her money for years.

Beyond the intimation that Mrs. Forbes was connected to Sedgwick's social circle (possibly through to W. Cameron Forbes, the banker, diplomat, and fellow Harvardian with whom he later toured Spain as Franco's guest), there is no record of these sponsors' ties to Boston or why it was chosen over New York or Chicago. They may well have been readers of the *Atlantic*, which had a significant Los Angeles circulation, and perhaps they viewed Boston, with its transcendentalist traditions, as an apt destination for this winsome nature writer. Or perhaps the choice was Whiteley's, as she moved steadily closer to her imagined European homeland. Lodged among how-to manuals on making money from writing and from collecting butterflies, her papers at the University of Oregon include a pamphlet for the "Sea Pines Home School for Girls," a private girls' school in Brewster, Massachusetts. That it was in Whiteley's possession hints at upper-class longing, turned eastward, that exceeds merely professional aspiration.

Far more purposeful in plotting her career than the other writers I discuss, Whiteley did not have a dedicated go-between to broker her work, no literary intermediary akin to Stewart's Mrs. Coney, Rose's Dr. Hobart, or Harrison's Miss Morris. While Mullen confided to Sedgwick, "I was so worried before she left Los Angeles it was almost a temptation to accompany her," Whiteley traveled to Boston alone, and thereafter she made her own appointments and called on publishers unaccompanied.[29] First she tried Houghton Mifflin and next *Youth's Companion*. Although the comment about Forbes's offices suggests an alternative explanation, the usual story is that the editor of *Youth's Companion*, Henry Chapman, directed her to Sedgwick.

Whiteley sent Sedgwick a letter of introduction in which she not only described *Fairyland* as incorporating "part of the journal of my childhood" but also promised to bring that journal with her to their meeting. Nevertheless, Sedgwick always claimed that she first mentioned it only after her vivid memories led to his questioning her:

> "If you remember like that, you must have kept a diary."
> Her eyes opened wide, "Yes, always. I do still."
> "Then it is not the book I want, but the diary."

His solicitation of the diary is invariably noted. Yet no one ever questions, why the quick dismissal of *Fairyland*? Had he chosen, he quite possibly could have shaped it into something with *Atlantic* appeal, especially considering the qualities it shares with *The Story of Opal*. There is something rather perverse about his unequivocal rejection of a text in hand in favor of a text in scraps. Perhaps the problem was not, as usually charged, that the nature book was too amateurish for his taste. On the contrary, it may have been too complete, lacking the infinite possibilities of a text not yet composed. Sedgwick liked discovering untraditional authors and open-ended manuscripts, and he liked the creative work both entailed.[30]

The Story of Opal

The other writers in this study published books about new phases of life in new places: Rose and Stewart on their homesteads, Harrison abroad. Their texts, consequently, either pass over or conceal impoverished childhoods, whether in rural Oklahoma, industrial Illinois, or segregated Mississippi. They also elide the choices and acts whereby they left these communities of origin behind. *The Story of Opal*, in contrast, depicts its author where she started. The book documents that original life, even as its existence proves her move away from it.

According to her neighbors, Whiteley literally wrote the diary for her mother. Ora Read Hemenway relayed, "Mrs. Thompson ask [*sic*] her if her mother knew she was writing the story of her life. Opal said 'No she was going to write it and then give it to her some time.'" Yet even without knowing this history, *The Story of Opal* reads as written "for" Elizabeth Whiteley, as Opal's passionate accusation of the woman who raised her. Moreover, it can be read as a book *about* her, in that *The Story of Opal* records the deeds and views of not one but two discontented, ambitious Whiteley women. Like Juliet Coney and *Letters of a Woman Homesteader*, Mrs. Whiteley is still another obscure figure whose acts drive a "faraway woman" tale, with traces of the process preserved in the text. Her behavior could be as erratic as her daughter's. "All of former neighbors remember Mrs. W. peculiar woman—much like Indian in temperament, one said," Bede noted. She occasionally hid from visitors, and in the last months of her life had "sudden fits of wild unreasonableness" (the phrase is Sedgwick's) that led her to move her children from house to rented house. Offering another view, according to Bede her grocer observed that she was "of reticent temperament but her command of perfect English and her evident refinement was something astonishing and unexpected." Several commented on her pressuring her eldest daughter to abandon her career goals in favor of becoming a housewife, as an achievement that would confirm the family's middle-class status. In a letter to a sister, Whiteley herself stated, "We know that your mother Lizzie Whiteley tried hard to put an end to her foolish interest in nature." The published book is unrelenting in its depiction of her abuse.[31]

The first sentence of *The Story of Opal*, "Today the folks are gone away from the house we do live in" (5), establishes its abiding premise, that Opal's textual practice hinges on family absence, both actual and emotional. As the diary proceeds, Whiteley continues to represent writing as a response to punishment, confinement, or neglect. "The mamma is gone for a visit away," she states (141). "Before her going, she did set me to mind the baby. I do so. In between times I print." She also claimed that the diary itself became a focal point of family antagonism, targeted by her sister Faye: "I caught her in the act of tearing it up several times. I would hide it in another place in the woods and when she found it she would tear more up." Hemenway stated that she and her husband "remember distinctly when she was in high school and she came to our house and was so heartbroken over her diary being torn up."[32]

The Story of Opal features both the Oregon parents of Opal's daily life, whom she refers to as "the mamma" and "the papa," and the French ones of her fantasies, "Angel Mother" and "Angel Father." Mr. Whiteley is scarcely visible in the text, but as a stern cruel taskmaster Mrs. Whiteley is ubiquitous. Garfield offers a useful schema: whereas "the mamma" is associated with American labor—the household drudgery to which she subjects Opal—"Angel Mother" is linked to European knowledge, and both Angel parents are "an endless, if deferred, site for [Opal's] desire."[33] The book's action consists of a series of Opal's outings in the woods, coupled with her mishaps at home and the punishments that follow. When afield, she is invariably attended by one or more of her animal companions—dog, horse, pig, mouse, cow, or toad—who bear lofty names like Brave Horatius, Elizabeth Barrett Browning, and Lucian Ovid Horace Virgil. In their company she engages in incantatory rituals, as when she commemorates the "borning day" of her presumptive ancestor "Louis Philippe, roi de France": "I did have prayers. Then I did light my little candle. Seventy-six big candles Angel Father did so light for him, but so I cannot do, for only one little candle I have" (SO 43).

Whiteley's introduction to *The Story of Opal* identifies both her erudition and her writing as a French family legacy: "There were walks in the fields and woods. When on these walks, Mother would tell me to listen to what the flowers and trees and birds were saying. We listened together. And on the way she told me poems and other lovely things, some of which she wrote in the two books and also in others which I had not with me in the lumber camps. On the walks, and after we came back, she had me to print what I had seen and what I had heard" (1). She secretly studied and transcribed lessons from the "Angel Books," she maintains, passing them on to her animal friends in songs, chants, and lectures. Scenes from the book depict the practice: "I do spell over and over the words in my two books Angel Father and Angel Mother did make. I sing-song the letters of the words when I go adown the road" (SO 141). This rich linguistic legacy is juxtaposed with the Whiteleys' meager literacy. Her real parents had "rows and rows of books," but the Whiteleys have only three—"cook-book," "doctor-book," and "almanac" (SO 53). *Our Babies Bible A.B.C.*, the oldest book in Whiteley's childhood collection at the University of Oregon, is the likely source of the "Angel Books" delusion. The copyright is registered to K. E. Boland, but "An Angel mother" is the nominal author. There is a kind of logic here, naming the author of the book that taught her to read as the source of all she knows.

The first entry of *The Story of Opal* poses a special challenge to the reader invested in the text's child authorship, in that it systematically introduces Whiteley's surroundings in a manner unlikely for a diary. It surveys the district's physical terrain—roads, hills, rivers, railroad. It glosses her social environment—neighbors and school. It offers a succinct history of her family's residency, from their arrival by wagon to the temporary housing that followed and finally their small house: "By-and-by, we were come from the tent to this lumber shanty" (*SO* 5). It even offers some natural history, that "woods used to grow, where now grows grain" (*SO* 7).

The text then takes on a more conventional diurnal cast, chronicling events in the writer's life. However, there are many moments that strain credulity. Opal often pleads ignorance even as readers know exactly what's what—why her newlywed neighbors had a baby so soon, why the handwriting of another neighbor is identical to that of gift-bearing fairies. The text is studded with carefully preserved (or introduced) precious spellings, like "screwtineyes" (*SO* 104), and pedantic interjections that are hard not to read as an adult's, especially as they occasionally echo *Fairyland*. These include "yellowjackets are such interesting fairies, being among the world's first paper-makers" and even "When I grow up, I am going to write for children—and grownups that haven't grown up too much—all the earth-songs I now do hear" (*SO* 15, 36). Some chapters conclude with reflections on the preceding events, such as "The back part of me feels a little sore, but I am happy listening to the twilight music of God's good world. I'm real glad I'm alive" (*SO* 13). *Atlantic* reader Helen Carson well expresses the effect of these moments in a letter to Sedgwick: "My mother declares no child of her age could have written as she did. For pages I am sure she could and then comes forth an expression and sequence in writing that impresses me that only an adult writer could produce." The letter concludes, "If Opal could write as she did at six will you not let your readers see what she is able to write at twenty-one? Please."[34]

Yet the source of the dissonance of *The Story of Opal* lies deeper than its seeming commingling of child and adult perspectives. The more one studies *The Story of Opal*, the more it unsettles, suffused with disturbed language and disturbing events. "The mamma" doles out "most hard spankings" for the smallest infractions, "with her hand and the hair-brush and the pancake-turner" (86, 154). The rituals are incessant and uncanny. And the text repeatedly references the voices Opal hears—wind songs, earth songs, star songs, potato songs. Of a melancholy walk, she recounts, "There was grayness everywhere gray clouds in the sky and gray shadows above and in the canyon. And all the voices that did speak—they were gray tones. 'Petite Françoise, c'est jour gris'" (89).

Equally arresting are the text's urgent rehearsals. In answer to a question her teacher posed the class, for example, Whiteley recalls, "And I did say in a real quick way, 'A pig is a cochon and a mouse is a mulot and a baby deer is a daine and a duck is a canard and a turkey is a dindon and a fish is a poisson and a colt is a poulain and a blackbird is a merle.' And after each one I did say, teacher did shake her head and say, 'It is not,' and I did say, 'It is'" (SO 28). She then repeats the full sequence twice more: her retort in which she lists the French terms, the punishment that followed, and then again, "But I do know a pig is a cochon, and a mouse is a mulot, and a baby deer is . . ." (SO 29). Her close to fifteen-hundred-word description of the "necessary things that the mamma has not knows of" (SO 275), treasured objects that she hides in a hollow log, reads as even more compulsive. Commencing with "my two books that Angel Mother and Angel Father did write in and I do study in every day" (ibid.), she submits an incantatory inventory:

> And there is four old horse-shoes of William Shakespeare that the black-smith did have allows for me to have when he was putting new shoes onto William Shakespeare. And there is the thimble of Dear Love that she has given me to carry drinks of water to the folks in the hospital. And there is the little bell of Peter Paul Rubens that he did use to wear to service in the cathedral. And there is Elsie's baby's little old shoe that got worn out and she gave it to me for Nannerl Mozart to sleep in. And there is the lid of Sadie McKibben's coffee pot that she did give me when it came off. (SO 277)

The collection's actual contents are telling, too. None of the "necessary things" retain their original use, and none originate in the Whiteley household. The hoard consists exclusively of outside donations, small discards that denote Opal's tissue of social support.

Whiteley situates her keeping of the diary among a range of other writing acts. Even as the text reads as an extended letter to her mother, charging her with injustice, it depicts actual epistolary activity: mournful messages to lost relatives and lost companions that are penned—somehow—on literal leaves. "This day it was a lonely day," she announces.

> I did have longings all its hours for Angel Mother and Angel Father. In-between times all day at school I did print messages for them on gray leaves I did gather on the way to school. I did tell on the leaves the longings I was having. Too, on the leaves I did tell of William Shakespeare and our talks as we do go walking down the lane. . . . I did tell of how on many days in gray-light-time I have had going on searches for the kisses of Angel Father. (*SO* 122)

Sometimes laid in her hiding place, sometimes attached to trees, these lonely, elegiac epistles are all addressed to the dead, a one-way communication. In addition to her bygone French parents and grandparents, recipients include the family horse (worked to death), pet crow (shot), blind friend (died in a fire), and loyal pig (slaughtered). Following a harrowing account of the butchering of this last, Opal states, "I do print a message on a leaf, and I tie it onto the highest limb I can reach. And I leave it there with a little prayer for Peter Paul Ruben" (*SO* 89).

The third level of writing activity in *The Story of Opal*, which shows neighbors assisting her efforts to write, most clearly forecasts Whiteley's transactional adult practice. Just as Sadie McKibben supplies her with "wrapping-papers . . . to print upon" (*SO* 13), pencils come courtesy of the benefactor who intercepts the supplicating letters she deposits. She recounts,

> I did have thinks about that letter I did write on the other day, for more color pencils that I do have needs of to print with. I thought I would go to the moss-box by the old log. I thought I would have goes there to see if the fairies yet did find my letter.
>
> I went. The letter—it was gone. Then I did have joy feels all over—the color pencils, they were come! There was a blue one, and a green one, and a yellow one. And there was a purple one, and a brown one, and a red one. (*SO* 32–33)

The only person aware of this activity, Whiteley states, is "the man that wears gray neckties and is kind to mice. He has knowings of the letters I do print on leaves" (*SO* 34). The exchange is repeated in the text, with the same elements—box, letters, surrogate—and the pattern recurs in Whiteley's fledging literary career, too. Sedgwick, ushering her into national authorship, was her adult version of "the man . . . kind to mice." Their relationship, however, was far more fraught.

Whiteley and Sedgwick

Once the diary project was under way, Whiteley became Sedgwick's unofficial ward. He gave her money for food, and his wife took her to the dentist and the doctor (the latter for treatment of a back injury incurred, allegedly, when she leaped out of her El Alisal bedroom window to escape Lummis's advances). He also solicited his acquaintances for part-time teaching jobs. Most important, he removed her to his mother-in-law's Brookline estate to give her a secure place to work on her book.

On Whiteley's first arrival in Massachusetts, she had stayed with the Forbes family, as arranged by her Los Angeles associates. She then installed herself in a boardinghouse in Cambridge, lodging that from Sedgwick's perspective was alarmingly spartan. "Her morning and evening diet was unvaryingly mush from the family pot," he divulged, with meat rarely featuring.[35] The several letters this prominent editor wrote to the affronted "two Misses Salter on Lancaster Street" defending his decision to remove her from their establishment read as a remarkable act of appeasement.

The move freed Whiteley from financial worries and domestic tasks, while Sedgwick gained more control over a text that, as he expressed it, "involves an enormous amount of work which ought to be done under my own supervision."[36] However, his choice to take Whiteley in made her later repudiation sting all the more. In *The Happy Profession*, he enthuses about zesty relationships with working-class writers "poised on the very threshold of your friendship" (*HP* 198), editor and authors interacting "at a safe distance." Yet Whiteley's winsomeness overruled his usual class instincts, and he literally took her across his threshold.

During the months Whiteley lived with the Cabots, her insistent greetings to the Sedgwicks (sometimes with small gifts for the children) read as rather forced. She clearly did not enter this upper-class family's inner circle. Beck maintains that she found her ambiguous status trying, neither family guest nor paid *Atlantic* employee.[37] We can imagine that the discrepancy between her past and present surroundings took an emotional toll of its own, as she re-created scenes of abuse in the crude cabin of her Oregon childhood while living on this commodious suburban property with its gardens, servants, and cloistered mistress.

Sedgwick had the boxes of diary fragments shipped in from Los Angeles, arriving mixed with "an indescribable quantity of old books, papers, clothing, nature studies." (Whiteley's freight bill reveals she also retrieved "7 CS BOOKS & SEA SHELLS.") Of the fragments, Sedgwick recounts in his introduction, "Some few were large as a half-sheet of notepaper; more, scarce big enough to hold a letter of the alphabet. The paper was of all shades, sorts, and sizes: butchers' bags pressed and sliced in two, wrapping-paper, the backs of envelopes—anything and everything that could hold writing. The early years of the diary are printed in letters so close that, when the sheets are fitted, not another letter can be squeezed in." He often presented these material conditions as proof of the diary's authenticity, precluding any alien text from being "squeezed in." At the same time, however, they prove the gulf between the original manuscript and the published book.[38]

Sedgwick oversaw the diary's reconstruction, and he alone determined which of the assembled sections were to compose the book. Reporting on her progress, Whiteley wrote him, "You spoke of desiring to see soon some of the completed incidents that you might get some idea of the journal as a whole. So I looked around on the floor and decided to select five or six of the incidents there partly pieced to-gether. . . . This is a very slow process—hours and hours of work showing only a few pieces pieced in—but I think it is achieving what you wanted to see soon." (She also complained, "When I am sleeping the little bits of paper all come dancing along.") Sedgwick had instructed her to concentrate on single events, to be ordered by age. "However," he also advised, "to tell your story chronologically may sometimes interfere with pursing a particular episode to its natural conclusion, and in case this difficulty arises, I suggest that while you adopt chronological order as a method, you do not subject yourself to it slavishly."[39]

This counsel to not "subject herself" to chronology is telling: despite its promotion as a genuine diary, the book is no record of daily events. It also belies Sedgwick's depiction of the process as primarily one of transcription. "No editing has been done or changes made," he promised *Atlantic* readers, but then allowed, "other than omissions and the adoption of adult rules of capitalization (the manuscript has nothing

FIGURE 3. Opal Whiteley with diary fragments in Brookline. *Collection of the Massachusetts Historical Society.*

but capitals), and punctuation (of which it affords no single trace)."[40] As "fragments of episodes" were "fitted together," they were typed onto index cards by an *Atlantic* assistant (*SO* xi). "Finally the cards were filed in sequence, the manuscript then typed off and printed just as first written, with no change whatever" —with the signal exception of those "omissions," capital letters, and punctuation marks. His very assurances delineate the massive overhaul the manuscript underwent.

For Hilda Rose's *The Stump Farm,* as the next chapter shows, the archive offers a clear view of the path the text followed from manuscript to serial to book. Such is not the case for *The Story of Opal.* The surfeit of records notwithstanding, it takes a leap of faith to conceive how the text fragments became an arresting book. To use Judith Plotz's characterization, *The Story of Opal* is "brilliantly inventive, metaphorically attentive, vocationally writerly," but these qualities are not evident in any of Whiteley's other extant texts, including her letters, adolescent journal, nature book, and even the progress reports she sent Sedgwick.[41] None of them intimate the haunting power of *The Story of Opal.* Her letters are rambling and repetitive, reflecting her deteriorating mental health. *The Fairyland around Us* shares some subject matter (and phrases) with *The Story of Opal,* but the prose is often belabored. And the 1911 journal is absolutely prosaic:

> Dear Old Diary I did not neglect you on purpose yesterday but I went down to Row River at 10:30 and did not get back till 4:30. . . . I took Mrs. Scites and Mrs. Hankens Papers to them.
>
> Mrs. Hankens was so friendly. She is feeling much better this spring. Her boy is getting along nicely in his studies she said. She invited me to stay for dinner but as I had ate my dinner before I started I thanked her and went on my way to Mrs. Gillespie. Grandpa sent me a lawn dress for May on the train. I read a pretty Easter Postal from Aunt Anna.[42]

My aim is not to insinuate that Sedgwick was involved in the actual writing of the text, which gives off not a whiff of his garrulous, metaphor-crowded prose. Rather, it is to demonstrate that the outcome of his profound intervention—selecting, cutting, arranging, editing—was something wholly new. *The Story of Opal* was like nothing either Whiteley or Sedgwick had written before.

The "textual condition," John Kevin Young reminds us, "expresses contingency, illuminating through manuscripts, drafts, and different published editions the range of versions a particular book could have inhabited." At seventy thousand words, *The Story of Opal* accounts for scarcely more than a quarter of the reconstructed text: Sedgwick excluded the bulk of the assembled manuscript. Regarding his principles of selection, I have argued elsewhere that they support a portrait of a timeless forest fairyland rather than a regionally specific, industrial landscape. Yet he also, with far greater deliberation, sought to keep *The*

Story of Opal from reading as too foreign. It was to smack neither of Oregon nor of France.[43]

As the diary began to take shape, Sedgwick believed he held a document that—entirely unknown to Whiteley—verified her identity as an exiled French aristocrat. The manuscript included "references so direct that they cannot be misinterpreted," proving "Angel Father" to be "none other than Henry of Bourbon, famous geographer and explorer." The "extraordinary story . . . came little by little, a bit here, a bit there." As the serial ran, *Atlantic* readers descried further corroborating details. Sedgwick's credence was also boosted by "curious letters from the West" that accompanied photographs labeled "Opal's Real Father, Opal's Uncle, and Opal's Grandfather." Stating the photos were "unquestionably of gentle people," he noted that their physical resemblance to Whiteley "has done much to support my belief in Opal's mysterious origins." As he confided to Frances Lee, the director of a private girls' school in Boston who would soon make, and later angrily rescind, an offer for Whiteley to organize "outing classes" for her students, "I only know that if she is a Whiteley her performance is far more remarkable than under the other theory. Moreover, I myself have seen Mr. Whiteley's letters, which are entirely illiterate and the letters of Opal's reputed sisters, who write like servant-girls." (Here he ignores the fact that Opal had actually worked as a servant.) As late as July 1920, he was convinced the family had accepted money from strangers to care for her, with "quite extraordinary" evidence "point[ing] to Mrs. Whiteley's having been the responsible person."[44]

During the course of their work, he chose not to tell Whiteley of the putative disclosures, since "once she knew, further revelations from the diary would, for obvious reasons, have far less weight." He also sought to keep them out of the published text. His motives were multiple. At first, he was concerned they could "give valuable hints to persons interested in defrauding Opal of her birthright." With greater self-interest, he also feared fanning suspicion about the diary's authenticity. But on a deeper level, he believed they would distract readers from the literary qualities of *The Story of Opal,* which in his view transcended its author's biography.[45]

To further minimize distractions, he counseled Whiteley to ration her French. Similar to Mary Antin and her Russian terms seven years previously, author and editor negotiated over what foreign material would make the cut, with Whiteley mollified by a promise of more to come in a second volume. In a note to an *Atlantic* assistant, she specified, "I wrote in 'Petite Francoise' where it came twice. I left it out in the other places. Only one fleur and one bird song I put in. . . . All other sings I left out as Mr. Sedgwick desired all things having a special reference should be left out."[46]

A great deal of sensational material got "in" nonetheless. The "bird song" to which she alludes, for example, is an acrostic that spells out "Robert d'Orlns" [*sic*] de Chartres in itemizing "*roitelet* and *ortolan* and *bruant* and *étourneau* and *rossignol* and *tourterelle*" (*SO* 139) and so on. A song about rivers likewise references Henri d'Orléans: "*Le chant de Seine, de Havre, et Essonne et Nonette et Roullon et Iton*" (*SO* 108). "I sang it as Angel Father did teach me to," Whiteley claims. Sedgwick extolled *The Story of Opal* as "the most illuminating chronicle of childhood that I have seen in twenty years of reading manuscripts." There is "nothing in the language more naïf and directly expressive of the spirit of childhood." Whiteley, however, was bent on expressing something more personal: her emotions as a girl haunted by memories of life in a different family, country, and class. This other "chronicle" kept erupting, with every wind song and every showing of "Françoise."[47]

As a consequence, Sedgwick felt obliged to school readers on the correct approach to Whiteley's diary. Instructions for reading the text pervade his promotional materials, correspondence, and memoirs. The first *Atlantic* installment is coupled with this didactic pronouncement: "There are many ways of liking to read. Some people read for the delight of it; some for knowledge; and some, again, to learn whether they cannot find out something about the author. Now, the right way to read *The Story of Opal* is for the delight of it." Similarly, his introduction to the book urges readers to focus on the text itself: "The authorship does not matter, nor the life from which it came. There the book is. Nothing else is like it, nor apt to be. If there is alchemy in Nature, it is in children's hearts that unspoiled treasure lies, and for that room of the treasure house, the Story of Opal offers a tiny golden key." Close to three decades later, he inserted these passages verbatim in *The Happy Profession*'s "An Opalescent Chapter," still trying to corral the book's waywardness and control its impact.[48]

After the *Atlantic*

For all of the "faraway women" texts I discuss, *Atlantic* serialization contributed to not only the market success of the volumes that followed but also the intense reader responses they evoked. "I lend my Atlantics over and over, but I want my Opal all in one piece to have and to hold till death do us part," one ardent reader announced, a statement later used to advertise *The Story of Opal*. As scholars such as Michael Lund and Patricia Okker have argued in respect to novels, serialization promotes especially strong attachment. A text is consumed over the course of not hours or days, but weeks and months. The intervals between excerpts allow for suspense and anticipation to build, and they create the sensation of living with the characters as their plots unfold.[49]

Compared to serial fiction, we can surmise that life narratives make for even greater engagement, as readers encounter real people whose lives appear to play out on the page in the same temporality as their own. This heightened attachment inspired *Atlantic* readers to send *Atlantic* writers gifts and money, to initiate epistolary friendships, and even to visit in person. The *Atlantic*, of course, was invested in fostering such ties, which fanned circulation. ("The Story of Opal" was said to have attracted many new subscribers.) Even those who disliked Whiteley's text framed their response as that of good *Atlantic* citizens. "Because I have loved the Atlantic long and well I am now emboldened to write a protest . . . against the preposterous and odious Opal," wrote "Jane Doe" from San Francisco.[50]

Like Sedgwick, many readers initially accepted Whiteley's claim of being an orphaned aristocrat. This judgment stemmed from the beliefs they held about working-class girls from the West: her erudition and sensibility proved she could not really be a Whiteley of Cottage Grove. The view expressed by Sarah Elizabeth Forbush Downs (a.k.a. Mrs. George Sheldon, the prolific dime novelist) was typical. *The Story of Opal*, she claimed—in a telegrammed order for six copies—was "a marvelous study in heredity."[51] The book quickly went through three editions and spent several weeks on Boston's best-seller list for nonfiction. In addition to her advance, Whiteley received a 10 percent royalty on the first five thousand copies, 13.5 percent on the next five thousand, and 15 percent thereafter.[52] Sedgwick reported that in its first month,

The Story of Opal had made its author "$2813.10 in this country, and for us practically the same."[53]

He once hoped sales would exceed fifty thousand copies.[54] However, almost at the moment of publication, his relationship with Whiteley imploded. He recalled, "I had sent her a copy of the book fresh from the press, and was expecting a note expressing delight when I heard the news of her disappearance."[55] He was soon contacted by her lawyer, threatening a suit. Its premise was that the book misidentified Edward Whiteley's father as Opal's grandfather, thereby implying she was truly a Whiteley.

Whiteley had been collected from Brookline by new acquaintances who took her by car to New York, first for a long weekend and then for good. She remained in the orbit of "Outer Court of the Order of the Living Christ" founder Genevieve Ludlow Griscom, the equally prominent theosophist Ernest Temple Hargrove, and the pair's acolytes for more than a year. Griscom, the enormously wealthy widowed daughter-in-law of shipping magnate Clement Acton Griscom, owned a rustic compound of cottages in the Bronx that Whiteley loved visiting (later the site of an opulent mansion rumored to have been built for Jesus on his return). Her movement emphasized the mental reform of its disciples; while displaying her usual hyperbole, Whiteley's later claim of having been "under complete restraint" may have had some truth to it.[56]

Sedgwick reported, "With a sudden and extraordinary prejudice, which at times seems to me to border on insanity, she has come to distrust, and certainly dislike, her group of friends here with a degree of intensity that is hard to understand." He long strove to pinpoint the source of her animosity. The matter was not just professional, about a text that bore his name. It was also highly personal. He repeatedly protested his kind treatment—"I have never done so much personally for any contributor"—and the generosity of "the contract which I made with this unknown waif for an exotic and curious book." Long after most would have recognized her as delusional, he was still worrying the cause. Whiteley's hostility was utterly unlike the deference and gratitude he had come to expect from his *Atlantic* cohort, especially the women.[57]

Although he came to doubt the veracity of many of Whiteley's claims, Sedgwick never intimated that hers was a witting deception.

I see his decision eight years later to publish Wilma Frances Minor's patently absurd "Lincoln the Lover," an imaginative biography based on a secret trove of letters between Lincoln and Ann Rutledge, as speaking to his conviction of Whiteley's good faith; his statement regarding Minor's collection, that "a hoax is not . . . within the realm of possibility," seems scarcely feasible from a man who suspected he had once been tricked.[58] In a 1945 letter to Bede about Whiteley's diary, he insisted, "I shall die in the absolute personal certainty that the story so far as it is printed in the *Atlantic* expressed Opal's personal convictions. I do not think that it was true, but I know that she believed it to be true and I also know that her life was the strangest medley of fact and fiction that I have ever come across."[59]

In an effort to sift "fact" from "fiction," he painstakingly assembled Whiteley's life history, which he conveyed in paratextual materials, private correspondence, and his formal "Record of Opal Whiteley." This work was in part a form of self-defense, against not only Whiteley's charge of personal mistreatment but also the larger charge of *Atlantic* fraud. Yet it also displays the zeal of a detective for cracking a confounding case. A reviewer of *The Story of Opal* demanded, "Are all the forces of modern authority to be confounded by the simplicity or duplicity, the innocence or guilt, of a mere child?" This question helps us recognize Sedgwick's investigation of Whiteley, and the reports that followed, as exhibiting a desire to discursively control an unruly figure. Her person and story would not yield to "the forces of modern authority" this leading Boston editor represented. His quest for a definitive history of Whiteley displays, moreover, a distinctly gendered cast, as he enlisted male doctors, psychologists, lawyers, publishers, journalists, and others in the cause. His letter to the nature conservationist Ernest Harold Baynes is revealing: "Sometimes I think that every male reader, at least, has two men under his skin, and that one of them is a sleuth."[60]

For his sleuthing, Sedgwick had to rely on the mail, sending out countless inquiries. If faraway women suffered from their distance from literary markets, then this distance also shielded them from scrutiny. "What little we could glean of her past apart from the diary came from scores of letters from persons, many half illiterate, who had known her in the rough Northwest" (*HP* 262), he recalled, a characterization that surely would not have pleased these willing informants. He paid Whiteley's friend Nellie Hemenway twenty-five dollars to question local acquaintances.[61] He also consulted Edmund Conklin, a professor of psychology at the University of Oregon who specialized in "the foster-child fantasy." His chief agent, however, was Elbert Bede, the Cottage Grove newspaperman. Bede clearly felt honored to correspond so familiarly with Sedgwick, confessing to "a peculiar feeling of friendship which seems quite unusual when it is understood that we have never seen each other" (a response in kind was not forthcoming).[62] Bede was so close to Whiteley's circle that his daughter was a friend of one of her sisters.[63] He labored to identify events, people, and places referenced in the diary, and he interviewed friends, family, and neighbors, research that forms the core of his rather snide 1954 biography, *Fabulous Opal Whiteley: From Oregon Logging Camp to Princess in India*. The carbon copies of the letters that circulated among Bede, Conklin, and Sedgwick make for an entertaining archival spectacle, a record of their hot pursuit of what were literally figments of Whiteley's imagination, sumptuous garments and shadowy followers. (Sedgwick once telegrammed Bede, "Have reason to suspect genuine conspiracy. Urge you avoid communication with correspondents seeking to know too much.")[64] The team labored to solve the mystery of this girl with "her dark eyes and dark hair and her smallness and the dimple in her chin"[65]—to use her own words—and utterly failed.

After their rift, Sedgwick wrote his former charge, "The care which I have given to your interests ever since that first day in September, a full year ago, when you came to my office, has been quite exceptional." With some perspicacity, she retorted, "I believe you had persuaded yourself that you were being both kind and generous, but I also believe that you thought of me as a sort of tool, which you could use for your own purposes and profit." Since its inception, countless writers had vied to contribute to the *Atlantic*, valuing its prestige over the relatively low financial compensation. Whiteley, however, was oblivious to the honor. Instead, she focused on how Sedgwick had used her to mint *Atlantic* coin, insisting that his use of her as a "tool" mattered more than any gracious conduct. Her behavior recollects another disruptive woman from the *Atlantic*'s past, Mary Abigail Dodge, who had sued editor James Fields for income denied her due to the magazine's policy of paying women less than men. For all its good offices, the *Atlantic* was a business structured by financial transactions, as dissenting contributors like Dodge and Whiteley underscored.[66]

In the same letter, Whiteley further argued, "You speak of your belief in the genuineness of my diary, as if that were also an act of kindness on your part, which ought to put me under obligations to you. But I cannot see this as an act of kindness, because you know that my diary is genuine, and so you could not think anything else." But by this point, Sedgwick was not sure what he believed and what he knew. As his last attempt at certainty, he asked for an affidavit attesting that "her story . . . was absolutely true." As this was not forthcoming, in the spring of 1921 he sold the book rights to G. P. Putnam's, "lock, stock and barrel," and he also forbade the further use of his preface.[67]

For Stewart, and even more so for Rose, *Atlantic* authorship resulted in not only writing income but also largesse from distant friends. Whiteley, however, reversed this movement: on receiving her first *Atlantic* income, she methodically began making restitution for past support, paying more than $1,000 toward debts she had incurred for *The Fairyland around Us* as well as giving $1.50 and $2.00 refunds for copies of the book never received. Willard James in Los Angeles, for example, received a check of $100 to go toward the $650 she owed him, along with best wishes for "success with your Little Rock Fruit ranch."[68]

Less explicably, over the course of several months Whiteley family members received costly gifts, mostly silverware, from an anonymous benefactor. They also received letters, purportedly from Opal's former guardians, explaining that the gifts were compensation for her care. The letters were easily traced to Whiteley through the rented typewriter she used in Brookline. Each of her three sisters received, in installments, a ninety-three-piece silver set that included a tea service and items like cold meat forks, a nutcracker and picks, and a tomato server.[69] Her father got a gold watch and silver shaving mug and her young brother, an Erector set. It is likely she sent the family money, too, since her sisters began attending "business college" in Portland and "dressing above the average," according to Bede.[70] And all this began before she got any money from the *Atlantic*. Sedgwick was confounded. "If Miss Whiteley actually sent the silver, how in the world did she pay for it?" he asked. "When I saw her first, she was in apparent destitution. I know she was hungry."[71] To comic effect, at his behest Bede strove to catch a glimpse of "the watch number" on Edward Whiteley's present, which he refused to reveal.[72]

This flow of silver from East Coast to West is still another odd turn in a story that usually features not the acquisition of objects, but their loss. Whiteley's history, both imagined and actual, is studded with disappearing things, including royal heirlooms, family photographs, the Angel Books, and the diary itself: destroyed, deposited, restored, and then vanished. Sedgwick often referenced the physical artifact as proof of the text's authenticity: "Of the rightness and honesty of the manuscript as the *Atlantic* printed it, I am utterly convinced; more certain am I than of the authorship of many another famous diary, for I have watched the original copy reborn" (*HP* 263). However, none of the manuscript is extant, and there is no record of its fate. Sedgwick's papers include an imploring note from Bede: "May I not have a page of the original diary? Fourth request."[73] In the note's margin, an editor's hand answers, "No."

The diary's disappearance may have its source in Whiteley's efforts to extend her writing career. Like Stewart and Rose, she sought to ride the momentum of her *Atlantic* success with immediate further publications, and she likewise sought to expand her generic range. Much less dependent on *Atlantic* connections, she had already developed her own marketing strategies with *Fairyland*, which she repurposed to self-publish a volume of nature poetry, *The Flower of Stars*, in 1923. By then she was living in Washington, D.C., where she had moved after leaving New York. She mailed copies of the book to prominent people across the country, who could opt to either return it or send payment (recipients included Amy Lowell, who declined graciously enough that Whiteley continued to write her). She also made plans for a memoir and outlined a novel, "The Impossible Man." Proving she had learned the rudiments of western cliché, the latter featured the wealthy Richard Livermore, "a little weary of the world," who flees New York City for Oregon to take up life as a humble lumberjack.[74]

Most important, Whiteley had a contract with Putnam's to publish the second volume of her diary. Now possessing the rights to the sensational *The Story of Opal*, they were eager for a sequel. Yet not only did they renege, but they also urged her to hand over the original diary manuscript to Richard and Ella Cabot. Cousins to Mabel, "Uncle Richard" and "Aunt Ella" had assumed Sedgwick's guardian role. A 1923 letter informs them she has mailed it off: "A lot of the Diary goes by express to-day. It is inside the suit box."[75] On this it dropped out of circulation, perhaps destroyed.[76]

From D.C., Whiteley moved on to France, briefly, and then India, with the intention of researching Henri d'Orléans's activities. Beck gives the fullest account of her ten months there, a welcome corrective to the usual stories (derived from Bede's and Sedgwick's embellished accounts) that have her feted by royalty and plumbing the kingdom's secrets, an-elephantback, no less.[77] While more pedestrian, the real story is still remarkable. In her usual way, Whiteley arrived in Udaipur entirely out of funds. Rather than have an almost countrywoman live in destitution among them, the British civil service put her up in a hotel. She began an intensive study of the region, and she came to know its deposed ruler Fateh Singh. She also entered into a possibly romantic relationship with a young Indian man later imprisoned as a con man, one Swami Duetenland. The growing scandal prompted the British to pressure her to leave, which she finally, reluctantly, did, sojourning in Rome and Vienna before reaching London.

Whiteley's "Story of Unknown India" was published as a six-part series of illustrated articles, November 27, 1929, to June 1, 1930, in the British travel magazine the *Queen*. But she had first approached the *Atlantic*. In a series of letters that reveal a shrewd awareness of her past value, she badgered Sedgwick to accept her latest work:

> Trusting that I may soon recieve [*sic*] money from you for the Indus River articles, also for the others which I sent 11 days ago on Udaipur in Jajputana river which by your long letter of August 6th you were so eager to have. . . .
>
> Also I trust you will pay me very well indeed because of course anything you publish from me will bring you a very large sale of extra "Atlantics" because of the interest they had in the Diary.[78]

She also took the opportunity to reflect, in a way, on past hostilities:

> I cannot hope that you will fully understand about my not wanting any more of my life story published until I had seen my beloved ones in France and elsewhere—you ought to understand in part—but you see I felt it belonged to them—I had poured into the diary what I had thought and felt for them & my dear little friends of the woods. I had put my soul into it and it was all I had to bring back except my character of a good girl. And it did n't matter that they were in fragments—they had all the feeling in them & there was no need for the piecing nor for the public to have them.

"Linking my true name with the nom-de-plume and sad life of 'Opal Whiteley' in America might cause a great sale," she wrote the following month.[79] Surprisingly, given their turbulent history, Sedgwick was tempted to publish one of the articles, whose "natural sympathy" he admired. He made inquiries to contacts in India to verify her experiences, and he asked Whiteley for documentation to "prove beyond a doubt that you have taken this extraordinary journey: that you have lived with Indian princes, that you have hunted and roamed through the most fascinating country in the world."[80] This was not vouchsafed, and he backed away. "Do you think the child is entirely herself?" he queried his staff.[81]

In *The Happy Profession*, he muses over Whiteley's final submissions: "The hard sunlight of middle age beat down upon a world that everybody sees only too clearly. The fairy kingdom was now the playground of other children. Its gates were closed, and Opal stood without" (266). By attributing the change in her writing to her "middle age," he affirms his steadfast argument: that *The Story of Opal* was the expression of the universal child. He also summons that urtext of women's class transformation to maintain, "At the heart of every little girl Cinderella sits enthroned" (264). The assessment reveals more about Sedgwick than Whiteley. If this *Atlantic* contributor is Cinderella, poised to regain her birthright, then her editor must be the prince. Sedgwick relished rescuing his faraway Cinderellas, elevating working-class women by making over jumbled manuscripts into polished texts. Yet in this tale, the princess comes to scorn the prince.

CHAPTER FOUR

ATLANTIC EXCHANGE

Hilda Rose and The Stump Farm

> The person to whom the writer addresses himself normally is
> not present at all. . . . he must not be present. I am writing a book
> which will be read by thousands, or, I modestly hope, by tens of
> thousands. So, please, get out of the room.
>
> —Walter Ong, *Orality and Literacy:*
> *The Technologizing of the Word*

While in Montevideo, Uruguay, in the course of his 1923 tour of South America, Ellery Sedgwick was in a quandary over how to change money on a bank holiday. The problem was solved when he chanced upon a man entering a closed branch office of American Express. He confided to his travel journal, "He is the manager of the company, and comes from Lynn, Mass. I am building a house in Beverly and we are in complete rapport. Mr. Clark—as his name is—was for years in the Philippines under Governor Forbes—'a fine man as ever was.' This makes us chummier still. 'You don't happen to know Peter Bowditch?' asks Mr. Clarke. 'Know him?' say I. 'I taught him at school.' A nice little, tight little world, isn't it" (TJ, March 27, 1923). This anecdote about encountering such chumminess so far afield is a little too smug for comfort, as Sedgwick savors the "complete rapport" his social connections induced in distant realms. Yet we should recollect that he made writers in "the outlying territories of Literature" (*HP* 197) feel like they, too, dwelt within his "nice little, tight little world." As Hilda Rose wrote him from far northern Canada following her *Atlantic* debut, "Instead of dreading the coming winter, I am looking forward to it. . . . I can read all the books and magazines that have come and think about the friends out there in the busy world. They were there all the time, they just didn't know about me before. What a nice friendly world it is. How much I owe to you and the Atlantic. You took away all my loneliness, made me happy and gave me a winter grub-stake with that big check."[1]

Rose is by far this study's most faraway woman. She never met Sedgwick and never went to Boston (although a family of *Atlantic* readers did pay a surprise visit to her cabin, only to stay on for the whole winter). Nor did she meet face-to-face most of the recipients of the letters that compose her only book, *The Stump Farm: A Chronicle of Pioneering*. Burntfork, Wyoming, and Cottage Grove, Oregon, seem centrally located in comparison to her adopted home of Fort Vermillion, Alberta, four hundred miles north of Edmonton. As Rose describes it, "It's such a big, wild country—big lakes, rivers, and muskegs; no trails and no people. Less than two human beings to each thousand square miles, and that means Indians, too. I won't admit out loud that I'm lonesome, but it's a Robinson Crusoe existence. Like being alive yet buried. Books will save my reason, and letters" (*SF* 149–50). Her isolation spurred her to a prolific correspondence, which ultimately resulted in *The Stump Farm*. A near emblem of the seamlessness of her textual and lived experience, one of her long-distance friends sent her a copy of *Robinson Crusoe*.

A selection of Rose's homesteading letters was first published across four issues of the 1927 *Atlantic*.[2] The *Atlantic* introduced "the author of these valiant letters" as "once a young and ardent school teacher in Illinois; but tuberculosis sent her to the highlands of the West, where after five busy and health-giving years of tent life she married a man much older than herself and, as a farmer's wife on a stump farm, gallantly shouldered his burdens and her own."[3] It then reveals how her correspondence was brokered by still another print institution, as a direct result of her paucity of cultural access: "Followed years of hardship and intellectual dearth, until at last, one bitter winter, she 'had the courage' to write to the Chicago *Tribune* for something to read—'the books that nobody cared for any more.' Her modest appeal brought her friends as well as books, and the letters which we print were written to those

FIGURE 4. Hilda Rose in Fort Vermillion. *Manuscripts and Archives Division, The New York Public Library.*

friends." The introduction concludes with the familiar insistence, "That they were ever to be printed was farthest from her thought."

Collectively entitled "The Stump Farm," the February, March, and April installments are composed of letters Rose sent from northern Idaho, although by the time of their publication she had already emigrated to Canada. Most were addressed to one Mrs. Austin in California, "a dear old invalid past 80" whom she never met in person.[4] Indicating how the letters themselves sealed the relationship, the series commences with the declaration, "We are friends now."[5] April's installment ends with Rose's move to Fort Vermillion and her early experiences there. After a four-month hiatus, a final contribution, "The New Homestead: Letters from Fort Vermillion," opens the September *Atlantic*. This consists of letters addressed to Dr. Mary F. Hobart in Needham Heights, Massachusetts, the retired obstetrician who would soon assemble a larger number of letters into *The Stump Farm*. Rose's impressions of life on the Peace River made for an astonishing second *Atlantic* act, the hills of Idaho succeeded by an almost trackless wilderness. The *Atlantic* itself advanced the plot: her payment from the magazine went toward supplies to survive her first long winter in Alberta. Boston's interest in her faraway home helped her establish an even remoter one and, as a consequence, produce for its consumption even more gripping tales.

In "The New Homestead," Rose guides her Massachusetts friend — and her *Atlantic* readership at large — stage-by-stage to Fort Vermillion:

> I see by one of your letters that you have no conception of how far north I am. Calgary is a large city crowded with cars. Farther north is Edmonton, also a big city. Next comes Peace River, a small town at the end of the railroad. . . . We went north all the way until we came to the Great Slave Lake Region. We got off just this side of it in the wilderness. . . . Get a map and find the Great Slave Lake. A little south of it — that's here.

Atlantic readers, educated by contributors such as Mary Hallock Foote, Mary Austin, Zitkala-Ša, Elinore Pruitt Stewart, and Opal Whiteley, were used to looking west. North, however, was a new direction. In accord with Rose's injunction to "get a map," Sedgwick imparts, "on our office map a blue star on the white waste area of northwestern Canada marks the frontier home of Hilda Rose."[6]

In April 1928, the serial was expanded into *The Stump Farm* under the imprint of Little, Brown, and Company, which as of the previous year published all *Atlantic* books. Further embedding the text in an elite Boston cultural milieu, Samuel A. Eliot, renowned Unitarian minister and son of former Harvard president Charles W. Eliot, contributed the foreword. The book went through five printings, two in 1928 and one each in 1929, 1931, and 1935. The *Atlantic* promoted Rose as a representative working-class American, a woman whose "struggle, although it seems almost unparalleled, doubtless has its counterpart in many an unchronicled life." Eliot likewise identified her as among the "Forgotten Millions," while an advertisement simply characterized her book as "The diary of the pioneer woman." Years later, the *Atlantic* reiterated, "The hardihood and resourcefulness required of every pioneer are brought home to us in the letters of the little housewife."[7]

As we shall see, in addition to Rose's "hardihood," literal donations from *Atlantic* readers enabled her family to stay on the land. This chapter delineates the socially enmeshed conditions of her textual production and tracks its passage between private hands and the marketplace. Following an overview of the life events that led to authorship, it traces the history of *The Stump Farm* — evolving from letters to serial and finally to book — and shows how the text itself inscribes it. Generated by cross-class relationships, Rose's writing displays a calculated exchange of personal disclosure for material gain, even as this operation is punctuated with sentiment. The *Atlantic*, moreover, out of self-interest and altruism alike was invested in her forming rewarding relationships with its readers, as the quintessence of *Atlantic* fellowship.

I also discuss how contemporary readers received *The Stump Farm,* yielding a more nuanced account of who read regional writing, and why. Amy Blair's *Reading Up: Middle-Class Readers and the Culture of Success in the Early Twentieth-Century United States* has helped me recognize *The Stump Farm* as having been expediently "misread." While it originated in letters directed to a select number of relatively privileged Americans, most of its readers were further down the socioeconomic ladder. Through processing the book in communal, conversive contexts (in schools, churches, clubs, libraries, offices), they both boosted their cultural capital and extracted the inspiring lessons they craved. Countless hundreds wrote directly to Rose, restoring the epistolary origins of her literary production, and a significant number sent her forms of material aid. We see a different kind of authorial economy emerge: not a writer selling an imaginative work to anonymous readerships, but one exchanging, at the individual level, her textual life for the goods she needs to perpetuate it. For decades, Rose enjoyed membership in an attenuated community formed by readers' devotion to *The Stump Farm* and the magazine that introduced it to them.

Hilda Marie Gustafson was born in 1880 in the industrial city of Rockford, Illinois. Only several months earlier, her parents, Carl Otto and Anna Mathilda, had emigrated from Sweden—"in a cattle boat," she relayed[8]—with their two young sons. They would soon have five children, including another son and another daughter. As in Chicago, the Swedish population of Rockford was booming, making it the second-largest city in Illinois and the nation's second-largest furniture manufacturer. By the end of the century, many of its factories were cooperatively owned by Swedes who had brought with them their traditional cabinetmaking skills,[9] men like Carl Gustafson. In 1900 he and his oldest son were employed as hardwood finishers, while the other children, including the twenty-year-old Hilda, were still in school.[10] The family, however, did not prosper. Rose mentions contracting polio as a child and living in a dire tenement with a punishing mortgage.[11] Suggesting her cultural aspiration, she also claimed she was a dedicated *Atlantic Monthly* reader by the age of fourteen.[12]

In her early twenties, she worked as a kindergarten teacher at Jackson Elementary School, not far from Kishwaukee Street, the main artery of Rockford's Swedish district. During this time she was saving for college, but illness disrupted her plans. Her education fund went to doctors, and in a family effort at recuperation, she, her father, and her brother Carl moved to Kootenai County, Idaho, in 1905. (She apparently made a full recovery: despite midlife complaints of a weak heart that "did not want to beat," she lived to be eighty-seven.)[13] They bought, on installment, ten acres of irrigated land just east of Coeur d'Alene, and her mother and sister joined them.

While Rose identified only climate as the draw, the Gustafsons' choice of destination may have been influenced by the pending implementation of the Allotment Act of 1906, which made vast tracts of the Coeur d'Alene Reservation available for homesteading. She recollected that she "took part in a land stampede" there—with no success—and did the same in Montana and Washington: "There were three reservations opened and I tried all three for I had come West with T. B. and my money was about gone. I was living in a tent in Idaho. We were short of food the coming winter and the next summer I took over the job of making our living so to speak. My father was broken in health and so was my brother. We three were here far from home to see if I could get well in a dry climate." Making the transition from artisans to farmers was difficult for the family, who had spent the past twenty-five years in a teeming city. Anticipating the conditions of her marriage, Rose maintained that their maintenance fell to her, traveling "9 miles to town for 4 years" to peddle the vegetables they grew. The year 1910 sees the Gustafsons in Prairie, Idaho, in a boardinghouse run by Mrs. Philomene Lippert, a French divorcée, as the census reports. At twenty-nine, Rose was a "Housekeeper," while her mother and sister were "Farm helpers." Carl the elder and Carl the younger were farmers, with the former employed by a fruit farm.[14]

Hilda married Charles W. Rose, twenty-eight years her senior, the following year, and their son, Karl Otto, was born in 1917.[15] A native of Quebec, Rose had emigrated with his Canadian mother, British father, and younger siblings to the United States in 1877.[16] The family "mov[ed] steadily westward" in a trajectory that included a long interval of farming in Oronoco, Minnesota.[17] From at least 1900 to 1910, Charles farmed with his brother Simeon in the hills of Rimrock, Idaho.[18] (Although Rose never mentions the couple, as of 1920 Simeon was married to her sister, Anna, twenty years younger than he.)[19] Charles and Hilda likewise settled on a so-called stump farm in Rimrock, having first to clear the land before they could begin cultivation. Yet the area soon entered a period of prolonged drought, a statewide agricultural crisis that continued through the 1920s. The Roses saw many of their neighbors leave, and in July 1926 they did the same, to begin homesteading in Alberta. While Charles yearned to return to his Quebec birthplace, filing on land in Fort Vermilion was much more affordable.

A full half century after Rose's arrival, the area was still utterly remote, as Will Ferguson's recollections of his 1970s childhood there attest: "The rest of the country seemed so far away it might as well have been an imaginary place. Canada lay far to the south, beyond the curve of the horizon. Canada was the place the radio signals came from." Fort Vermilion was established in 1788 by the North West Company, later becoming a Hudson Bay Company stronghold. "Peace River Country" was opened to settlement in 1905 just as agriculture was beginning to supplant fur, enabled by new steamboat service. In this land of forests, lakes, and bogs, the river long remained the primary mode of transport, for both people and goods. The area saw an influx of homesteaders through the 1920s, a transition Rose records. It became an important farming district, as the northernmost arable land in Canada—and the world. The first road, however, was only built in 1947; during the long winters, residents received mail only by dogsled.[20]

Rose once announced, "I am strong on eugenics."[21] Her belief in the need to safeguard and improve human genetic stock is much on display in her published and private writing, in respect to both her own family and the Native peoples among whom she lived. For example, she often commented that she married Charles—whom she called "Daddy"—because she knew he would sire a good son. "Daddy's ancestors are the finest in Scotland and England," she maintains in her book. "Therefore my boy is more receptive and by instinct chooses the better things because I chose for him a father of that type" (*SF* 66). She also made disparaging comments about her "half-breed" neighbors in Peace River. *The Stump Farm* recounts her crisis of conscience over having encouraged a white girl to marry the Métis man she loved, championing romance without considering the miserable children to come. Rose states, "For I don't want breed grandchildren myself. I can't think of anything more horrible than to have grandchildren with strong backs and weak heads" (*SF* 109). With their disclosure of personal, vested interest, such comments go well beyond reflexive participation in dominant racist ideologies. Rose's beliefs about the necessity of staving off reproductive folly aligned her across class lines with some of her white readers, including her key supporter Dr. Mary Hobart (on whom more later), and with Sedgwick, too, who expressed open distaste for miscegenation.

Proclaiming Rose to be the "flower" of "pioneer virtues," Eliot makes an implicitly racial endorsement in his foreword to her book: "There is no indication in these letters that we have reached an age of lotus-eating or that American life has grown soft and luxurious and prosaic." Rose herself, however, extols Charles's pedigree but omits her own contribution to the gene pool, a choice consistent with her usual silence about her Swedish descent. While her father and brother often went by the anglicized variant "Charles," on first inspection she seems to have recovered the original family name in deciding on "Karl Otto" for her son. Yet in response to a query from Sedgwick, she identified a different source and other reasons: "Daddy's name is Charles Worcester Rose which was his father's name. I wanted Boy named for him but Daddy said a short name would be better in case the Boy became a doctor or went into politics. 'We'll change Charles to Karl, spell it with K and he'll have a universal name, known in many nationalities.'" She then tersely divulged, "I was born in Illinois, my parents came nearly fifty years ago from Sweden"—and changed the subject. Her disinclination to identify either of the elder Carls as her son's namesake intimates her sense of distance from the Gustafsons' native country. *The Stump Farm* underscores her American identity, even as it depicts still another act of emigration, that which made her the *Atlantic*'s "friend in the Far North."[22]

The Stump Farm: Overview

The Stump Farm originated in Rose's need for women's community while living on her isolated farm in the hills of Idaho and even remoter homestead on the Peace River. Foregrounding this genesis, Eliot's fore-word concludes with "grateful acknowledgments to those whose radi-ant good will penetrated to the remote stump farm and elicited these letters, addressed at first to strangers in California and New England, and then, with growing confidence and affection, to true-hearted friends."[23] Rose's receptive first readers played a generative role, "elic-iting" pungent letters that led to friendship. *The Stump Farm*, accord-ingly, emphasizes Rose's persistent desire to "see and talk to a bunch of women once more, for it almost drives me wild to be alone" (*SF* 34). From Idaho, she divulges, "I have no woman to talk to, so I will write to ease my brain" (*SF* 30). In Canada her isolation drastically intensified, a condition she represents as a crucible for her art.

Justifying the decision to emigrate, she once stated, "One thing a writer must be and that is himself," continuing, "Daddy said he was going to take me so far from the world that it would never spoil me, so far from the world that it would never hurt me. So I can be myself without fear and have all the quiet needed to think in and write."[24] She suggests both that her solitude enabled her to write and that it compelled her to. Even as she founded a women's club in her home community, her developing correspondence created the sensation of companionship in the world at large, twinned undertakings that proved decisive for her literary future.

The Stump Farm spans January 1918 to October 1927 and is divided into two sections. Part 1 ranges over eight years in Idaho. Part 2 is more compressed, describing Rose's first fifteen months in Fort Vermilion. Sometimes the narrative leaps forward, due to wide gaps in the chronology. At other points it stalls, as Rose expresses the same sentiments and tells the same stories to different recipients. Fort Vermillion's postal service informs the book's structure, in that Rose wrote letters in concentrated bursts to catch the infrequent mail boat. Her finances were also a factor: she hesitated to begin a letter unless she had the stamp.

From its opening line, *The Stump Farm* represents Rose as displaced from her customary environment, and thus as more akin to her readers than one might expect: "It's thirteen years since I taught school, and I have gone through a great deal since then" (3). In the Idaho section, she stresses the marginal "far" aspect of her location in referring to it as "the backwoods," "up here in the mountains," or simply "out here" (36, 42, 30), and she invokes a range of other sites at various degrees of remove from her. These include "the prairie" below, a scant seven miles away but psychologically a whole other realm. She often makes the long walk down, to collect the mail, cultivate rented land, work for wages, visit her brother, or attend a rare social event. There is "the city" of her past and her foreboding, to which she has resolved never to return. There is Canada, for which Daddy longs. And last, there is "the world"—the dwelling place of the women to whom she writes—which she conceives as a heady realm of leisure and culture: lemonade, gardens, and college towns. An early entry succinctly represents her yearning with two comments, the exhilarated, "At last! At last! I am going to have friends who will be glad to see me when I go back to the world for a visit or to stay," and then the anguished, "I want to go back, I don't care where, and have friends once more" (6, 8).

Many passing remarks indicate her hardship. She is two years behind on taxes and in debt for seeds. She is obliged to send her elder foster child back to a Spokane orphanage, where she died. Charles's sister in New Haven, Connecticut, makes a bid to adopt Karl, promising a college education in return. She breaks a finger while picking apples and sets it herself; Karl loses part of one of his to a hay cutter. The long gaps between some of the letters tell their own story.

The Stump Farm records her daily work while mapping plans for a brighter future. She and Charles raise livestock and grow oats, wheat, fruit, and vegetables, and she supplements their income with day labor that includes berry picking, canning, and work on a chicken farm. Charles is "already broken in health" (*SF* 13), so his contribution is limited. Adding to her responsibilities, her parents come to live with them. "Father is partially paralyzed," she explains, "Mother is too feeble to be up all day. . . . And Daddy is so tired he goes to sleep if he sits down anywhere" (*SF* 16–17). Conditions worsen with the drought, and she struggles to feed them all. What began as Daddy's quixotic notion, "to die on Canadian soil among the Indians" (*SF* 20), hardens into a plan.

Once *The Stump Farm* reaches Fort Vermillion, her experience takes on a fantastic dimension, as she describes disembarking from a steamboat on a wild riverbank with her elderly husband and young son and a freight car of household goods, farm tools, livestock, and piano (why not?), unsure of her next step. She files on a claim and erects a tent, in which the family is still living when winter sets in. Of her life there, she had envisioned, "I thought I would get some traps and try for some furs up there; live like an Indian; shoot and fish and trap" (*SF* 24). (She also hoped that Karl could study Greek and Latin with some well-educated priest.) She learns, though, that there is no fur to be had; she also discovers that to go out of sight of her home is to risk becoming permanently lost. Revealing the perspective of a born-and-bred urbanite, she describes her son on his horse as looking like "a Wild West movie show" and a mounted policeman as "just stepped out of a story book" (*SF* 103, 110). Her portrait of a bygone age is textured by the domestic objects she uses, pioneer hand-me-downs like "Grandma Rose's old cards to comb the wool with," "Grandma Rose's big black iron kettle," and "Grandma Rose's old cook stove that she used fifty years" (*SF* 107, 119, 166). "I have gone back to when the world is still young," she avers. "Civilization is gone and only the little band of lonesome women here remember it" (*SF* 143).

Her sense of authorial vocation grew more pronounced in Fort Vermilion, keen recompense for the daunting challenges she faced. Even as she chronicles her homesteading efforts, she shows herself undertaking a new kind of work, writing. Before her move, she had exclaimed, "Won't there be lots of things to write about in a new country way out on the frontier!" (*SF* 78). This prediction proved true, as her hardship itself became her literary coin.

The Stump Farm: Composition

"Are you Discouraged?" Thus queries Charles B. Driscoll in his review of *The Stump Farm*. The widely syndicated panegyric urges,

> In case you ever feel that your affairs have come to about the worst possible pass, and you feel that a jump into the nearest and deepest river is about the next move, please do me a personal favor and read "The Stump Farm."
>
> It isn't fiction nor poetry. Hilda Rose, who wrote it, is a real woman. . . .
>
> Hilda Rose wrote letters to her friends of school days, and one of these friends was so much impressed that she sold the letters to the Atlantic Monthly, sending the proceeds to Mrs. Rose, who had no notion that she was producing literature as a by-product of her struggle. Now these letters, with some others, have been made into a book, and Hilda Rose is an author![25]

We will shelve for now the questions of how her text was received and whether Rose had "no notion that she was producing literature," to trace the chain of events that led to *The Stump Farm*. Her epistolary network, rooted in women's benevolence projects and spanning the continent, little resembles a simple exchange with "friends of school days."

As the *Atlantic* relayed, Rose first began corresponding with distant well-wishers after writing to a Chicago newspaper to request secondhand reading material. This growing network supported an altruistic venture of her own, the women's club she founded in Rimrock in 1923. Thanks to the federal Smith-Lever Act of 1914, which required state and local governments to match federal funding for agricultural extension work, such clubs were booming across the Midwest and the West. Rose launched her "Civic Club" both to assist her desperately poor neighbors and to give herself a social project. She was aided by the University of Montana Extension Service, which arranged occasional workshops on subjects ranging from nutrition to hat trimming. The club flourished, joining the state federation two years later (*SF* 76).

Charles disapproved. As an "aristocrat," Rose disclosed, he believed the "so fragile, so nice, so dainty and everything" Hilda should shun the women she lived among, warning, "If Mrs. T. and this club lady knew what sort of women you have taken up with, they'd have nothing more to do with you" (*SF* 46). Moreover, she herself had reservations about her neighbors, whom she viewed as sexually rampant; she feared entering their company would thwart her plan "to go back into the world some day and take my place and associate with cultured people once more" (*SF* 49). Yet as her loneliness mounted, her standards lowered, as she reveals prior to cataloging their reproductive choices:

> So for twelve years I have minded him, and then I couldn't stand it any longer. I started this club. It has twenty active members and they are all living straight now. The club is keeping some of them straight, they are so anxious to belong. Here is what some of them are: (1) Mrs. C. has two children and almost kills herself once a year to avoid a baby. (2) Mrs. T. is not married, but says she is. We all know better. She lives with Mr. T. and has two children, and does what Mrs. C. does every year. She has wretched health like Mrs. C. (3) Mrs. S. left her husband one winter and lived with the hired man several months. Her husband told her to get a divorce, and she did, but married, not the hired man, but the Greek cook at a railroad construction camp east of us. . . . I could go on like this all night. (*SF* 48)[26]

While Rose depicts her inclusive organization as providing essential community services—fund-raisers like a box social and a spelling bee, visits to new mothers, emergency aid after a fire, and a successful petition for better postal service—her largest claim is that the club kept its members "straight."

In 1910 Mary Woolley, president of Mount Holyoke College, described the burgeoning club movement as creating "common ground" that connected "California, Illinois and Boston."[27] Far from the ostracism Charles predicted, the Civic Club yielded just these kinds of national affiliations for Rose. Socially, it made for new contacts with distant middle-class acquaintances (it probably led, for example, to her association with Hobart in Massachusetts, who was dedicated to women's causes). Textually, it gave her a writing subject that strengthened her bonds with them and made for the semblance of equitable relations. Like Stewart before her, she could demonstrate that she herself did charitable work, placing herself on the same level as the women to whom she wrote. Her sense of reciprocity is suggested in comments like this one: "The magazines you sent me were very interesting, especially as I am working on somewhat the same line with the women up here in the mountains" (*SF* 42).

Her correspondents passed her letters on, a practice that resulted in forms of material aid for Rose and, eventually, publication. In hindsight, this trajectory is signposted in her April 6, 1925, letter to Austin, the primary recipient of the letters that form the *Atlantic* serial. Suggesting how closely she associated the topics, the letter moves swiftly from club news to Austin's proposal to distribute her letters and finally to a package of clothing she had received:

> I am glad you get the same point of view in regard to my Club up here as I have. I have written to the State Federation of Clubs and I'll have something for them to do next meeting, I think. I gave them a little talk last week and got them interested in "better laws" and "better homes." In regard to my letters you may do as you like. I didn't know they were interesting, but I suppose they are a contrast to the life of the city. The reading won't hurt me if you leave my name off, just say it's a friend of Mrs. Austin's.
>
> It was very kind of your friend Mrs. Meserve to send me what she did. I cannot but accept gratefully because I have to or go without clothes. . . . It's a fine dress for this climate. And the cream wool skirt will make me two skirts or one whole dress.[28]

Rose identifies herself as sharing Austin's "point of view" about the less privileged, even as Austin served as her own benefactor. Austin collected reading material and clothing for her from her friends, surely the same people with whom she shared the letters. Indicating the process by which her epistolary circle broadened, Rose goes on to specify where she should forward her letter: "This is Mrs. Sturtz's address. I owe her a letter since last fall and her friend Mary's last letter must be answered soon. Mrs. Blanche Sturtz 3014 E. Sixth, Kansas City, Mo." (Sturtz was active in local politics, elected to a Missouri state committee position in 1952.)[29] Rose would conduct this manner of exchange throughout her life, proffering tales of rural strife and striving that, circulating within a diffuse and increasingly eminent social network, elicited essential goods, services, and connections. Yet for a heady period, she was an author as conventionally conceived, with actual sales.

The "Publishers' Note" to *The Stump Farm* identifies Florence Fisk White as the first to submit Rose's letters to the *Atlantic,* which Rose corroborates in alluding to the efforts of "Mrs. W." on her behalf. As life grew grimmer in Idaho, her correspondents had dwindled to Austin alone, who urged her to persevere so that, some far-off day, she could mine her letters for fictional themes. Rose presents her literary efforts as a direct result of women's friendship. She had "quit writing" (*SF* 138), she states, "But this little old lady persisted. So I kept on with my diary to please her." Austin acted on her faith in her talents by showing

Rose's letters to White, a service that made for her first connection to a social elite.

White's parents, Robert E. Fisk and Elizabeth Chester Fisk, had been lead actors in the business, social, and cultural enterprise of Helena, Montana, during the city's early years. The couple met through the "Autograph Quilt": signed by its many makers (including Elizabeth's younger sister) and donated to the United States Sanitary Commission, the quilt covered Robert's hospital bed in North Carolina as he convalesced from a war injury, prompting the correspondence that led to his engagement.[30] In Helena Robert ran the *Helena Herald,* and Elizabeth spearheaded education and civic reform efforts. The latter enjoyed a writer's reputation for the vivid letters about pioneer life, commencing in 1867, that she sent her family in Connecticut. By encouraging Rose to circulate frontier narrative, White extended her own western maternal legacy.

The Fisk family had relocated to Berkeley, California, by the time Rose herself came west. Florence went on to marry Clarence White, scion of a wealthy family of industrialists whose products included the White truck and the White sewing machine. Clarence and Florence's 1931 funding of the Redlands Bowl in Redlands, California, a public amphitheater for outdoor concerts, proves their affluence. In a resonant encounter, Rose met her crucial intermediary for the first and last time at the Spokane train station, just as she began her migratory journey. To the acquaintance they shared, she wrote, "I am glad Mrs. W. liked the two adventurers she met in the railway depot for forty minutes. I was very tired, worried, and depressed, so I didn't look my best, but I surely felt good when she actually kissed me and Boy good-bye. She did like me a little, and me a perfect stranger too" (*SF* 99). In a letter to the *Atlantic* that Sedgwick printed in the "Contributors' Column," White situates her dealings with her new homesteader acquaintance as an extension of her leisure activity in the West: "This summer I made occasion when returning from Yellowstone and Glacier parks to meet Hilda Rose."[31]

With White, Rose gained an advocate who sought to market her work, and she began to recognize her experience as literary capital. She claimed that she knew nothing about her forthcoming publication until she received a copy of the February 1927 *Atlantic* along with her first check. Arriving at her "blackest hour" (*SF* 136), the money was much welcomed, but in time the serial's greater impact came from the new correspondents it drew: both the voracious fans, whose letters Rose dutifully, if resentfully, answered, "for if I don't they will not buy my next book," and a select group she identified as honorary family, among them "a teacher in Michigan who is a Communist, a teacher in N.Y. An old doctor in the Indian Service, a woman who had almost a billion but has them no more, a congressman's wife, and six aged but brilliant old maids."[32] The "brilliant old maids" she cherished (despite ruing their choice not to propagate) included Margaret G. Emerson of New York City, a member of an illustrious family of scholars with close ties to Europe and Japan whom I introduced earlier as one of Stewart's supporters. Jack Jensen, an elderly veteran in Los Angeles whom she assisted in writing a memoir, was another important new friend, and this chapter will revisit them both. Through the *Atlantic*, Rose boosted her economic capital (slightly) and her social capital (considerably).

She also continued to write to her early *Atlantic* liaison Hobart, whom she always addressed as "Dear Dr. Lady." One of the first women to graduate from an American medical school, Hobart was retired from a long career at the New England Hospital for Women and Children. She had also been a physician for the Boston Children's Aid Society and Boston Juvenile Court. On behalf of the latter, she conducted gynecological examinations of girls suspected of "sexual misconduct," an activity that, with its whiff of eugenic policing, suggests some of the common ground on which she and Rose met. Making for another link between Stewart and Rose, Hobart was the attending physician at the death of Mary Hannah Graves, sister to Stewart's primary correspondent, Juliet Coney. While this is certainly a coincidence, it also demonstrates the narrow span of the *Atlantic's* inner circle.[33]

The "Publishers' Note" gives White and Hobart equal credit for *The Stump Farm*, commending their "generous interest," "valuable suggestions," and "friendly services" (*SF* v). The archive suggests, though, that Hobart was the more involved. It was she, for example, who informed Rose of the book's inception—scant months before publication—as Rose's letter to Sedgwick reveals: "The Doctor lady told me how you were planning a book and I was very glad. If only one edition sold it would ease the hardships here a little."[34] During production, she served as the intermediary through whom Rose requested small changes.

Hobart has a second book about women's frontier experience to her credit, owing to her custodianship of the diary kept by her own great-great-grandmother Martha Ballard. A midwife in Hallowell, Maine, for close to thirty years, Ballard turned to her diary to record hundreds of deliveries along with the events of a developing community. Laurel Thatcher Ulrich compiled excerpts from the text, with exegesis, to form *A Midwife's Tale: The Life of Martha Ballard, Based on Her Diary, 1785–1812,* a pathbreaking study of an unknown woman and her work that was awarded the 1991 Pulitzer Prize for History.

Ballard's manuscript reached Hobart as "a hopeless pile of loose unconsecutive pages." Arranged and bound, it became "a source of vital interest" to her colleagues and herself. Ulrich attributes Hobart's attraction in part to the "problematical relation with the medical establishments of their time" that she and Ballard shared. Yet she may also have recognized in her ancestor's narrative of female frontier endeavor the ongoing challenges her friend in Canada presently faced. In 1930, close to fifty years after inheriting it, she donated the journal to the Maine State Library. While she stated only that she wished to make it available to historians, I would submit that the surprise popularity of *The Stump Farm* at exactly that time, a text that braced and heartened so many, helped her recognize its wider significance. Rose's frontier settlement in Alberta resembled Ballard's in Maine more than a century earlier, right down to the river's annual thaw being a major event. But more than this, the two texts are themselves akin, each a labor history of a seemingly ordinary woman that reveals much about not only her individual life and sensibility but also her economic, cultural, and social world.[35]

Rose did not write directly to Sedgwick until July 1927, and then with much humility: "Dear Mr. Sedgwick, Mrs. White says I may write to you. I have nearly done so several times but was afraid it would bother you. You must be a very busy man. Quite a job to run a big magazine." Sedgwick sent her a camera so that she could take photographs for the book, a service the "Publishers' Note" disclosed. Characteristically, he also asked for greater personal disclosure, "disappointed," Rose recalled, by the "short and formal" letter she had sent that "gave him no details." He published the additional letter she furnished in a "Contributors' Column," commencing the *Atlantic*'s protracted staging of Rose's dialogue with its readership beyond the limits of her contracted articles. With Sedgwick himself, Rose never reached the level of familiarity that inspired Stewart's gifts and notes or, for that matter, Whiteley's angry rebukes. (Is it telling that she regularly misspelled his name, addressing him as "Ellory" or adding an extra *e* to Sedgwick?) However, her connection to the *Atlantic* community at large—"all the *Atlantic* folks," to use her phrase—was profound and abiding.[36]

On receiving *The Stump Farm*, she happily informed Sedgwick, "The Book came and Boy and I looked at it. It is so much larger than I expected and because it is about us it seems so intimate and friendly."[37] She continues, "I'd like to thank each one who helped on the book. Surely no author ever enjoyed his book like I did. When I read it I discovered letters written to strangers that I had forgotten I ever wrote. I lived over the past again for I have never read nor seen any of the letters after I mailed them." At least in this statement, Rose seems so removed from the project that she scarcely recognizes the book as her own (we will return later to her casting of authorship as male). Her reaction accords with the official presentation of *The Stump Farm* as an anomaly in her life, the felicitous creation of a visionary editor and charitable friends. Yet while it is true that her *Atlantic* showing was her first time in print, it only accelerated her along a course she had long since begun: through minutely local life writing, cultivating the far-flung social network that afforded her a margin of survival.

Rather than the author's personal relationship with one cherished friend, *The Stump Farm* displays the process whereby she constructs a patchwork of emotional and economic support from countless benefactors, friends and strangers alike. We cannot identify all of the original recipients of the letters that compose it, since the editors chose to omit salutations and use pseudonyms. Austin, Hobart, and White are among them, the archive shows. After the *Atlantic* serial commenced, Emerson became Rose's most important correspondent, and the book includes some early letters to her. Rose also alludes to letters to "N. and the girls" in California and to an old friend in Illinois. But *The Stump Farm* reproduces letters to still other recipients, including "strangers" whom Rose said she did not even remember writing.

The Stump Farm lacks not only the sentimental freight of *Letters of a Woman Homesteader* but also its crafted, semifictional tales: Rose confines her narrative focus to daily events. This very adherence to epistolary convention, however, makes for the book's disorienting quality. A letter is inherently partial and open-ended. It starts without introduction, assuming considerable prior knowledge. Nor does it offer closure, as the events it recounts are always "to be continued." Moreover, a series of letters typically responds to another series of the same. For at least the semblance of a complete story, both sides of the correspondence must be available. The difficulty is compounded in *The Stump Farm* by its multiple anonymous recipients and by the way it sometimes approaches journal. Single letters can span weeks, divided into individual dated entries. "This is my diary. It is true" (*SF* 30), Rose insists. "This letter is part of my diary, so keep it" (*SF* 170). A diary is usually conceived as a private record of days. But only the assurance of outside readers— coupled with the prospect of future gain—motivated Rose to marshal the events of her life into narrative. It is revealing that, having stated of *The Stump Farm*, "It isn't fiction nor poetry," reviewer Driscoll was at a loss to name the genre it actually was.

The Stump Farm: "I Live Like an Indian"

Throughout *The Stump Farm*, Rose assesses what she has lost and gained by emigrating. "Not a day passes that I don't question myself whether I have done right by coming so far away," she confesses (*SF* 102). Happy to be back in his native country, Charles does not share her ambivalence. Yet it is too simple to say that she was coerced by him into a life she did not want, given the comments she makes about their move, such as "I wanted to keep my self-respect and raise the boy to be a real man" (*SF* 103). She shared his view that their location shielded them from vice, and she repeatedly alludes to the advantages conferred: material, social, and, not least, authorial.

Her son helps her make the case for the North. "He needs to be in here" (*SF* 163), she insists. "Boy will grow up, like Lincoln, in the wilderness." He learns to hunt and ride and is befriended by the Native men he emulates. In an unpublished letter, Rose queries, "What would Karl be without his horses and dogs and guns and all this great wilderness to roam in[?]"[38] But how would she have evaluated Karl's life had he been a girl? As we know, Stewart, too, used her child to argue for frontier prospects; portrayed working by her side, Jerrine buttresses her book's leading claim, that women can flourish as homesteaders. Rose's project was less straightforward. While through Karl she could intimate the nature of the ideal frontier man, she was at a loss to descry even a functional frontier woman. The white women in her book appear irrevocably damaged by rural hardship. In reference to her Idaho neighbors, she writes, "You

don't know how anxiously I look in the glass as the years go by and wonder if I'll ever get to look like the rest of the natives here. You have seen
overworked farmers' wives, with weather-wrung and sorrow-beaten
faces, drooping mouths, and a sad look" (*SF* 7). Women fare even worse
in Alberta: "The white women were elderly—wives who had followed
their husbands here . . . [a] lonesome sisterhood. They held my hands so
long; they didn't want to let them go. They were nearly all from the
States. One had gone insane—not very bad; you could see her mind was
shattered. You know it takes some mental calibre to come in here and live
alone and not see a white woman more than once or twice a year" (*SF*
124–25). The frontier does not offer her any viable models, or even any
women friends. She cannot turn to the local "northern girls," the "wonders" whose competence she admires but whose morals she deplores.[39]
She feels even less kinship with the district's Native women, noted but
unrepresented. That she cannot recognize that they, too, are women
drives her sensation of inhabiting an exclusively masculine world.

In the absence of female role models, Rose assumes male identities
to conceptualize her experience. "I live like an Indian [man]," she comments. "Shoot and fish and trap" (*SF* 48).[40] And while Native men help
her assess her labor, iconic figures like Robinson Crusoe and Abraham
Lincoln serve to orient her undertaking at large. On first reaching the
North, she maintains, "I felt like Robinson Crusoe as I stood on the
shore of this mighty river and looked at the swamp that edged it, so
dense and luxuriant that I had never seen anything like it," and she later
confides, "It makes me think of Lincoln's early life" (*SF* 89, 102). Yet her
sense of affiliation with masculine practice is most pronounced in her
claim to authorship. Even as she rues the "queer way" she must live,
so unbefitting for a "little lady," she revels in occupying territory that
enlarges her authorial identity.[41] In this district primarily inhabited by
men, she embraces a vocation she views as equally men's domain. We
have seen her use of the generic "he" to represent authorship: a writer
must be "himself." More significant, her formal literary influences are
exclusively male. She mentions studying Walt Whitman, Robert Burns,
Sinclair Lewis, and Jack London, and she alludes to Shakespeare,
Byron, and Zane Grey. In all her correspondence, I have encountered
only two references to work by women—an anthology Emerson sent
her included "verse" she had "never met," by Emily Dickinson, and
four Mennonite sisters recollected *Little Women*.[42]

Nevertheless, women's voices permeated the texts she read most, given that letters and popular magazines constituted the bulk of her reading material. While books were hard to come by, periodicals sustained her, including the *Ladies' Home Journal, Good Housekeeping,* religious papers, farm papers, and the *Atlantic,* which she and Charles "enjoyed" (of course) "the most" (*SF* 28). With their topical subjects, lower prices, and less durable materials, magazines were much more likely to be passed on by their first owners than books, and they were also exempt from customs tax. Once read, Rose used them to paper over cracks in her cabin—another reminder of the sheer materiality of her print-culture activity.

But even more than magazines, Rose read letters. Correspondents such as Austin, Hobart, and Emerson were writers as well as readers, producing a series of texts on her behalf. Their letters prompted her own and—in ways we cannot know, given their absence from the archive—helped determine their composition. Suggesting at least the imaginative uses to which she put these records of greater privilege, in one instance she acknowledges a correspondent's "many beautiful letters to me" and requests further detail: "And what do you do in California all summer long? Do you read and tatt and go to the movies? What a life!" (*SF* 16, 18). Her account of a miserable week spent weeding in the blazing Idaho sun, which rather aggressively contrasts her lot with her correspondent's, is revealing. "I'm not used to that kind of work; it takes a Jap to do it" (*SF* 53), she states. "I pictured you and the girls drinking iced lemonade on the deck of a beautiful ship, and J. foxtrotting with a handsome lieutenant, going out to the islands. My water jug didn't taste half so lukey after that" (*SF* 53–54). The glamorous scenes of white upper-class activity such letters purvey help her endure her own grinding hardship, even as racializing her work as fit for "a Jap" underscores the racial identity she and her correspondents share. Her comments recollect the outlook of another homesteading Swede, the fictional Alexandra in Willa Cather's *O Pioneers!* When her friend Carl, rootless in the modern city, pontificates on the solace he takes in envisioning her home on the farm, Alexandra demurs: "If the world were no wider than my cornfields, if there were not something beside this, I wouldn't feel that it was much worth while to work. . . . [I]t's what goes on in the world that reconciles me."[43] Rose expresses the sentiments voiced by Carl and Alexandra alike: her satisfaction in escaping "the world" is matched by her craving to hear of it.

Like Stewart and Whiteley before her, Rose portrays two forms of labor in her book, manual and literary, along with her hopes of developing the latter. She references numerous plans: "learning the poetry" (*SF* 6), taking a fiction writing course by correspondence, sending commissioned reports about homesteading to the Canadian government, saving up for a degree in journalism. "Do you think I'll ever be able to write for a living?" she implores (*SF* 142). However, until it was actually realized, she did not recognize the commercial potential of the letters themselves. According to her early assessment, "They don't amount to much. Just the struggle for existence on a farm" (*SF* 139). "I never thought you'd ever sell those old letters," she tells White. "So I never asked about them, as I felt so sorry for you because you'd be so disappointed after trying so hard" (*SF* 129).

The Stump Farm chronicles its own route to publication. "I am making three wool-filled comforters now out of my check" (*SF* 154), Rose notes after receiving her first *Atlantic* payment. In her formulation, the stories she purveys literally replace another frontier resource: "I was disappointed not to find fur to trap but the Atlantic texts have bought food for a whole year ahead" (*SF* 171). Reminiscent of Stewart's serial, the book includes a letter to Sedgwick, thanking him for his "good letter and check" (*SF* 167). (The original letter addresses him by name, but as published it becomes "To the Editor of the Atlantic Monthly," putting the emphasis on the institution.) She confides to White, "Last night I kept thinking about you and the good old editor. At first I thought he was a young man, but now I believe he must be old, for age makes folks kindly and loving." She continues on to happily muse, "And it's going to be a book. What color will the cover be? And some day I will hold it in my hand, and Daddy will be happy forever and ever" (*SF* 175–76).

The Stump Farm: Reception

While her vision of perpetual royalties remained only that, *Atlantic* publication did invigorate Rose's personal economy. The circulation of her private letters had already primed her social intercourse, and after publication her support network expanded to include not only friends of friends of friends but also people with whom she had no personal connection at all. *The Stump Farm* intimates the beginnings of the persistent, if occasional, assistance from readers that over the next two decades would prove so significant: she was "swamped with letters" (*SF* 144), and although most asked if she needed reading material, "two enclosed money, making $30 in cash." An early letter to Emerson shows just how substantial and diverse this aid could be: "The Publishers sent me $313 last fall for a grubstake. It wasn't enough. . . . But an Atlantic reader sent 350 lbs. of groceries which arrived in October. Another one is paying for hired help. . . . So an old trapper is in the woods now getting up a load of wood."[44] She continues, "I could ask some Atlantic readers to buy me a home in Quebec and then I would pay it back to them as a last resort if the book doesn't sell. One has already offered it." The following year, yet another reader hired a man to plow twenty-five acres of her land, so that she could prove up.[45] Even prior to the book, a newspaper in Canada had looked to boost the nation's new resident, appending the following plea to an *Atlantic* excerpt: "So runs this epic of our Frontier. Can not some of our readers mail a few books or some other magazines to Mrs. Rose, Fort Vermillion, N.W.T., to help her in her task of making a home in the far west. Surely it is not much to do and would be everlastingly appreciated. Be sure there is sufficient postage on anything you send. Do it now."[46] (Suggesting its efficacy, Rose commented, "Canada woke up this time. That made me happy to get such a welcome from them.")[47] Edward Weeks, Sedgwick's *Atlantic* successor, relayed, "'Letters from a Stump Farm' which ran through several seasons, brought forth many gifts from tenderhearted readers, some of whom did not realize that electric toasters were no use without electricity."[48] Recollecting the diversity of antebellum literary income—which could run to items like "clothes, kisses, and copyrights"—over the years payment for her frontier narrative took myriad forms, including loans and actual cash, essential services, and both new and secondhand goods.[49]

There is some truth to Little, Brown's claim that her letters "aroused a response nationwide and seldom equaled in the experience of the editors." *The Stump Farm* recurs in discussions of Sedgwick's revival, as one of the key texts to exhibit the *Atlantic*'s newly inclusive profile. We know, from Sedgwick's history with faraway women, why he would have liked Rose's story. But why did it resonate so deeply with readers, and why draw so many into the *Atlantic* fold? Rose's fans little fit the stereotype of the genteel *Atlantic* adherent. In a telling reply to Jensen's first letter, Rose writes, "So you think my book is a good cure for the discouraged. Bless your heart, most of the letters say the same thing. They even sent a copy of it to the mother whose only son was to be hanged. . . . Pass your copy around, it is a pleasure to help even in a small way the misery of this world." In 1935, at the height of her financial troubles, she reported, "Most of the friendly souls who read the Atlantic could spare but little from their own needs and sent each a dollar."[50]

The evidence about Rose's readership confirms the insights of scholars including Nancy Glazener, Charles Johanningsmeier, and Emily Satterwhite, who have shown that consumers of regional texts were more heterogeneous than usually conceived, among them rural and working-class people whose lives and communities resembled those the texts portray. Consequently, it undermines the binaries associated with the genre, which is too often understood, as Christine Holbo formulates it, as "constructed upon an opposition between elites and subalterns, an opposition frequently supported by their alignment with a series of further oppositions: between urban and rural, whites and minorities, men and women, realism and regionalism, Boston and Elsewhere." "I have just finished 'The Stump Farm' by Hilda Rose," a woman in Wisconsin stated, "and think, our farm life was a bed of roses by comparison." Perhaps for their original recipients—women like White, Hobart, and Emerson—Rose's letters did indeed induce nostalgia for a bygone era or confirm their own status and success. Many of the readers of *The Stump Farm*, however, registered the book quite differently, as an inspiring demonstration of courage and perseverance in the face of familiar ongoing problems. Beloved cowboy actor and cultural commentator Will Rogers pronounced it "as fine literature as ever I tasted."[51]

The Stump Farm also potentially confirms Glazener's observation, that regionalism, rather than solely satisfy the desires of an urban elite, "had the potential to swivel in its orientation and serve the periphery" by "testifying to the exploitative consequences that certain national policies had for rural Americans." As much a tale of protest as pluck, the book transmits Rose's view of an oppressive, monopolistic system that kept small farmers down. Her rationale for emigrating reads as an indictment: "The only way I could see to make a living was to go where an old man, a tiny woman, and a young child could get food easily. Hunt, trap, and fish is what we can do yet, since farming has failed here in the West" (*SF* 81). She demands to know "why there is so much made in the world and yet one must not have it to use" and predicts, in an unpublished letter to a Clara and Blanche in Redlands, California, "I'm afraid something will happen if things don't get better. But these hard times have shown the farmer that he belongs to the proletariat and he's going to stand behind the worker when the revolution comes. You bet!" However, neither Rose's official spokespeople nor her readership at large acknowledged, much less endorsed, this dimension of her work and thought, the intimation of systemic exploitation. (An *Atlantic* editorial pencil marked the statement about "the revolution" with "Um?" and rejected it for the book.) Blair has discussed the persistence with which aspirational readers ignored the complex moral and aesthetic propositions formulated by authors such as Wharton, James, and Howells in favor of searching out useful lessons, a practice she identifies as a form of misreading. Despite her quite different generic location, we can see something analogous in the reception of Rose. Her contemporaries made no comment about those aspects of *The Stump Farm* that may now give us pause, including its eugenic convictions, naive recklessness, and odd family dynamics. (An example of the latter: her son resembles his father, and so, Rose gloats, "I'll have Daddy from the cradle to the grave" [*SF* 177].) Rose is always cast as admirable, never bizarre. Reviewers and readers followed the *Atlantic*'s lead in accepting her as an ordinary woman of uncommon fortitude, battling the elements.[52]

This stance—which at first inspection seems almost willful—is more explicable on consideration of genre. Reception theorist Hans Robert Jauss's notion of "horizons of expectation" is illuminating, "the set of cultural norms, assumptions, and criteria shaping the way in which readers understand and judge a literary work at a given time." Johanningsmeier, glossing Jauss, explains that "a reader judges a text based on an implicit comparison between his or her expectations of that type of text, formed from previous reading, and the reading of the new text." *The Stump Farm*'s "type of text" was the pioneer chronicle and as such was to yield a tale of endurance and self-reliance. The communal contexts in which the book was read further directed interpretation and contributed to the popular consensus about it. Readers, Janice Radway expounds, "approach any text with a set of assumptions about what a text is, what its relation to them might be, how it should be read, and what it could possibly mean."[53]

Rose provides a revealing view of how her book circulated, in conditions that suppressed sales but enlarged readership:

In regard to Little Brown and Co They are a very big concern and the reason my book did not sell well was because the younger generation like fiction better. But it will be alive for a long time for it will have a revival when my next book comes out. I already have become quite well known because no one reading it forgets the name of the author and it is such a good lender that frequently people have to buy a new copy to replace the one worn out. This all is advertising of the best kind, also there is hardly a woman's club in the land that has not had it read aloud to them but it means only one copy sold though my name is becoming fairly well known in that kind of circles [*sic*]. I am only biding my time and all will come out right I think.[54]

The culture of uplift in which *The Stump Farm* was embedded mirrored the culture Rose herself had entered as a fledgling correspondent, right down to the role played by women's clubs. The actual transmission of the book, moreover, passed from reader to reader, recollects its earliest iteration as private letters. It became a form of shared property: loaned to friends, borrowed from libraries, discussed in clubs, studied in schools, distributed in offices.[55] *The Stump Farm* was released only two years after the advent of the Book-of-the-Month Club and just after the Literary Guild's, and although neither of these mail-order organizations featured it, it would have been appropriate for their lists, which often showcased self-improvement and advancement.

The publication of her book sparked a keen public appetite for more Rose. "Folks are funny, aren't they," she complained (and boasted) to Sedgwick. "Hundreds of letters in the last mail and all expecting an answer at once." Indicating the diverse uses of *The Stump Farm* and the diverse requests she fielded, she reported in 1929:

I still get a big mail. More letters than I can answer but when I read them I see that nearly all are from Public Library patrons. Also teachers, College students, scientists, doctors and Club-women predominantly. The Clubs and College classes buy one book and all read it or it is read aloud. Then each one writes me a long letter. I answer by writing one to be read to them at their meeting or in class. This letter is quite often printed in their Club or College paper. It often takes me quite a time to write these letters as I want them to be good. The scientists and teachers often ask for Indian baskets, rare orchids, mosses plants stones etc. I send them as fast as I run across them.

Reports of her life were akin to the exotic "Indian baskets" and "rare orchids" northern Canada also furnished. As late as 1933, the *Atlantic* commented on the "continuous stream of letters from people who demanded to know the latter-day adventures of Hilda Rose." Rose relayed that same year, "The letters are increasing instead of diminishing as the Stump Farm is a good lender if not a good seller. Several report their copies as well as the letters I send them in reply are literally worn to tatters." Here she indicates the permeable membrane between *The Stump Farm* and her ongoing correspondence. Readers lent out their books, and they also wrote to its author, who replied. These responses were themselves distributed, until—just like the books—they, too, were in "tatters." Rose learned to specify when she wanted privacy: "P.S. Don't send my letters around. They are only for you."[56]

She opens an early letter in *The Stump Farm* with "I have no gifts to give, just myself, and I will write you a letter and try to put myself in it" (67). Yet once the barrage of fan mail commenced, she learned to write with greater reserve. She viewed many of her fans as her social inferiors, as a rather startling assertion in the book reveals: "If I lived Outside and met these people and they talked like that, I'm afraid a washtub wouldn't make me a hat. But in here I just say, 'what a kind letter,' and go out and hoe the beans" (164). (*Atlantic* readers sent her so many letters grousing about their spouses' extramarital affairs, she maintained, as to constitute a genre of their own, "Broken Hearts.") She appreciatively responded to Jensen's first overture, "Very seldom do I receive a letter that tells me something. They all want to know what I do and what I eat and how I like it here." The grim persistence she brought to answering such letters—"a task I loathe"—intimates the calculation that must have informed the earlier correspondence that resulted in *The Stump Farm:*

> I have a terrible task with my letters that must be answered. They accumulate until now there are nearly 700 to answer in spite of buying stamps to the extent of 18 dollards [*sic*] every year. I dig away at them for if I don't they will not buy my next book though I daresay most of them have read the Stump Farm at the library. All authors answer their fan letters but most of them have secretaries or else they don't have to do housework. I expect to clean them up this winter unless the publication of my diary brings a flood.

Rose's resentment of her readers' demands reflects one of the fundamental ironies of her book. Her literary achievement originated in conditions of not only economic exigency but also cultural dissatis-faction. Her decision to homestead was informed by a desire to pre-serve her family from the masses, and she developed long-distance friendships with women whose intellectual and social level she viewed as closer to her own. Yet the book that ensued was embraced by the very population she sought to escape—whose favor, moreover, she felt obliged to cultivate.[57]

Friends and Patrons

The fifth sentence of *The Stump Farm* succinctly expresses the difficul-ties Rose faced as a farmer: "We are far from markets" (3). Her western locations made for equal difficulties as an author. Like Stewart, while her adopted homes offered rich subject matter, they posed formidable obstacles to a writing career. Her life was perilous: grinding labor, extreme isolation, severe weather, no cash. Moving to Canada com-pounded the difficulty, as she attempted to write across the border to American friends and for American markets. She concurred with Emerson in New York that it was "harder to get a letter in and out of here than halfway around the world."[58]

In the *Atlantic* "Letter to a Young Contributor" that, famously, inspired Emily Dickinson to begin writing him, Thomas Wentworth Higginson urged, "Use good pens, black ink, nice white paper and plenty of it. . . . An editor's eye becomes carnal, and is easily attracted by a comely outside." We are likely to attend to Higginson's equation of a manuscript with an alluring female body while passing over the actual advice as banal. However, financially strapped writers like Rose show just how much the material conditions and costs of writing matter. She wrote by the light of a "butter-bitch," a wick in a saucer of oil. She had to choose between stamps and sugar. Postal access was a perpetual concern: the rush to get letters to the mail boat, the long winter with almost no contact with "Out-side." And the first need was paper. Of a later project, she allowed, "The depression makes queer bedfellows and many other queer things so why not a book written on scraps," but also mused, "Yet if it had been written on good paper it would have perhaps received more consideration." Like the other faraway women I discuss, Rose literally had to assemble fragments to write. Such improvisation, at the material level of writing, is an apt metaphor for their authorship at large.[59]

Her correspondence itself generated solutions to sustain it. At the most basic level, the letters she received often included money or postage to facilitate replies. In her first letter to Jensen, she bluntly instructed, "Tuck in an American dime now and then and I will talk with you." The following anecdote well demonstrates this manner of exchange:

> I was answering some fan mail, total strangers, I have a bunch every mail, and in two of them I said "I will close now for my fingers burn so bad with the mosquito bites and there is a lot of them hovering over my hands while I write." I always put my thoughts into words no matter how they sound and if it is true that is all I care about, I never think that my letter may shock. These did and both sent mosquito netting as a gift so the boys as well as Daddy and I have nets over our beds. . . . They sure surprised me but one might as well say that God looks after us.

Frontier experiences like being swarmed by insects make it almost impossible to write, but the narrative she manages to produce nonetheless is especially pungent, a "shocking" account to which readers respond with heaven-sent "surprises" that expedite further efforts.[60]

We can see from Rose's letters her affection for many of her correspondents; we can also see how carefully she managed their aid — belying her assertion, "I wait patiently when there is a need." She gradually established some forms of habitual support. "I wrote out to my good friend and expect to hear from her soon. She will I know take care of the groceries for the winter," she assured Jensen, and factored into her budget the small sum another friend sent her each Christmas. Other assistance was more occasional. She recounted the efforts of a Mrs. Sweezy: "I received a letter last fall saying she was on her way to buy a bank draft. When it did not come I thought perhaps the poor lady had been hit by a car or had found she was overdrawn. I am writing her in this mail." In response to her query, Sweezy promised to send the check again. "It is providential isn't it that it will come for this fall's expenses," Rose marveled — with who knows what measure of ingenuousness. A recurring phrase in her lexicon is "the nick of time."[61]

Her most consequential epistolary relationship was with Margaret Emerson, Sorbonne graduate and former professor of languages at Japan Women's University in Tokyo. By the time of their acquaintance, Emerson resided on the Upper East Side in Manhattan, supported by her rental income. She was a published writer (her 1905 eyewitness account of Lafcadio Hearn's funeral appeared in the *Critic*), and she was an *Atlantic* devotee. The file of her letters from and about Rose, archived in the Emerson Family Papers at the New York Public Library, includes two stray 1915 letters from Elinore Pruitt Stewart and her young daughter, Jerrine. Stewart thanks Emerson for a box of gifts (including candles and a "little Jap picture") and, indicating the vital role she came to play in her writing, states, "It seems to me that I must tell you something or show you something a dozen times a day. I haven't Mrs. Coney now." Attesting to the links Emerson made between western *Atlantic* contributors, her 1924 Christmas present to Jerrine was a copy of *The Story of Opal*.[62]

The common ground Rose shared with her *Atlantic* homesteader predecessor must have inspired Emerson to contact her, too. She and Rose began corresponding during the "Stump Farm" serial, so volubly that a portion of the book that almost immediately followed is composed of the letters Rose wrote her. Despite never meeting in person, they grew very close, exchanging countless letters up until Emerson's death in 1948. Emerson assiduously organized aid for her distant friend, buying, collecting, and mailing essentials such as coal oil, medicine, and clothing along with small luxuries like books, tea, and raisins—and an annual *Atlantic* subscription. She also served as her *Atlantic* intermediary, negotiating with Sedgwick and Weeks on her behalf. In 1938 Rose granted Emerson power of attorney as her literary agent.[63]

Her form of address grew more intimate over the years: "Dear Margaret Emerson," "Dear Miss Emerson," "Dear Margaret," and finally "Dear, dear Margaret." Each letter thanks her for the most recent "pkg." and alludes to further desires and needs—lemons, bitter chocolate, "[shoes] anything from 2½ to 6 and any heel except French high," "1/4 inch white rubber tape for my bloomers." Rose often voiced her concern about burdening her, especially as Emerson grew older and, apparently, less affluent. A 1944 letter opens, "It is sad to know you have to work—not because of the loss of caste—but because you are too frail to work." But it also includes a handwritten postscript: "Fruit— dried—is the most needed. I'm just longing fruit—all the time."[64]

Increasingly, the responsibility was shared, as Rose entered into correspondence with a number of Emerson's friends who became her own, including among others Blanche Randolph in Mount Vernon, New

York; Christine Fowler in Batavia, New York; and Frances Gaston in Somerville, New Jersey. These women, while not necessarily wealthy, were upper middle or upper class. Gaston's family, for example, was as eminent as Emerson's, as the Gaston Family Papers at Rutgers University attest. Conversant with the minutiae of Rose's life, they exchanged news about her activities, worried about her prospects, and circulated her letters. It is an odd sensation to see the fussy Fowler use Rose's epithet to disparage a "half breed"—in green ink on personalized stationery—or assess Karl's prospects of making it as a laborer in New York.[65] The *Atlantic* began referring concerned readers to Emerson, and some of Rose's supporters, including women on the Boston school board, even called on her at her home.

Such exchanges, set into motion by the magazine, themselves became *Atlantic* grist, featured in new essays by Rose and in "Contributors' Column" items. "Christmas at the Ranch" and "Pioneering on Peace River," a December 1933 and January 1934 diptych composed of a selection of Rose's letters to Emerson, highlight Rose's evolving relationship with the *Atlantic*. The next year saw "Long Distance Calling: New Letters from the Stump Farm," a piece Emerson had brokered without Rose's knowledge (and to her dismay) that was coordinated with an appeal to *Atlantic* readers to assist her.

"Christmas at the Ranch" opens with Rose's statement, "There is not time enough to answer all the letters that come and all the questions people ask. I will try to answer them in this diary." The essay that she seems to write expressly for publication is ostensibly a diary (although in fact originated in letters) meant to replace a daunting correspondence. *Atlantic* publication had expanded her epistolary network to the extent that she must publish once more to "answer all the letters" she owes. Rose inventories the donations her narrative prompted, ranging in magnitude from flower seeds to "a new stove, a gift from an *Atlantic* reader." She also reveals that she has been joined in the flesh by a hapless family who took her book as a literal emigrants' guide: "The father lost his job and they read 'The Stump Farm' in the *Atlantic* and decided to pioneer in the Far North."[66]

"Long Distance Calling" further develops the theme of patronage. Well-wishers fill minor needs: "One teacher keeps me in paper and pencils, another in typewriter ribbons, one old lady sends me a roll of adhesive tape." An American high school, we learn, sent Karl a pair of binoculars and a radio. Rose complains about a naive friend who marked a package as containing money, which got pilfered as a result, and refers to another, more substantial, missing offering: "The coal oil you tried to send us last winter is famous now. Such things grow like a snowball rolling downhill. We heard that there were ten gallons of coal oil at the end of rail for us, held up by the river being frozen early last fall. We thought someone else, name unknown, had sent it." Her exchange with Emerson about a coat for Karl suggests how she directed the charitable process. Having been informed, "A man's raincoat, no matter how old-fashioned or shabby, would be a great gift to the boy," Emerson apparently proposed a "rain cape." Rose continued to press for the actual coat, tactfully explaining, "[A cape] will be very welcome in this rainy land and just the thing on horseback, I should say. A raincoat has its uses too, as it can be buttoned up tight and affords more protection when it is windy and stormy at the same time."[67]

By publishing these later letters, the *Atlantic* not only spurred renewed support for Rose but also broadcast its institutional consequence. Rose willingly participated in the exercise with commentary like, "When I come to an article in the *Atlantic Monthly* that I do not understand I read it aloud to Daddy. He can usually explain it in simple words. If it is too deep for him, I read it to the boys. They listen intently, and if they too fail to grasp the idea, we lay it aside for the boy to take to college with him."[68] Offering novice readers like herself a model of cultural instruction, she affirms the *Atlantic*'s value as a tool for self-education and class advance.

Over a six-year period, the *Atlantic* shrewdly fostered the fiction of a personal relationship with Rose by staging an attenuated dialogue among author, editor, readers, and associates in the "Contributors' Column." Each *Atlantic* issue that includes an essay by Rose, and nearly every preceding or succeeding one, offers some kind of supplemental material: another letter or poem from Rose; a letter, poem, or even telegram from an acquaintance or reader; an editorial update on her life. Thus, we have the following, from Rose: "May I send a Christmas message to your readers? 'If you leave the concrete highway / And go in the lanes and byways / You'll find many Hilda Roses / Digging spuds and picking posies.'" A reader supplied a long limerick: "And a Rose of her species blooms once and is done. / She has only Daddy and Boy—that's her son." In a pointed commentary about the motives of her readership, a disaffected viticulturist remarked, "Your glutton for punishment, Hilda Rose, has gone into new pastures where the hardships are really abounding" and proposed she venture into her own, "a rich field, beset with all the hardships and disappointments to satisfy the most exacting readers of the *Atlantic Monthly*."[69] Margaret Beetham notes that "one of the characteristics of the periodical press" is the use of such forums to encourage "readers to become writers."[70] The "Contributors' Column" afforded *Atlantic* readers opportunities to see their words in print, further promoting a sense of community among them.

The *Atlantic* stressed that Rose attracted reams of solicitous inquiries: "An almost daily duty in this office is to answer questions about Mrs. Hilda Rose—how she fares and what she needs." It also promised, "A recent letter from her (just four weeks on the way) will answer many queries." The epistolary genre in which she worked made this manner of dialogue the natural next step, "corresponding" with the *Atlantic* at large, and the rationed delivery of seasonal updates was part of the appeal. As a point of reference, Gertrude Stein's *Atlantic* serial, "Autobiography of Alice B. Toklas"—which overlapped with Rose's 1933 letters—was accorded only meager commentary, and that which does appear is much less energetic and invested: "Readers who have inquired curiously how it was possible for Gertrude Stein to write the autobiography of Alice B. Toklas will find the riddle explained in the last paragraphs." Rather than the worldly Stein, it was Rose who captured *Atlantic* readers' imagination, and it was she whom the *Atlantic* embraced as its own.[71]

Well before her *Atlantic* showing, Stein had informed Sedgwick of the dire financial straits of Mildred Aldrich, one of his pivotal early contributors, as a prelude to urging him to solicit *Atlantic* readers for donations to a fund.[72] Sedgwick readily agreed, grateful to Aldrich for having bolstered the magazine's fortunes at a critical juncture with her popular hit, "A Little House on the Marne." Readers responded so generously to his 1925 *Atlantic* call that "very soon Mildred Aldrich was safe," to quote from *The Autobiography of Alice B. Toklas* (241). This success prepared Sedgwick and Weeks to participate in a like operation for Rose ten years on, similarly preserving a household and way of life that once knew *Atlantic* fame. A flood had drowned the Roses' stock and ruined their farmland, leaving them in urgent need of a new homestead. The October 1935 *Atlantic* includes this cryptic notice: "S.O.S. Miss Margaret G. Emerson, 325 East 72nd Street, New York City, has information from Hilda Rose that she will be pleased to communicate to those who plan to send Mrs. Rose letters for the approaching Christmas."[73] Note the belief that it was superfluous to identify Rose further; *Atlantic* readers knew who she was.

By the following month, the plan—coordinated by Emerson—was fully formed, as announced in the November issue:

> Her letters, written to three close friends in New York, help to keep her going; thanks to a friendly "round robin," they remind the *Atlantic*'s circle of the hardihood and spirit which our great-grandparents must have had on their frontiers. It seems only fair to repeat this caution uttered by one of Mrs. Rose's correspondents: "I only wish the readers knew she did not volunteer all the sad details. These had to be got out of her by insistent inquiries." Should any readers wish to send a Christmas remembrance, they may do so direct by letter to the above address or through the agency of the T. Eaton Company, Winnipeg.

Mild though it was, the invitation drew ardent response. Rose reported that the Christmas mail brought "seventy odd" packages, and thirty more arrived in January. Necessities, luxuries, and hard cash poured in from not only middle-class readers but also the working poor. The total monetary contribution came to $586.47, meeting expenses that, as Rose cataloged, included "Sit [*sic*] of Sleigh 15, Washing machine 8, Harness 15, Team 160, Seed Wheat 28, Seed Oats 22, Feed Oats 30." With the surplus she got two teeth pulled, and Karl could turn down an arduous job hauling freight. Sedgwick also set up an account for her at Eaton's department store in Winnipeg. That she was ordering her groceries from this massive emporium—whose distribution spanned the continent—with money collected from equally dispersed *Atlantic* readers testifies to her immersion in national systems. The personal system of exchange that had long helped her survive exponentially expanded. Even as she was promoted as a pioneer, her experience was institutionally structured—by federal homestead policies, the U.S. and Canadian postal systems, and the *Atlantic* itself.[74]

Practically speaking, as Rose pointed out, the event should have been held in the summer, when the river allowed regular mail service. To carry all the packages over the snow, the government was obliged to hire two additional dog teams and an oversize sled.[75] But by casting its appeal as an act of sentiment—soliciting "Christmas remembrances"—the *Atlantic* masked the economics of the venture along with stirring up enthusiasm for its important December issue.[76] Rose responded with a similar discursive maneuver in figuring it as a "party," as evident in her several letters of thanks to Sedgwick. "The surprise party you folks planned was a real surprise," she wrote. "We are all happy for we know we have friends Out there who care what becomes of us and to them all known and unknown goes out our love."[77] The following winter she confided to him, in a letter signed "Lovingly":

> A year has gone by since the wonderful Christmas, a year that changed my life in some ways but more to be treasured in memory because in this year I have been allowed to share in so many lives, have felt the very pulse of the readers of the Atlantic. It touched my heart to read this from a little old grandmother left alone with two young grandchildren because of an acci-dent, "we lived on mush all day so we could send you this dollar bill." And from a stenographer, "I saved ten cents a day from my lunch-money this week for you." Another said, 'I was going to buy myself a little potted plant for Christmas and then I thought of you." I would write to each one tonight if I could and say, "I think of you as I sit here in the candle-light and it is not only the candle that dispels the gloom but the love you give that comforts and brightens my way."[78]

Rose viewed this project, which put rich and poor on equal footing, as exposing "the very pulse" of *Atlantic* fellowship. Sedgwick put his usual spin on it: "By that time Hilda Rose's friends were legion and the dog sled which formerly carried a dozen letters as its pack now staggered forward piled high with sweaters, blankets and comforts of every kind. *Atlantic* subscribers felt as I did about the Stump Farm" (*HP* 200).[79] For Rose's benefactors, the satisfaction came not only from having a per-sonal stake in her frontier enterprise but also from joining communal efforts on her behalf, which reinforced a sense of group membership, whether club, school, nation—or magazine. Amplifying their activity as *Atlantic* citizens, such efforts demonstrated that they shared in its sensibility: in Sedgwick's evaluation, showed that they "felt as I did."

"If I Fix Up Another Book . . ."

In her 1925 letter to Austin, the woman first to propose sharing her let-ters, Rose cautiously allowed, "The reading won't hurt me if you leave my name off." Eight years later, she was making shrewd assessments of the order of "the less I publish the more interested people seem to be as to what is become of us." Following the precipitous advent of *The Stump Farm,* she commenced lifelong efforts to support herself and her family through writing. It is likely that she placed some small pieces, given the currency of her name; she once informed Sedgwick, "There is seldom a mail comes in that does not bring a letter from some editor asking why I don't write some more." However, whereas her epistolary network took on a life of its own, ever richer and more intricate, her writing career was fitful. Despite her resolute pursuit of them, she fell far short of realizing her literary dreams.[80]

Displaying a creative, entrepreneurial energy of the same order as that which drove her farm and homestead practice, she tapped every writing income vein she could find. She was especially enthusiastic about poetry, for which she dreamed of winning the Nobel Prize. "I thought that when I get it rhymed up right it might get me ten dollars towards another horse," she noted of one poem. "I am wild to get after some of my poems and finish them up and see if they will sell." She aspired to make Karl an author, too. When he was young, she copied down his speech to submit to the *Atlantic,* contending, "He often talks in real poetry and does not know it." In his teens, she urged him to "start sending out little sketches of his life in here to the Boys' magazines" and to sell folk songs he collected and other songs he wrote himself. She boasted, "He is a genius if there ever was one, and will be a writer of stories and books. Next winter we hope to get him started writing and sending out some." The family invested in a gasoline lamp so they could work on their writing projects during the long winter nights. Karl's daily work was typical for men in northern Canada: hunting, trapping, chopping wood, tending stock. Yet he was also immersed in U.S. print culture, as reader, editor, and aspiring author. (He does not have an evident publishing record.) In reference to one of her submissions, Rose relayed, "[Karl] is going to try to make 30 dollars so we can send it to a good critic before we send it to the prize judging."[81]

Her activities also included her faithful pen pal Jack Jensen. By the time of their acquaintance, Jensen lived in a veterans' home in Los Angeles, but he had served under William Cody (Buffalo Bill), taken part in "land stampedes," and had other frontier experiences that at least in retrospect could seem colorfully romantic. Surely inspired by Rose, he began writing a memoir himself. Rose assumed the duties of tutor, typist, editor, and agent. Urging him to capitalize on the "Wild

West" aspects of his life, she advised, "Horses and cows and cowboys. Leave out the women," and she proposed he call the book "Caballero West." "It means a Western gentleman on horseback. Or a knight of the West." Her work with the manuscript was folded into her seasonal labor. "I shall get to work again on your book as soon as I have fixed up some warm quilts for us," she promised. Her plans for it included writing competitions and submission to the *Saturday Evening Post*. Any profits were to be shared, an agreement she broached formalizing: "If you want to fix it legally it is up to you. If not or unable to don't worry over it. . . . [T]he book is a labor of love."[82]

Rose's advice to her friend reveals much about her own workman-like practice. She urged him to write a poem a day, study famous authors, and invest in a rhyming dictionary. "Borrow books that deal with writing from the public library. Like 'experiments in writing' —by Cook. 'Writing the short story.'" (The former is Luella B. Cook's 1927 *A High-School Textbook in Composition*.) "The only book I want you to read is Babbitt, the author won the world prize for it, the celebrated Noble [*sic*] prize of 40.000 dollars." She also dictated, "Make a poem about the boys in the Home and about what you have to eat and look out of the window and tell what people look like that go by. . . . You have the gift and that is wonderful but to sell it must be more personal, Get me." With striking assurance, she states, "I can write songs about anything at all and some must be good is the way I figure. You ought to read some of the rot some great writers like Byron and Shakespeare wrote sometimes. Some of it was good and was printed but some was awful. So we may strike lady luck some day when we least expect it." Everyone has the potential to write like Shakespeare —on a bad day— and success is sometimes sheer luck.[83]

"Caballero West" did not, as she had hoped, become her "next grub-stake," as it was never published.[84] Her compensation was Jensen's habit of folding dollar bills into his letters and sending Karl presents like chaps and a hunting knife. Of the dollars, she told him, "While they lasted they helped the rugged road more than you can ever realize."[85] Her domestic, social, business, and authorial roles all overlapped in the project she named a "labor of love."

The steadfast focus of her own literary enterprise was a second book that began as a homesteading memoir. While it bore the ambitious working title of "The Land: An Epic of Today," she always referred to it as a diary, proposing to contain epic themes within this quotidian, feminized genre. The manuscript is not extant, but her observation that it was "hard on the capitalistic system and stressed co-operation" indicates it developed the political views discernible in *The Stump Farm*. She explained, "The main idea is the terrible conditions of agriculture and how it is being solved by the people on the land. I'm right in it here and it's a terror and just beginning."[86]

At first, given that *The Stump Farm* came into being so felicitously, she was confident of an easy success. "If I fix up another book in the coming year and sell it all will be well," she assured Hobart. Originally, she planned to recycle old letters that had not made it into *The Stump Farm*. Soon, though, accepting a heavier workload and longer time line, she began writing new material. She assessed her prospects for an *Atlantic* competition thus: "I haven't got much chance to win the prize at the Atlantic because it is open to the world and thousands will try for it, Learned proffessors [*sic*] in big universities. One of them won the last prize but I think mine will be accepted and published as a regular book." Whatever else it may have lacked, the subject matter was apt. *Jalna*, the inaugural volume of Mazo de la Roche's enormously popular Canada family saga, won the Atlantic Monthly Press's first $10,000 Atlantic Prize Novel award in 1927, Rose's own debut year. Even more germane, in 1935 Mari Sandoz won the magazine's nonfiction prize for *Old Jules*. By honoring this Nebraska chronicle of family pioneering, the *Atlantic* made official its commitment to women's stories of rural hardship and reward.[87]

Rose can reveal a greater concern with accumulating text than with structuring and polishing it, as when she remarked of "The Land," "I still have a lot to write. I planned to have 200 typewritten pages as full as I can cram them and I have 126 done now and they must leave here on the first of February." Partly this stemmed from a view that writing was at heart a matter of transcription. In reporting on her progress to Sedgwick, she consistently represented it as a by-product of life events, oddly autonomous: "I am keeping a diary and am wondering what strange happenings it may record in the days to come." The perspective evident in statements such as "When I take up my pen it is a perpetual surprise to me to see what it writes" accords with Sedgwick's pet notion, that in premodern societies, urgent experiences "wrote themselves."[88]

In her account of what she believed to be her husband's final sickness, she maintains that crises made for inspired prose: "Daddy lay dying for weeks and I wrote steadily while taking care of him, sitting up nights and writing with one hand while with the other hand I held a butter-bitch to see the keys with. Yet writing under such stress and just as the thoughts came makes many of those pages inspired and I know it is true what the editor said he debated long whether to print some of them." The same outlook led her to recruit her casual correspondence to energize more studied efforts; thus, she asked Jensen to copy and send back those sections of her letters he thought strongest. Nonetheless, she actively cultivated her writing style, as she reveals: "I have practiced for years writing longer sentences, starting them without 'I' and filling notebooks with words that were beautiful of expression and conning them over and over." Her prose may have been celebrated for its "unconscious power," but she was deliberate about her effects.[89]

Artistic ambition as well as economic calculation led her to resist publishing excerpts from "The Land," lest the concession suppress the masterpiece she hoped to create. Informing Sedgwick, "I can get rid of all I write," she continues, "but the help would be so temporary and the writing would not live." Richard Brodhead's comments about Louisa May Alcott at the onset of her career describe Rose equally well: she "begins envisioning herself as a writer in a highly distinctive idiom: in the language of hierarchies of merit . . . exalted vocation . . . the gradual attainment of high proficiency . . . and culminating achievement." "You will realize that I am very sensitive and very impulsive," Rose predicted to Jensen, "two reasons why I think I will make an author in time." However, in ways analogous to Alcott's reassignment as a writer of juvenile literature, the marketplace did not support the version of authorship she pursued.[90]

While Rose never lost her commitment to publishing a second book, its identity shifted over the years. She was long confident that a contract for "The Land" was imminent, once commenting that it was "practically sold to Houghton Mifflin Co. Boston."[91] By 1938, however, she had turned her attention to another book of letters, "Pioneering on the Peace," a project Emerson directed. She dedicated the manuscript to "the editors of the Atlantic Monthly and to the readers of the Atlantic Monthly without whose kindness I could never have carried on."[92] After this effort also stalled, she began work on a conventionally structured autobiography, which opened with the life of her woodcarver grandfather in Sweden. She made the leap to fiction in 1940, recasting her personal history as a novel featuring a schoolteacher protagonist named Sandra. Later, she resolved to separate out her work in progress into two books, the novel and a memoir.[93] Yet through all these vicissitudes, her commitment to the *Atlantic* did not waver.

The publication trajectory of another Canada writer, L. M. Montgomery, presents a useful contrast. Prior to the sweeping success of the "Anne of Green Gables" series, Montgomery methodically placed her work in increasingly prestigious organs, publishing in more than seventy magazines before reaching her personal apex, *Pictorial Review*.[94] A modern, fresh women's magazine featuring a blend of fashion, fiction, and progressive issues, *Pictorial Review* serialized Edith Wharton's fiction throughout the 1920s, including *The Age of Innocence*, no less. Yet Rose commented with only limited enthusiasm that since the *Atlantic* wouldn't bite, she was "seriously thinking of trying the Pictorial Review"; her book was "somewhat in their line." Having started at the top rung of the periodical ladder, she was loath to descend, her elitist impulses at odds with her democratic appeal.[95]

References to such alternatives had dropped out altogether by 1935. Rather than search out more receptive hosts, Rose tried to refashion her writing for the *Atlantic*, adapting tone, topic, and theme to more upbeat end. She once promised Sedgwick, for example, that she would excise "all sarcasm and bitterness" from an excerpt he was considering.[96] Recalling the counsel of her early agent, she remarked, "There is so much that I have never dared to write about, I tried once and sent it to Dr. Hobart who is 84 years old now and she said it was too terrible for the Atlantic readers."[97] ("Terrible" in just what way, one wonders.) Her dilemma recollects Stewart's lament about frontier narrative, "I wonder what I *can* write of that won't be shocking" (quoted in *AWH* 193). Nevertheless, like Stewart she too held out for "our first love the Atlantic," to use Juliet Coney's phrase (*AWH* 34). Her intermediaries had a like narrow orientation, submitting her work exclusively there. This is especially surprising given that Emerson was a published writer and her niece, geographer and explorer Gertrude Emerson Sen, was associate editor of the influential *Asia* magazine. Sen had read *The Stump Farm*, and Emerson forwarded her letters to Rose, who often asked for news about eminent "Cousin Gertrude." Emerson would have well served her friend by urging her to broaden her search.[98]

For these misguided tactics, Sedgwick and Weeks bear some of the blame, stringing her along as they encouraged her about new placements. Just as Rose was reluctant to give up the *Atlantic*, so was the *Atlantic* reluctant to give up Rose. In July 1933 she wrote Sedgwick asking for the return of "The Land": "I think I have found a sale for it. . . . I realize every day that it does not appeal to the cultured Atlantic audience and this time it will go to the opposite." It was only then that he agreed to publish an excerpt, which she attributed to his fear of losing her to the competition. Yet after it ran, she complained, "I was disgusted with it rather with him for he passed up what had real meat in it." She also thought he rather missed the point of her need, having informed her, "The check will not be large but the prestige will make up for that."[99]

She stated the following year, "The Atlantic will from now on print life as I live it and that is a big order. But I live it." Sedgwick's injunction that she "print life" in real time struck a chord; months later, she iterated, "The editor says he will print more after I have lived it." Emerson eventually heard from Weeks that he was considering a "Stump Farm" sequel, with Sedgwick slated for the foreword. However, far from proceeding with the book, they decided to close her *Atlantic* run. According to Weeks, "There comes a time when, however reluctant he may be, an editor must put an end to a series of related articles on the same theme." Ten months later, from retirement, Sedgwick confided to Emerson, "I have read Mrs. Rose's manuscript myself, for I could not bear that another should make a decision when my own feelings were so strongly engaged. But, alas and alack, I cannot see these additional letters in a book." The problem, he said, was that such a book would interest only those who already knew her. Conceding her son's point, that "to keep a serial running more than 10 years was preposterous," Rose allowed that their decision would get her out of her "rut" of relying on the *Atlantic*. Nevertheless, she subsequently corresponded with Weeks about her novel, and she even mentioned saving up money to visit him in Boston, insisting, "I know he will want to see me and talk to me about it." Suggesting he was indeed interested, Weeks recommended to Emerson that they both review the novel's early drafts. And over all this time, Rose's friends forwarded her letters for *Atlantic* perusal. Celebrating the length of their association, in his memoir Sedgwick stated that she "long held *Atlantic* readers and the *Atlantic*'s editor under a spell of mingled interest, affection, and admiration" (*HP* 200).[100]

In December 1934, Rose happily updated Jensen about Karl's love life:

He is now writing to a girl his own age near Boston, an editor's daughter. Well his letters are corking and shows he can write. He dictates them to me and then signs them. The grammer [*sic*] is alright in spite of not knowing a rule. . . . Natalie writes him, all she can see when she sits down to write is rules and more rules until she's scared to set down a sentence and all Karl thinks of is the most expressive word to tell what he feels. The girl is talented and her father is training her in his office in Boston to be a thorough Newspaper woman. . . . Karl has a picture of her framed and hung in the center of a deerskin as a background, in his cabin. She I am sure kisses his picture every night before she goes to sleep. The letters are flying fast, the trail is kept hot between Fort Vermilion and Boston.

"We think he will marry the girl he writes to," she reported the next month. "She is coming out here as soon as she is 21 to see him if he doesn't come to see her first." Rose's expectation that Natalie and Karl would marry, sight unseen, attests to her belief in the power of letters. Had the marriage come about, we would have had a near-literal union of Boston and Fort Vermilion, the *Atlantic*'s "faraway" project made flesh. (The identity of this editor is unknown, but at the least it was not Sedgwick, father of Theodora and Henrietta Ellery.) It is tempting to read the satisfaction Rose displays as reflecting not only maternal pride but also a sense of one-upmanship on Boston's literary establishment—especially its editors—which after her first surprise success assessed her as falling short. Compared to the overeducated Natalie, Karl was the more naturally gifted writer, and the editor's daughter could not resist the prose of the homesteader's son.[101]

Weeks published one last letter from Rose, in 1939, conceding, "Her many friends in the *Atlantic* audience should know of her plight." Rose informs the recipient, a Miss Booth, "I am writing in the dark because I have been ill since April—and it affected my eyes so I cannot see, and to regain my sight must stay in the absolute dark room until sight comes back. It is nine months since I have seen my hand. I feel like a disembodied spirit." This letter appears literally out of place in the May 1939 *Atlantic*, which by then had a new look and format. The magazine was larger, to fulfill a promise to give readers three full novel serials a year, and its cover was bright red—in the words of one disapproving reader, "neurotic red." At this point, the line is entirely blurred as to whether Rose's letter was included in this issue to lend interest to the *Atlantic* or to sustain the interest of *Atlantic* readers in her.[102]

In January 1940, the Roses lost their home to a fire, and Charles died months later. Rose's vision continued to deteriorate until she was almost blind. (Her many illegible, precipitously slanting letters to Emerson during this period are heartrending.) One of the friends she made through Emerson, Blanche Randolph, stepped in to help Karl fund an operation in Edmonton. Her sight was entirely restored. Following her convalescence, Rose returned to Edmonton to work, write, and savor urban life—after years of wondering if she would ever get "Outside" again. The Emerson papers include a poignant photo of her, old, frail, and frumpy on a city street, captioned in her hand, "I look at a bright bewildering world."

The letters Rose wrote from Edmonton express her keen delight in having companions, clubs, and the University of Alberta at hand. However, lacking the necessary degree, she was unable to find the teaching job she had hoped for and instead took an onerous service position for a couple and their child, duties 6:30 a.m. to 8:00 p.m. daily.[103] From this she saved enough to rent a private room for two months and devote herself to her novel, a period that a timely twenty-five-dollar check from Ada Fitts in Boston extended by twenty-five days.[104] She studied writing guides at the library and paid a "critic teacher" for editorial help, the acclaimed Chicago poet Kathleen Foster.[105] (Frances Gaston supplied the funds.) But while she had hoped to move on to Montreal— realizing Charles's homecoming dream—she felt obliged to return to Peace River to assist Karl with his growing family. Thereupon she became a teacher in an "Indian school in the woods," grueling work that at least was good fodder for her novel, as she characteristically maintained.[106] Her friends in the East urged her to come live with them, but she met them only in imagination: "I am looking forward to the day when the novel is done and I board a train for the long dreamed of visit—not in an apartment but to take you and Christine and Miss Gaston if she wants to come away from the world and there we will sit in deck chairs and look at each other and talk and explain away all

FIGURE 5. Hilda Rose (*right*) in Edmonton: "I look at a bright bewildering world." *Manuscripts and Archives Division, The New York Public Library.*

problems and ask each other questions and draw a deep breath of relief that this struggle is over."[107]

Rose never lost faith that she was on the verge of a breakthrough. Her letters are studded with statements such as "After awhile there will be another book and it will be a big one I'm afraid," "Do not worry about my selling the novel. It is so good that no publisher can turn it down," and "This will be the last winter of hard times for us for as soon as my book is accepted we can live." She also never lost her sense of powerful connection to the *Atlantic*, both as an institution in which she had professional standing and as a community that fostered caring ties. In her words, she had "studied" the *Atlantic* for "almost half a century — started when I was 14 and that's 50 years ago." "I enter a different world when I read it." Shortly after Charles's death, she wrote two letters to Emerson, sent in the same envelope. The longer one informs her of his passing and describes the funeral. The other gives instructions for the first: "The enclosed letter is not very legible I'm afraid but if you think best you may send it to the Atlantic as there are so many readers who would like to learn that Daddy has left us." While Rose did not achieve the success she dreamed of, through her enduring relationship with the *Atlantic* she had the rewards of authorship nonetheless.[108]

CHAPTER FIVE

JUANITA HARRISON

AND

MY GREAT, WIDE, BEAUTIFUL WORLD

Rhetorical Lives

It is not simply that the white story teller *will not* do full justice to the humanity of the black race; he *cannot*.

—William Pickens, *The Vengeance of the Gods, and Three Other Stories of Real American Color Line Life*

I have thought and written about Juanita Harrison and *My Great, Wide, Beautiful World* for many years, following my felicitous introduction to the text in Margo Culley's *A Day at a Time: The Diary Literature of American Women from 1764 to the Present*. In the past, I identified Harrison as an African American traveler and writer from Mississippi, and I described her book as "a compilation of over two hundred journal entries describing new places and experiences as Harrison slowly circles the globe."[1] Other accounts of Harrison, both in her time and in ours, offer similar formulations. I have come to recognize, however, just how much this summary obscures the complexities of her text, experience, and identity. That the representation of Harrison has been so uniform testifies to Sedgwick's editorial control. It also, more broadly, reflects enduring critical habits. Some revisions are in order.

Harrison did indeed travel extensively, passing through thirty-three countries over the eight years *My Great, Wide, Beautiful World* represents. However, the book is not a travel diary. Rather, it is a collection of letters to friends and former employers, edited and arranged so as to appear like a journal. She did leave the United States on the Atlantic Ocean and return to it on the Pacific. The experience, however, was hardly an around-the-world trip as usually conceived, as it consists of a three-year period of working as a maid, cook, or nurse, punctuated by bursts of travel in Europe and the Middle East; a five-year residence in France; and finally an eight-month journey through Scandinavia, Russia, and Asia. Not least, Harrison subordinates her African American identity and elides her Mississippi origins to claim citizenship in a global community of women of color.

Given her feats, it is no surprise that her critical reception has always had a celebratory ring, dominated by accounts of how far she came from her actual and socioeconomic places of origin. She made over domestic service, close to the lowest rung of women's occupational ladder, into an exportable, liberating trade. She rendered the racial identity that was a liability at home an asset overseas, her indeterminate dark looks supporting her quest to mingle with local peoples. And as a direct consequence of her dearth of formal education, she produced a text that reads as if it's about to burst into speech. Even had she enjoyed a comfortable middle-class upbringing, her book would be an inspiring travel romance, featuring a canny, carefree, supremely self-possessed wanderer, one confident enough about her abilities and prospects to spend her money while she has it. Her enthusiasm about her choices unqualified, Harrison exhibits none of the doubt and boredom that can dog the long-term traveler. Add her exuberance about the people she meets and the places she goes, and the formula is beguiling.

However, such admiring assessments can shut down the actual text. Attention is confined to the author (her strategic self-fashioning, multiple subject positions, and picaresque tactics) rather than the book (its composition, style, and arguments). By now, enough preliminary work has been done that we can both narrow and broaden the purview to make more incisive readings of *My Great, Wide, Beautiful World*. Uncovering the conditions of its publication advances the project.

I am interested in the text's identity as at once an outcome of and a commentary on distinctive labor and social relations. Expressing a persistent desire for unbounded leisure, Harrison proffers a resounding success story of managing her own labor and time. Yet, as the pages that follow discuss, her travel and textual projects alike were fostered by her relationships with middle-class and upper-class white women employers, and the majority of the book is composed of letters she wrote to them. As much by her travel history and responses to new destinations, *My Great, Wide, Beautiful World* is structured by her work history and responses to new employers. Her pattern is to travel until her money runs out. Then she finds another position, which she keeps only until she can afford to move on, her relief as pungent as her employers' dismay. "I always get a job when I go out to get one," she states, "but never feel any to glad no matter how good it is. Its when I am ready to give it up that I have the grand feeling" (*GWBW* 254). (Her orthography was not amended, an editorial choice whose implications I will soon assess.) Leaving most of her employers behind, she maintains relations with a select number: from a distance, through writing. This practice led to her book.

There is a marked discrepancy, then, between Harrison's narrative of the unfettered solo agent who embarks "happy that I had no one to cry for me" (*GWBW* 1) and the behind-the-scenes story of enduring ties with women who offered emotional and material support. This discrepancy is akin to that between Elinore Pruitt Stewart's public image as the independent "woman homesteader" and the reality of Juliet Coney's involvement, or between Hilda Rose's plucky reputation and the assistance of her many *Atlantic* fans. The actual histories of these authors and their texts may be less viscerally satisfying than the simpler fictions about "pioneer virtues" and the like.[2] They are, however, more instructive.

Just two installments of Harrison's narrative appeared in the *Atlantic,* in the October and November 1935 issues (the latter also featured Rose). *My Great, Wide, Beautiful World* was published the following year, May 1936. It sold so well as to go through nine printings in ten months, and then another in 1939, prompting Harrison to casually refer to it as a "best seller." She alluded to agents in New York and San Francisco, her desire that the book be sold "for much less," her publisher's promise that she would soon be reconciled to her celebrity, and the many autographs she signed (FL3). The prominent African American newspaper the *California Eagle* proudly reported, "Miss Harrison's book is the first work by a colored author to get on the 'best seller' list of the New York Herald Tribune."[3]

Authenticity, predictably, was the keynote of her publicity. Even as readers were assured of Harrison's authorship—recollecting the authenticating discourse of the past century's slave narratives—they were also informed that Harrison was not an author as conventionally understood. The introduction to the second *Atlantic* installment opens, "As readers of the October *Atlantic* know, Miss Harrison's diary is entirely genuine." *Kirkus Review* described the book as "primarily a unique human document"; the title of the *New Republic* review is simply "Natural." Katherine Woods, profiling *My Great, Wide, Beautiful World* for the *New York Times,* praised it as a "spontaneous, shrewd, and unselfconscious story of the Odyssey of an American Negress." Yet the middle adjective rightly calls into question the other two: Harrison's literary enterprise was more deliberate than most evaluations suggest. As we shall see, while her racial identity dictated her publishers' choices and her readers' responses, her writing career and text itself undercut their assumptions.[4]

My Great, Wide, Beautiful World includes two references to its origins. The first is the dedication to Myra K. Dickinson, the woman who had employed Harrison in Los Angeles not long before she left the United States. Harrison insists, "If You hadnt been interested in me I never would have tried to explain my trips." The other is her disclosure that the Morris family for whom she worked in Paris, also American, advised that "my travellers should be put into a Book, just as I have written them misteakes and all" (*GWBW* 243). I will revisit these statements and their larger contexts, but their implications can be succinctly summarized: Dickinson made her a writer, and the Morrises made her an author. Similar to *Letters of a Woman Homesteader* and *The Stump Farm, My Great, Wide, Beautiful World* is both engendered by and represents the author's cross-class relationships with other women. But further complicating the textual dynamic, Harrison's were interracial, too. We might recall that for Stewart, becoming a homesteader meant she no longer did work she associated with African American women; she was no longer a "washlady." For Harrison, crossing the Atlantic made for a literal departure from racialized American labor relations, a change she implicitly celebrates. Nevertheless, these relations deeply inform her book.

There is another key player in Harrison's literary production, Alice M. Foster, whose presence disrupts any simple readings by showing it did not solely revolve around white associates. Foster was a friend, an African American who had emigrated with her husband from Mississippi to Pasadena some two decades prior to Harrison's arrival in California. On beginning work on her book in 1931, Harrison asked Foster to send to Paris all the letters she had written her during her international travels, to be assessed for inclusion in the volume. The two women's history is preserved in papers that Foster's granddaughter, Ann Cunningham Smith, donated to the University of California–Los Angeles in 2009. Their correspondence ranged from 1927 to 1936, and the collection includes three of Harrison's letters to Foster. Two were written in Paris in early 1931, as she was working on the book, and the third in Honolulu in 1936, just after its publication. While few in number, they are rich in content, highlighting key subjects: the process by which the book was composed, Harrison's conflicted views about authorship, and the potent influence of Myra Dickinson and her husband, George. Throughout this chapter I draw on them as a biographical source, and I assess their implications more critically in its latter stage. As the only substantive texts we have from Harrison that did not undergo editorial processing, the letters are invaluable. Among other important functions they indicate, by way of contrast, the contingency of the narrative persona and racial stance we see in *My Great, Wide, Beautiful World.*

Despite their less than mainstream status, the other writers I discuss are well documented. Whiteley's activity can be minutely tracked through papers at the Massachusetts Historical Society, the University of Oregon, and the University of London. Rose's correspondence is archived at the MHS and the New York Public Library, while Susanne Bloomfield's research materials at the Sweetwater County Historical Museum richly express Stewart's life. But aside from the small UCLA holding, Harrison's personal and publishing history must be gleaned from public records, her book and its paratexts, and the remarks of editors, reviewers, and journalists. Even the Ellery Sedgwick Papers yield no traces. In contrast to the other faraway women, Sedgwick did not enter into personal correspondence with Harrison, nor did the *Atlantic* preserve her manuscripts, fan mail, or reviews.

One result is that the identities of the published letters' original recipients are shrouded. In respect to retrieving the letters for review,

Harrison explained to Foster, "I have written to all the People that I wrote to and have many but cannot have to many as some may have only a page that's worth while" (FL1). Passing allusions in *My Great, Wide, Beautiful World* indicate that her correspondence was various and extensive. Yet without manuscripts, we can identify only a small group of recipients: the Dickinsons in Los Angeles, the Morrises in Paris, and Helen Rose on the Cap d'Antibes.

It is telling that Harrison's sole repository is a family legacy as opposed to an institutional one. Any archive, Carolyn Steedman comments in *Dust: The Archive and Cultural History*, is composed of "selected and collected rememberings and forgettings." Eric Gardner notes that due to "the grasp of white power on much of American print culture and American memory," African American texts were more likely to be dismissed as "ephemeral," resulting in a dearth of resources. John Kevin Young argues that the paucity further stems from a conception of them as racial documents rather than art. Essentialist views about black people result in essential views about black writing, rendering superfluous any preservation of the "material forms on which the 'inner' text depends." Scholars working in all periods of African American history and literature, among others Lois Brown, Frances Smith Foster, Marisa J. Fuentes, Gardner, Saidiya Hartman, Laura Helton, M. Thomas Inge, Joycelyn K. Moody, and Young, have shown the challenges of African American archival study and recovery, and they model an array of scholarly tactics to address them—in Brown's words, "the strategic and necessary ways in which we must read what we have" in the face of "rhetorical ruptures and biographical caesuras." My discussion of Harrison attempts to repair some of those ruptures and caesuras in her text and her personal history.[5]

Harrison was born in Columbus, Mississippi, on December 26, 1887, to Jones Harrison and Rosa Crigler (which she variously spelled Creglar, Crutler, and Creagler). The 1870 U.S. Census enumerates the Oktibbeha County, Mississippi, household headed by her maternal grandmother, Lizzie Crigler, when her mother, Rosa, was just three. Originally from North Carolina, Lizzie worked as a cook to support her four young children, two daughters and two sons. While both she and an eighteen-year-old boarder, Manerva Nail, are listed as black, all the children are identified as "mulatto." The Census offers no clue about their father, the white man whose relationship with Lizzie dated back to at least 1864, the year the eldest was born.[6]

The 1860 population of Oktibbeha County was composed of 5,328 white people, 7,631 slaves, and just 18 "free coloreds." After the war, many of the county's African American residents who did not leave Mississippi altogether moved to adjoining Lowndes County, the site of Harrison's birthplace, Columbus. Either the Criglers did the same, or Rosa went there as a young adult, perhaps with Jones. In her introduction to the reprint of Harrison's book, historian Adele Logan Alexander comments that her family were most likely sharecroppers and, if so, "wretchedly oppressed and dirt-poor."[7]

Columbus was always a small town during Harrison's residency, with a population of 6,500 in 1900 and 9,000 in 1910. Its *Atlantic* debut came in 1867 with Francis Miles Finch's poem "The Blue and the Gray," which celebrates the choice of a group of townswomen to adorn both Union and Confederate graves. Home to Mississippi University for Women, the nation's first public women's university, in some ways Columbus was a champion of class mobility. In advocating for the school, legislator Wiley Nash had pleaded, "Can we not do something for the poor girls of Mississippi[?]"[8] Tuition was free, each county had a quota of guaranteed places, and students could work off their board. Eudora Welty—another Mississippian whose writing career began in the *Atlantic*—was enrolled from 1925 to 1927. However, as demonstrated by its original name, "Mississippi Industrial Institute and College for the Education of White Girls," the school had nothing to offer Harrison. Columbus is now known for its preserved antebellum mansions, among them perhaps some of the homes she serviced.

Juanita lost her mother at the age of six. She reveals to Foster that she knew her mother's mother, Crigler, but that she was separated from her family very young (FL3). The bereavement was doubtless the formative event of her childhood, and when she tendered a minute recital of her "true life story" to her editor Mildred Morris, she began it then (FL2). Yet disappointing sentimental expectations, she insisted, "I am glad I went out from my dozen of Kin before I were old enough to know all their names" (FL3).

While Morris transcribed Harrison's oral history with care, all that remains is the condensed biography she offers in her preface to *My Great, Wide, Beautiful World.* Typical of discussions of Harrison, she opens by stating, "Juanita Harrison is an American colored woman."

Born in Mississippi, she had a few months of schooling before she was ten. Then began an endless round of cooking, washing and ironing in an over-burdened household,—labor that might have daunted a grown woman.

But the child at work, clothed in a woman's cast-off apparel, stiff basque bodice, long skirt and laced bicycle boots, lived with a bright vision of tem-pled cities in foreign lands which she had seen pictured in the stray pages of a magazine.

Out of the sordid life that colored her early years she distilled a resolution: "I will sail far away to strange places. Around me no one has the life I want. No one is there for me to copy, not even the rich ladies I work for. I have to cut my life out for myself and it won't be like anyone else." (MP, ix)

Morris is a reliable guide to Harrison and her text. Her focus on the natal workplace rather than family of this "child at work" aptly intro-duces a book that centers on navigating an array of work environments. She relays a formative print-culture encounter. She flags the utility of the racially ambiguous looks—"slight form, fresh olive complexion, long hair braided about her head" (MP xi)—that not only contributed to her being "accepted as a native" in the countries she visited but also brought her closer to a presumptive white readership. Forecasting the eclectic costumes Harrison donned overseas, she inventories a hybrid outfit that in addition to poverty attests to adaptability, ingenuity, and (with the restrictive Victorian clothing impugned by the bicycle boots) an impending embrace of distinctly modern mobility. She also calls attention to the critical role of the "rich ladies" who employed her. In her youth, their static lives inspired her to travel, and she went on to construct a book out of extended conversations with other women whose social positions resembled theirs.

According to the youthful memory Morris reconstructs, that "bright vision of templed cities in foreign lands which she had seen pictured in the stray pages of a magazine" (MP ix) kindled Harrison's longing for travel. Her comment to Foster that "at 11 years I planned my life" (FL2) suggests a possible age. The event is a key element in her personal myth of origins, the source of her desire to become not just a traveler but perhaps also a travel writer, too. Harrison resembles Opal Whiteley in making a print artifact an emblem of the life she desired, comparable to her "Angel Books," and her achievement is equally immense. Nei-ther woman aspired to join the social and cultural leaders of her home community; her sights were set on distant realms.

The magazine Harrison saw was perhaps *Century Illustrated Magazine* or *Harper's Bazar,* the most popular illustrated periodicals of the day. (It could not have been the *Atlantic,* which never had pictures.) Given that such a text was a middle-class luxury, her exposure may have been in an employer's home. Morris implies that only the drawing or photograph made the controlling impression, not any article it illustrated. If Harrison had seen the magazine at work, she might have had only a few moments to glance through it, and her meager schooling may have precluded the level of literacy to readily read it.

Her own text is silent about her home state and her past. "The South," Patricia Yaeger has noted, "is most conspicuous in its absence from her story: a travelogue in which almost every other place on Earth gets visited, celebrated, named." Devoid of allusions to family or friends, *My Great, Wide, Beautiful World* discloses almost nothing about Harrison's life in Mississippi. Perhaps it is significant that the most substantive reference to her past concerns aborted travel, a harrowing train wreck she recollects after another serious accident in Czechoslovakia: "I was in a Reck in 1903 on Sept. 1st when I was a little girl also a Monday but it was twice as bad about 100 killed and many wounded I didnt get hurt but many in the coch did so I knew just what to do" (*GWBW* 53). The accident actually occurred on Monday, September 1, 1902, when an excursion train traveling from Columbus to Birmingham derailed in Berry, Alabama. Harrison was fourteen, old enough to have learned "just what to do" to help survivors. The *New York Times* sensationally reported, "Railroad Wreck with One Hundred Victims: Twenty-One Are Dead and Twenty-Nine More Will Die—Negro Excursion Train Plunges over an Embankment." Said to have been "packed with passengers," that the train served working-class African Americans was surely a factor in its safety standards.[9]

Harrison's best Columbus prospect was leaving it, and there is no sign she ever saw Mississippi again, or wished to. Morris writes that she was just sixteen when she left, but the evidence suggests her departure was likely in 1910, which makes her twenty-two (adding to the confusion of her chronology, Harrison regularly took four years off her age). She crisscrossed North America while holding a series of service jobs, and she eventually established two western urban bases, Los Angeles and Honolulu. Her trajectory was in some respects typical, one among millions in the Great Migration of African Americans who left the South to "better their position," to use a favored phrase.[10] While the movement is often associated with men taking industrial jobs in northern cities, countless domestic workers participated, too, women who, as David Katzman shows in *Seven Days a Week: Women and Domestic Service in Industrializing America,* in their itinerancy resembled Harrison. Their ability to quit a job and soon find another was their most powerful bargaining tool.[11] Yet Harrison presents herself as invested in movement for its own sake and as more intent on culture and leisure than economic advance. Anticipating her habits overseas, she visited popular tourist destinations across the continent, including Pike's Peak, the Great Salt Lake, Niagara Falls, and St. Augustine. Claiming to have been "in nearly every state in the Union," she fondly reminisced, "I did what I wanted saved what I wanted and I traveled about from State to State City to City in the Union Canada and Cuba" (FL2).

According to her 1950 passport application, which asks for the years and places she "resided continuously in the United States," between 1887 and 1917 she lived in Mississippi, Alabama, Michigan, Illinois, New Jersey, Pennsylvania, Florida, and New York (in the latter state "for years" [*GWBW* 100], she notes in her book). From 1922 to 1925, she was in Louisiana, Texas, Kansas, Indiana, and New York once more. Following the eight years abroad, she resided in the "Hawaiian Islands," 1935 to 1939. The record is incomplete, however. The application does not give information about her 1917 to 1922 interval in Canada and Cuba, identify her American locations between 1925 and 1927, or reference her time in Iowa, Colorado, and California. Absent, too, is a prior residency in Hawaii: in January 1925 she had sailed from Los Angeles for Honolulu, returning to San Francisco six months later as one of only several U.S. citizen passengers not born in the Philippines. By this time, she had settled on the West as her lifelong U.S. region of choice.[12]

Morris reports that she lost a sum of $800, most of her savings, in one of Colorado's many bank failures of the 1920s. Yet the event led to a "happy turning point" (MP x) in her life, in that it was the catalyst for her move to Los Angeles. Harrison remained in Los Angeles for several years, largely in the household and employ of the Dickinsons, who were leading property developers. The city was booming, and they paid her well, according to George's report tendering above-average wages and many presents. They also invested $2,550 of her savings in mortgages, the same kind of investment that, on a miniature scale, undergirded their own fortune. Yielding 8 percent interest, this generated the annual income of $204 that subsidized the first stage of her world journey, up until the stock market crash of 1929. By then she had long since developed effective methods to get jobs on the move, traveling with uniforms and a growing portfolio of references, placing and responding to newspaper advertisements, and wielding a formidable skill set that ensured her a pick of positions.

In June 1927, she embarked in Hoboken, New Jersey, on a German ship bound for Plymouth, England. She returned to American territory in April 1935, settling in Hawaii. In December 1939 she renewed her passport to move on to Brazil. She remained in Brazil for a half year, followed by another half year in Uruguay, a year and eight months in Argentina, and three months in Chile. Returning to Argentina in January 1943, she commenced a seven-year residency in Buenos Aires. In 1950 she renewed her passport again to travel through Bolivia (by rail for "pleasure"), answering "uncertain" the question of when she would reside once more in the United States and—strikingly—identifying her profession as that of author. She may have returned to California in 1953, the year she applied, newly eligible for benefits, for a Social Security card in La Jolla. She died in Honolulu in October 1967, aged seventy-nine.[13]

My Great, Wide, Beautiful World

Morris states that Harrison planned her trip with circumnavigation as her goal, and the concept structures *My Great, Wide, Beautiful World*. It determines the choice of title (on which more later) and the choice of excerpts. Yet cordoning off this portion of Harrison's nomadic life as a discrete journey is an arbitrary division. With its multiple tours and sojourns, the decade the book records little differs from the one that preceded it—during which she worked and traveled all over North America—or the one that followed, when she did the same in South America.

Within this span, moreover, she spends nearly five years residing in southern France. The text does not represent this major disruption of trip and chronicle, beyond the terse editorial comment, "Because of the unsettled condition in China Juanita determined not to complete her journey around the world at this time but returned to the south of France where she remained until May 1934" (265). The anonymous voice insists on the actuality of an around-the-world trip, even as it gives information that exposes it as fiction. One can imagine alterna-tive handlings of the break, such as Harrison accounting for it or even relaying some events from these years. She was not in fact entirely sta-tionary, traveling to at least Belgium and Corsica. More important, this was when she returned to Paris to begin work on her book with Morris, a crucial act of agency that official histories of her authorship omit.

Touring China was far from the only way for her to stay on the road, and, indeed, on resuming her travels she went to Holland. The prob-able cause of the hiatus—which commenced in November 1929—was the collapse of her investments. In George Dickinson's words, they "fell down entirely."[14] The editorial choice to excise this financial setback reads as a reflexive gesture of class solidarity, which Sedgwick extends in *The Happy Profession* (along with disregarding Myra) in maintain-ing, "Under the kind guidance of her master, her savings were wisely invested" (211). Rather than undermine the narrative of benevolent white guidance, a major and surely traumatic life event was passed over. He also casually reifies racial hierarchies in identifying Dickin-son as her "master" rather than, to use Harrison's term, her cherished "friend."

Harrison conducted the final stage of her trip more swiftly. No longer intermittently employed, she moved through Scandinavia, Russia, and Asia in the space of eight months. By this time, having begun the book project, she was writing letters with the knowledge that they would feed into it, perhaps influencing both her travel itinerary and her nar-rative choices. On arrival in Honolulu, she took a service position with an American military couple, only to quit it upon receiving her first writing income. "That cheque from the Atlantic Monthly for my article gave joy," she reports. This statement opens the book's epilogue, which is dated "Now." "I got it on a Sat. and gave up my weekly job" (315). Once again, the *Atlantic*'s instrumental role in a contributor's ability to sustain the lifestyle she writes about is highlighted, along with the in-process immediacy of her text. Harrison used the money to have a capacious tent custom made for herself, which she erected on a plot of ground owned by a Japanese family, the Tadas. We will soon visit her there, in the company of Ellery Sedgwick.[15]

My Great, Wide, Beautiful World opens with her boarding in Hoboken: "Our cabins looked good. I always want a upper berth I don't want anybody making it down on me. I went to the 1st and 2nd Class. Their towels looked more linnen so I took two, the soap smelt sweeter so I took 2 cakes. I went up to the writing room and the paper was the kind you love to touch so I took much and tuked it away in my bunk" (1). At the moment her world journey commences, she literally elevates her status through this series of appropriative acts: claiming the top bunk in her third-class cabin, taking the nicer towels and soap from first and second class, and finally ascending to "the writing room" to pocket its fine paper.

While her attention to the paper indicates she considered quality writing essential to satisfactory travel, a late entry in the book makes a more deflating reference: "when I think of the good things I can get to eat for what the stamp cost I just stick these letters in my case" (293). One statement suggests a sensuous relationship to writing: the paper "you love to touch" gets "tuked" in her bed. The other humorously deflates its worth, as rather less than that of a good meal, and the letters are relegated to her suitcase, unsent. However, both commonly express a canny calculation brought to bear on the activity, as one whose costs and benefits must be weighed. "I had to send so many cards to many people about the world that have been kind to me which is a small bit to do. but it have amounted to dollars with stamps I wanted to stop at Heidelberg but cut it out so to have it for postage," she reports (262). Harrison relied on creative scavenging, both metaphorical and literal, to sustain her writing practice. Like other faraway women, she shows writing to be at once labor and luxury, as well as a necessarily piecemeal enterprise.

She more consistently represents her oral practice. Unique among this study's subjects, Harrison is a self-consciously adroit speaker, and her book is threaded with commentary on her speech acts and acumen. She bargains for rooms and goods. She flirts with and coaxes admirers. She wrangles concessions from transportation and immigration officials. Most important, she brokers acceptable work conditions. These exchanges, moreover, are often in languages other than English. Harrison was a committed linguist. She had learned Spanish while working in Havana, and she studied French both in that city and in Los Angeles. She started learning German on the ship that bore her to England, and she continued to work with it in Paris and beyond. She acquired a smattering of Russian and Arabic, too. Consequently, among other applications she could serve as a translator for her American employer in Spain or use French while traveling through Syria and Egypt. She gives regular updates on her prowess, as when she allows, "For my French I can put out the words but its the Frenchmans hard luck to get them round in the proper place" (*GWBW* 14), and she increasingly recruits French and Spanish phrases at moments when English proves inadequate: "I made a promise to come back in two weeks like the promise I made to Mrs. M. but I dont think it will be two years. But qu'n sabe (Spanish)" (*GWBW* 252). She even begins addressing Alice Foster in Pasadena as "Madame," a habit that persisted after her return to America.

The book also presents numerous scenes of reading, albeit exclusively nonfiction. Of the moment her train wrecked in Brno, she recounts, "I was studying the book that means everything to me, Bradshaws Continental guide all of a sudden I was throwd across the compartment and hit my head. . . . I was very dizzy but I thought about nothing but this book and kept calling my book, my book I was stunted" (50–51). Her dazed search for "my book" shows her intense connection to the texts she relied on for travel information and cultural orientation. In addition to popular guide books such as Bradshaw's, she pored over encyclopedias and histories to search out esoteric knowledge, such as the origins of Buddhism or the meanings of Egyptian tattoos. Yet the books that mean "everything" to her—those she "studies" to learn about her destinations—appear to be the only books that mean *anything* to her. *My Great, Wide, Beautiful World* is conspicuous for its near-complete absence of textual allusions.

Such absence confirms the past dearth of literary access that Harrison's nonstandard prose broadcasts. Her book includes no statements like Stewart's "I felt very like Leather-stocking" (*LWH* 26) or Rose's "It's a Robinson Crusoe existence" (*SF* 150), much less Whiteley's familiar references to the likes of Virgil and Mendelssohn. While these other women had limited cultural resources, they sufficed to yield models of authorship. Stewart was inspired by American writers including James Fenimore Cooper, Marietta Holley, Jack London, and Mark Twain. Rose educated herself with Shakespeare, the Bible, Robert Burns, Walt Whitman, and Sinclair Lewis. The Whiteleys owned only reference books, but public libraries afforded Opal a steady diet of popular fiction, and she versed herself—somehow—in ancient and European history. Harrison's early print exposure, in contrast, seems to have been confined to "stray pages." Yet this lack notwithstanding, she embraced the prospect of authorship along with a host of other life changes.

My Great, Wide, Beautiful World demonstrates her efforts to resist a fixed national, socioeconomic, and racial identity as an "American colored woman." Suggesting the deliberation with which she crafted her image, prior to departure she decided on California as her nominal home state since "every one know it" (192); its renown made her "proud." Numerous scenes in the book show her expediently adjusting her class and ethnic aspect, through language, clothing, acts, and gestures. In Europe her ability to move between social classes takes literal form in her habit of boarding trains on third-class tickets but then proceeding to "go forward to the front," while in India she can appear both so "high cast" she must argue for her right to travel second-class and as "low cast as a European can look" (50, 110). Her not infrequent invocation of her status as a "European" is intriguing, a deft way to distinguish herself from local populations in the Middle East and Asia without making either national, or explicitly racial, claims. In a 1923 essay, W. E. B. Du Bois stages a dialogue in which his narrator is asked how, given the nation's long history of racial mixing, a black "group" can be descried in the United States: "'But what is this group; and how do you differentiate it; and how can you call it "black" when you admit it is not black?' I recognize it quite easily and with full legal sanction: the black man is a person who must ride 'Jim Crow' in Georgia." According to Du Bois's theory, once overseas Harrison was no longer "black," to all appearances enjoying unfettered mobility. That she was "fascinated with her own ability to cross boundaries," Yaeger points out, surely stemmed from the policing of mobility she had endured in the South.[16]

In part due to her ambiguous dark looks, Harrison was variously deduced to be Chinese, Japanese, Arab, Cuban, Moroccan, Indian, Jewish, Spanish, Argentinean, Greek, and even English, misreadings she cultivated when they served her, and consistently reports. For example, she passes—or says she does—for French in Boulogne. "I looked so much like one of the Fishman wives," she states, "most of the women have long hair and dress it in two brads as I do all I laked was ear rings. I had two pairs in my case that Mme. gave me. Well I put on my correll ear rings and was a perfect Boulognesser" (*GWBW* 14). Her text neither conceals nor emphasizes her race. Of a group of African women, she remarks, "I think they saw I had some of their blood I couldnt fool them" (*GWBW* 19). (Who, then, did she fool?) She mentions turning "a dark chocolate" from the sun in Egypt even as she presents herself as a viable candidate for a job "open for a European lady only" (*GWBW* 177, 115). Her cycling between identities indicates the "pliability and instrumentality of race," to use Gayle Wald's phrase. We can recognize Harrison's activity in Wald's description of racial passing as "a practice that emerges from subjects' desires to control the terms of their racial definition, rather than be subject to the definitions of white supremacy" and a way "to negotiate the multifarious needs, fantasies, and aspirations that are mediated and expressed through the racial sign."[17] Her stance can be read as not a disavowal of African American identity but a claim to citizenship in a global female community of color. She may be a "European lady," but she is everything except white.

My Great, Wide, Beautiful World presents travel as a utopian venture, undertaken by a heroine who is never bored, never tired, never frustrated, never fearful. Consequently, as a key element of her enterprise, her racial or ethnic identity can only be a strategic asset, not a liability, and a condition over which she has full control. Whether this depiction entirely aligned with her lived experience is doubtful. Toni Morrison's statement in her essay "Home" is a potent reminder of the ubiquity of racial strictures: "I have never lived, nor have any of us, in a world in which race did not matter. Such a world, one free of racial hierarchy, is usually imagined or described as dreamscape—Edenesque, utopian, so remote are the possibilities of its achievement." Gene Andrew Jarrett quotes from "Home" at greater length in introducing his *African American Literature beyond Race: An Alternative Reader*, an anthology of texts featuring protagonists "explicitly or implicitly marked as racially white, neutral, or ambiguous." Vigorously arguing for the promise of travel, Harrison's narrative offers an additional platform to interrogate the significance of such authorial choices.[18]

Another possibility: an awareness of her first readers' sensibilities triggered self-censure, leading Harrison to subordinate her identity as an African American and perhaps suppress instances of discrimination. Or Morris may have literally edited out racial content in preparing her letters for publication. We know that Sedgwick, at least, considered it inappropriate for the *Atlantic*. In rejecting Zona Gale's story about an African American family moving into the fictional Wisconsin community of "Friendship Village," he explained that he "could not 'accept the implications' of the piece's plainly stated 'argument' for racial equality." He was loath, moreover, even to "take . . . up" discussions of racial subjects, as he indicated in response to a reader's objection to his calling Harrison a "Negress." The abundance of interpretive options and ambiguities produced by the multiple participants in Harrison's project demonstrates the truth of Jean Lutes's assertion, that due to their disruption of "convenient, familiar" ways of reading, periodical texts call for alternative analytic approaches.[19]

Although it is impossible to verify the psychological, social, or editorial sources of Harrison's racial depiction in *My Great, Wide, Beautiful World*, what we do know is that it is different from that evident in the Foster correspondence. While her letters to Foster were, of course, also written under specific conditions and for specific ends, they serve as a control for evaluating the published book. Harrison casually references (and criticizes) their shared racial community, stating, "In our race we will be kind up until we think that one count on us then we let you fall" (FL2). Moreover, as the same comment intimates, a different personality emerges, far less insouciant. While there are still moments of joie de vivre, she can also sound anxious, bitter, defensive, or weary, another indication of the constructed aspect of her more public persona and the relative ease she felt writing someone she knew outside of service relationships.

There is an even greater disparity between her position in *My Great, Wide, Beautiful World* and in a mid-1940s letter to notable drama critic John Mason Brown. The latest extant text we have from her, Harrison had written to Brown to support his endorsement of performing *Uncle Tom's Cabin* despite its racial stereotypes. Brown's remarks, which originally appeared in a 1945 *Saturday Review* column, were picked up by *Negro Digest* in a brief essay entitled "Is *Uncle Tom's Cabin* Anti-Negro?"[20] The magazine polled its readership on the same question, and while most white readers answered no, 60 percent of black readers said yes.[21] Openly political, in the letter Harrison expounds on her minority position, criticizing the choices of "we Negroes" and vigorously arguing for their greater representation.

> Why are the white people so careful not to include the Negro in the holy Literture [*sic*] and their textbooks? . . [*sic*] Mr. Brown, If the truth were told and had been told all along there would be no need for uncle tom's. . . . I am wondering if God know there are black people on earth? . . [*sic*] Or, are they to turn white before God will addmitte [*sic*] them. you want to show uncle tom's cabin for the sake of American culture. Why not show some part off

[*sic*] uncle tom in your American Chrisrian Literture [*sic*], and textbooks for the sake of culture? It may help the Negro, if no one else?"[22]

That she contacted Brown himself proves she had the self-confidence to assume the role of racial advocate and weigh in on cultural debates—and that she was still writing, although by now (enormously ineptly) on a typewriter.

Friends and Patrons

Another tantalizing disclosure from this late letter: despite never marrying, she signed herself, by hand, "Mrs. Harrison," surely a bid for the more serious consideration this marital status conferred. Whether an isolated instance or a habit we cannot know, but, returning to *My Great, Wide, Beautiful World,* we can ask how a similar motive might inform her depiction of her love life, censoring behavior or views that would impugn her in the eyes of the women to whom she wrote. While Harrison operates within a context of continual romantic possibility, her activity seemingly never goes further than a shared outing or meal. The book includes only one reference to an actual relationship, "For years in N.Y. I was a love of the Army" (100). She figures the men she meets on the road as a fount of favors, people to enjoy, profit from, and leave behind. With motives narrowly ranging from lustful to gallant, they procure her seats, tickets, rooms, visas, and food. Yet she is "man proof" (22), she claims, and always finds a way to dodge them—skipping rendezvous, skipping town. Her treatment can verge on the callous, as when she deceives an Egyptian suitor into believing she will go back to a private apartment with him, in order first to enjoy a lavish dinner at his expense.

Her interactions with men are zesty but undemanding. In high contrast, her interactions with other women appear charged, vexed, and invested. She focuses intently on them: their looks, habits, relationships, and ethnicities, along with the feelings of superiority, empathy, and obligation they evoke. Just as the men in her text consistently appear as benefactors, bestowing upon her presents, concessions, and guidance, the women consistently appear as supplicants, extracting *from* her material and emotional boons. Her portrayal of them, consequently, exhibits a host of contradictions: avoidance and attraction, solidarity and scorn, kinship and difference. Establishing fleeting bonds with women of many nations enables her to subjectively position herself within a world community, even as they shore up her identity as a "true rover" (*GWBW* 126).

She regularly records small acts of sisterly charity, like giving her share of a communal boardinghouse dinner to a "young, blonde dancer" who "looked so hungry" (*GWBW* 4) or planning to donate a winter coat to the African women she visits at the 1931 Paris Colonial Exposition. She also discloses her reluctant, and often distressing, emotional involvement in their lives, as in Syria, when she helps a woman get her daughter onto a train just as its doors close: "Well the mother cried and went on it made me cry" (*GWBW* 68). The most extreme instance occurs in the aftermath of the train accident, when a young German woman dies in her arms. She laments, "Had I been killed it would have been absolutely nothing compared to that girl" (*GWBW* 51).

Yet she also portrays the women she meets as offering negative models, showing her how not to live. She depicts them as confined to the domestic sphere, bound to homes and husbands, a choice that by contrast highlights her own liberty. In Spain, for example, she comments, "I told the women and girls if I was married I would be at home washing dirty cloths just as they are during" and "I teased Josefa the Young Wife she bought rabbit I said you have a husband so must eat rabbit I am single so can have turkey" (*GWBW* 192, 206). Attributing her autonomy to informed personal choices as opposed to larger social structures, she appears oblivious to the prerogatives that being an American afforded her, the multifarious forms of discrimination she experienced in her home country notwithstanding: to invest her savings, to carry a powerful passport, to make influential friends, and, perhaps most important, to stay single. Jessie Redmond Fauset, who also traveled internationally in the 1920s, provides a useful point of reference. Her "Dark Algiers the White," which ran in 1925 issues of the *Crisis,* displays Fauset's multiple and contrary subject positions as a middle-class African American woman in North Africa. "Both observing (as a tourist) and being observed (as a stranger)," Claire Garcia maintains, Fauset's "presence in Algiers opens up and confuses questions of national identity, class, privilege, and power."[23] Harrison's presence does the same, although she leaves it to her readers to ask these questions.

Her record of grudging attraction to other women also sheds light on the sensibility that led her to correspond with past employers, maintaining relations from afar. Inverting the usual hierarchy, she proposes,

"Its the Ladies should give me their references" (*GWBW* 244). "I dont need any to get a job I like written references more to go with my collection for if they are written nicely and kind they give joy. and the memories of the writer are sweet." She repurposes these testimonials, as sentimental mementos rather than employment aids. (And note her confidence in evaluating if they are "written nicely," with its double meaning.) We can read the "collection" she totes about as a version in miniature of *My Great, Wide, Beautiful World,* in that it attests to her emotional attachment to a select number of employers, through writing preserved under highly mobile conditions. Her report on the cache of "nine beautiful letters" that awaited her at *poste restante* in Marseilles conveys the blend of affection and pragmatism that characterized such relationships, as well as the role letters played in them: "So of the nine each had beautiful news. Two from Mrs. M. I worked for in Paris one forward from Bombay. She always enclose a new dollar bill I always kiss bills the minute I draw them out" (*GWBW* 166). The book includes a letter (presented as such) in which she thanks Myra Dickinson for a family picture. "[I] got the Happiest shock when I open your letter and saw the Photo," she assures her. "I feel highly horned" (149–50). She both stresses her emotional ties to the family and urges, "Write to me at Marseilles and if you have a little interest money will you send it if not kindly stick in a little love offering" (150).

Highlighting her avidity to write even as it obscures her authorial agency, a 1936 newspaper profile noted that she "records her observations in lengthy epistles which she sends in voluminous batches to several of her friends who were chiefly responsible for calling Juanita's talents to Mr. Sedgwick's attention."[24] While it was likely Mildred Morris who first approached Sedgwick with the "epistles," it was surely Myra and George Dickinson who received the largest share of them. Myra Kellam Dickinson was born in Kansas, and she and George came to Los Angeles by way of San Diego around 1899, just before Harrison's friends from Mississippi, the Fosters.[25] They prospered, hugely. A partner in the real estate investment firm Strong, Dickinson & McGrath, George was eulogized as a "pioneer Los Angeles realty man . . . responsible for the opening of some 200 subdivisions."[26] Like many others in their upper-class neighborhood, the Dickinsons employed a succession of live-in African American maids. Harrison was preceded by Labada Robinson, of Arkansas; Missourian Maude Mccaleph followed her.[27]

Harrison's ability to travel the world is invariably attributed to the couple's shrewd money management on her behalf, credited in her book's framing materials, reviews, and Sedgwick's memoirs as well as recent commentary. The interest her investments yielded gave her critical income and perhaps also the confidence to embark. However, given that she only briefly had returns on them and suffered a net loss, in the long run the Dickinsons' financial advice served her less than their sheer entrenchment in Los Angeles. Continuing to maintain the family home at 423 Lafayette Park Place even after she was widowed, Myra Dickinson's choice never to move made it easier for Harrison to continually do so. She paid her property taxes, forwarded her interest, and served as her emergency contact. She also provided the permanent U.S. address that gave her a legal claim to California residency. In 1950, after having lived in Buenos Aires for many years and with Myra close to ninety, Harrison still listed the Lafayette house as her residence.

The Dickinsons, she told Foster, were always "looking after my welfare," noting she could expect the letters that awaited her at each destination to include "a little bill 5. 10. 15. or 20. that I may enjoy my self more" (FL3). Characterizing them as "the Picture of Hope sitting up in the world in Their true hearted kindness never useing If" (MP x), she almost literally puts them on a pedestal. As with Stewart and Coney, the caretaking was surely reciprocal. They had lost their daughter, Martha Kellam, when she was only twenty-one—perhaps the reason Harrison perceived them as "all by their Lonsome" (FL2)—and then George died in 1936. Affectionate and effusive, Harrison must have been a source of comfort to her bereaved friend. That said, differences in class and, especially, race would have strictly constrained the relationship. She always addressed Dickinson as "Mrs.," just as the Morrises were "Mrs. Morris" and "Miss Mildred."

The dedication of *My Great, Wide, Beautiful World* reflects both the strength and the possible strain of Harrison's attachment to her mentor: "To Mrs. Myra K. Dickinson Your great kindness to me have made my traveling much happier if You hadnt been interested in me I never would have tried to explain my trips also your True and Kindness encourage me and made me more anxious to tell you the way I spent my time." The statement implies that without the other woman's "kindness" and "interest," she might not have been moved to write, with the lack of a period after "much happier" identifying the effect as twofold: a deeper satisfaction both in the journey and in writing about it. Dickinson's generous receptivity helped her render her experience as narrative. Or perhaps it compelled her to. Especially considering Harrison's usual composure, the phrase "made me more anxious" feels incongruous. One available interpretation is that it reflects a belief that Dickinson had a right to know "the way I spent my time," a remnant of the contractual obligation she once had as a maid in her home. Yet to overemphasize this possibility is ill-advised: Harrison in fact comes off as much less uneasy about past service than Stewart, with her defensive posturing as Coney's "ex-washlady."

A richer vein to tap is the anxiety the dedication itself engenders. After publication, Harrison insisted, "I care nothing about the rest of the world when it comes to the Book and from the time the Publishers accepted it I had a heavy heart for fear there would be something in it that wouldn't be just the proper reading and it being Dedicated to the only two people that were ever true and kind to me" (FL2). (Either Harrison later removed George from the dedication or her publishers chose to do so, thereby promoting a simpler story about women's support—which is always my temptation, too.) Like Stewart before her, Harrison worried that her book might cross some line of propriety, offending the devoted friends she so closely associated with it.

Although their relationship was not conducted at the same affective pitch, the Morrises in Paris were also steadfast supporters. The family was composed of Mary B. Morris and her two adult daughters, Mildred and Felice. Harrison identifies the elder Morris as "a very nice Lady of New York" (GWBW 16) and, about her first position with her, gloats, "I was looking for a place with lots of Francs lots of time off and little work and I have that." During her travels, Morris regularly sent her small sums and gifts. Harrison alludes several times to a treasured pair of "life saving" black tights: "You are so wise and kind to give me [them]" (GWBW 292). As references accrue in the book, this flimsy item takes on symbolic weight, an emblem of Morris's support through which its recipient keeps both her gratitude and her continued need on display.

Thoroughly international, the Morrises were all retired actors. Born in Missouri, Mary Morris had been married to Felix Morris, a well-known British vaudeville and character actor who established his career in London and Paris before moving on to New York. As a member of the Rosina Vokes Company, this "busy if unheralded comic" was praised for "the delicate quality of his talent in refined dialect parts," linguistic dexterity also evident in his much vaunted French.[28] Prior to Felix's death from pneumonia in 1900, Morris collaborated with him on musical arrangements and acted in his productions. (She was variously identified by her stage name, Florence Wood, and as Mrs. Felix Morris.) She also sometimes appeared onstage with Mildred, who had prominent juvenile roles in London and Broadway shows. Mildred's 1905 role as Wendy in *Peter Pan*—sharing equal billing with J. M. Barrie's original Peter Pan, Maude Adams—made her a minor celebrity.[29] She and Felice attended the Hillside Home School in Wyoming, Wisconsin, a progressive boarding school founded by two of Frank Lloyd Wright's aunts. Felice acted, too, and the sisters have a footnote in theater history for their collection of celebrity autographs, now at Princeton University.

By the time Harrison's association with the family began, Mildred worked as a writer and theater reviewer. "It was then decided," she explains, "that I should arrange her Odyssey for publication" (MP xi). Harrison seconds her, marking her route to authorship in the book itself: "One of the Daughters is a writer and the mother said my travellers should be put into a Book. I told her I would come back after my trip to India and work for nothing if Miss Mildred, the Daughter would help me" (*GWBW* 16). Felix Morris's work with "refined dialect parts" may have attuned them to the commercial potential of Harrison's vernacular; she states that Mrs. Morris urged her "travellers" be printed "just as I have written them misteakes and all" (*GWBW* 243). An important disclosure in Harrison's comments, here and elsewhere, is that from the outset she envisioned a book—in contrast to the other texts I discuss, which were conceived as serials but then evolved, thanks to Sedgwick's involvement, into bound volumes. In January 1931 she commented that she and Mildred Morris had a contract of some kind (FL1), but nothing was published before 1935.

They began the project just over a year into the long interval when Harrison's travels were suspended, with Harrison joining Morris in Paris. Far from accepting her offer of unpaid domestic labor in exchange for editorial help, the Morris family put her up as a guest in the spacious apartment just below theirs, breakfast brought down each morning, for the resonant period of forty days. "I gave the time to the Writer," Harrison states, identifying Morris by her profession. To complete the project she postponed her return to the Riviera household of

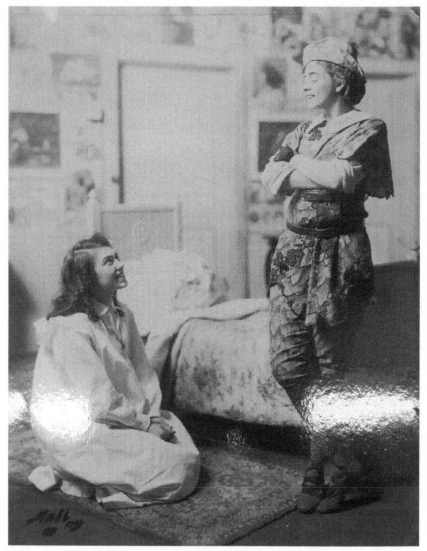

FIGURE 6. Mildred Morris (left) with Maude Adams in *Peter Pan*, 1905. *Billy Rose Theatre Division, The New York Public Library for the Performing Arts.*

a "French Lady" impatient for her service; she remarked that she was "being more of a Lady than she is altho she is Rich" (FL2).

The book's title page identifies Morris as having "Arranged and Prefaced" it. Promising the intact delivery of Harrison's original expression, the phrase both buttresses claims for authenticity and recollects

Morris's acting background, which surely served her well in editing the narrative into its most dramatic form. Her self-effacing editorial presence notwithstanding, the labor of collecting and editing a mass of letters to form a book must have been considerable.

According to Harrison's inviting account, "The Writer young and beautiful came down 9.30 a.m. We worked in a beautiful room with the restful view of the Seine and the Cathédrale Norte-Dame and the apt. was so delightful heated the water I could make tea from the tap. 9.30 to 12 noon then I was free for the rest of the day to do as I pleased" (FL2). Her record of their working methods suggests the shifting currents of power and authority between these two American women, born the exact same year:

> At the beginning the Writer thought that she would type a short sketch of my life for the interducting of the letters. but I knew that it couldn't be a short sketch because my life are like the saying to "never judge a book by its covering." . . . [She] became so interested that she said she could not do her other writings she was so anxious to get down to me to go on with my true life story . . . at the end said that She had never enjoyed writing so much as the month and 10 days. I also enjoyed it Because she is a brilliant intelligent Lady. And I enjoyed watching how Her beautiful brown eyes sparkled as I went from Six years old up to Jan. 1931. (FL2)[30]

Steedman has likened "telling someone else's story" to "the condition of servitude,"[31] and in assuming the role of amanuensis, now it is Morris who functions as the attendant, not only bringing her family's former maid food but also waiting on her words. A deeper reversal, of course, is that Harrison presently occupies an important place in American literary history, while the publishing record of "the Writer" can be detected only with effort.

Morris's preface to *My Great, Wide, Beautiful World* does not represent her and Harrison's collaborative process, much less the textured personal relationship they must have developed in its course. It does, however, set the stage for the book's focus on strategic, evolving relations with an array of employers: "Juanita never remained long in one place, though her employers invariably became her friends and raised her salary in the vain hope of keeping so excellent a servant" (MP x). Newly her "friends," these women offered their "servant" more money to stay on. For Harrison, in turn, this worker in a low-paying field, managing personal relations so expertly as to garner extracontractual benefits was essential practice. As she typically comments, regarding a position in Paris, "I wanted to give it up a week ago but they offered me some useful presents so I had to stay to get them" (*GWBW* 253).

Her account of a chance encounter in a Roman park references a different kind of employer relationship, along with the racialized culture of American service she left behind: "I notice setting down on one of the lower Terices a colored nurse about 40 and weigh about 200 lbs. I went and ask her if she spoke English and laughed when she answered 'I say I do' She was a joly old Girl I spent the rest of the afternoon. . . . [They] have 4 children she is so sweet and Gentle with them and they love her so" (*GWBW* 36). The nurse travels because of her job, and she seems attached to the family for whom she works. Harrison, in contrast, works in order to travel, and she stringently rejects the role of devoted retainer. While she portrays herself as formidably accomplished, always in demand, the magnitude of her competence is matched by that of her aversion. Longer tenure does not bring further satisfaction or even further material reward. She once remarks that she had worked for only four months the previous year: "Have just spent the time in the sun eating sleeping going to amusements and have just as many Francs as the year before as I can see" (*GWBW* 266). This disparity between months worked and money accrued had precedent: when she worked hard and saved her wages in Denver, the bank failed, and when she did the same in Los Angeles, not many years passed before the value of her investments plummeted.

The many scenes of employment in *My Great, Wide, Beautiful World* pose Harrison a narrative challenge, as she engages in the delicate exercise of furnishing detailed reports about her current employers to her former ones. She is circumspect about middle-class British and American women who share common ground with her correspondents. In an early entry, she states, "I knew the English servants very well I worked in a big house in Iowa with them and they were selfish and jelious I have often hear it that they were the heardest of all servants to get along with I also knew the English ladies I worked for one in Canada and one in Cuba. They have their servant problems here" (*GWBW* 11). To an extent the construction of this passage is parallel. She "knew the English servants" from working with them, and she "knew the English ladies" from working for them. Yet that likeness calls attention to where the lines diverge. While she openly criticizes the workers, she says nothing about their employers beyond the cryptic remark, "They have their servant problems here."

She reserves her more pungent stories for the conspicuously foreign or, if American, the very rich. Such women include "La Senora" (*GWBW* 5), a needy Bolivian in London who never bathes; a worldly Italian; and a wealthy woman from Santa Barbara who, Harrison lightly comments, treats her daughter "just like a black slave" (*GWBW* 27), racializing the abuse she observes. She exhibits a range of attitudes toward them, from pity to contempt, from admiration to affection. She sounds almost star-struck about the Italian: "She is my idea of a real Countess I look after her beautiful cloths and she knows how to wear them" (*GWBW* 12). None-theless, she comments, shortly before quitting, "Madam leaves for Paris in a few days to attend a wedding she will take me with her if I promise to come back I havent decided yet whether I want to go under those con-ditions" (*GWBW* 13). (They kept in touch, so it is possible she was one of the original recipients of the book's letters.) Her depiction of her attach-ment to two-year-old Joan in Spain, progeny of close-fisted Americans, is unusual for its sentiment. Of the child's parents, she concludes, "If Joan hadnt been so sweet I would not have stayed with them one week. I try hard to like them" (*GWBW* 216). Through her committed transience, she escapes the control of attractive and repulsive employers alike.

Her most trying position was with a Russian American woman in Paris, who once impounded her suitcase to keep her from quitting:

> This is my seventeenth day and I am just beginning to understand how to get along with her but it is not a pleasure to be with her altho. the pay is good and the work is light. one thing She doesnt go about the house nagging you but its when you go in to her dressing room. it have a large mirrow and while You are helping her to dress She stands in frount of it looking at You in the mirrow and calling You such auful things. One thing she like as She have travelled is to hear of my travelling and think its wonderful when I am so poor . . . so I say things to her it seems to help. (*GWBW* 246)

When considered in light of her first readers, this small scene of wielding travel stories to mollify an abusive boss takes on greater significance. Appeasing a woman in power with picaresque tales was Harrison's special skill, the exact skill her letters deploy. Even as she writes affectionate letters to supportive past employers, her subject is often present-day bad ones, who impede her, or indulgent ones, whose choices she directs.

As much trainer's manual as travelogue, *My Great, Wide, Beautiful World* educates readers about acceptable work environments for the women who manage their homes. It reminds them that they are observed; their actions, judged. However, only the book's epilogue includes any criticism of middle-class domestic conventions. Employing a rare use of second-person voice, Harrison states, "Well you have bring out your moth ball smelling cloths and no doubt feel very pleased with the world to be in a Caged up Building looking out on others more caged up. I have gone through the same and how greatful I am to myself" (318). Here she seems to address not a single acquaintance but her American readership at large.

Form and Reception

The steady attention Harrison accords a seemingly endless stream of new jobs, new acquaintances, and new destinations makes for a harmonious narrative. The text's jarring notes come from "outside" the actual record. The dissonance begins with the title, that crucial piece of text "half sign, half ad." "My Great, Wide, Beautiful World" has its source in the 1899 William Brighty Rands poem of almost the same name, "My Great, Wide, Beautiful, Wonderful World," and two of its verses constitute the book's epigraph. Featured in composition textbooks for older children and assigned to younger ones to memorize, the poem was once a grade school staple. The eponymous heroine of Houghton Mifflin's 1903 *Rebecca of Sunnybrook Farm* stands up in a moving wagon to declaim its opening lines:

> Great, wide, beautiful, wonderful World
> With the wonderful water round you curled
> And the wonderful grass upon your breast,
> World, you are beautifully drest!

Harrison never references poetry, of any kind, and it is unlikely that the nod to Rands originated with her. The choice harks back to the cultural agenda of the past century's *Atlantic,* an agenda evident in editor Horace Scudder's project of implementing a curriculum of American classics in secondary schools. Conferring both epigraph and title, the poem almost literally wraps Harrison's book in a reassuring mantle of middle-class associations, even as its nonstandard prose potently testifies to her denied access to formal education. Such alignment of her narrative with *Atlantic* sensibility is of a kind with the editorial emphasis on the "long hair" and "olive complexion" (MP xi) that narrow the gap between this black writer and an implicitly white readership. Angela Sorby has noted the racial arguments that underwrote the promotion of so-called school-room poets like Longfellow, and something akin is at work here.[32]

However, the dust jacket of the original edition of *My Great, Wide, Beautiful World* breaks out of the familiar cultural purview that Rands's poem conjures to make bolder claims. The cover design is a grouping of photographs of Harrison in different poses, settings, and costumes interspersed with cartoons, captions, and possibly snippets of her letters, seemingly all in her hand. The images include her veiled and holding a clay pot, playing a mandolin, and standing in a bathing suit on a beach.

The collage gets a lot done. It summons the original handwritten manuscript. It offers proof that Harrison went where she claimed. It replicates the text's attention to her looks. But most important, it supports her cosmopolitan identity. An assembly of costumes and props, her self-portrait is almost literally constructed out of allusions to other people of color, but the result is a claim to mainstream status. That she dresses up as an Oriental exotic proves she isn't one. As confirmation, we also see her as "herself," a modern American wearing a fashionable cloche in one picture and swimwear in another. One wonders, for whom did she pose?

The original outer cover has disappeared from the critical record, so completely that the introduction to the 1996 reprint claims "no photographs survive" of Harrison.[33] The loss is significant, given that this purposefully modern presentation, which positions drawings, photographs, and text on the same plane, does much to dissolve the residue of gentility that Rands's poem spackles onto the book. Even as the title of *My Great, Wide, Beautiful World* recollects nineteenth-century cultural hierarchies, its cover evokes a contemporary sphere of cultural relativism.

Presenting sometimes as diary, sometimes as epistolarity, the book's generic indeterminacy occasions a more subtle dissonance. *Letters of a Woman Homesteader, The Stump Farm,* and *My Great, Wide, Beautiful World*

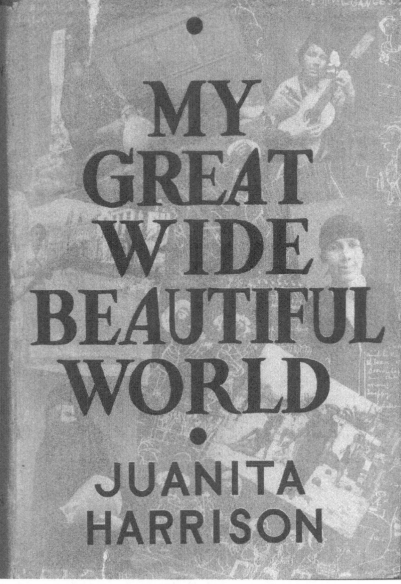

FIGURE 7. *My Great, Wide, Beautiful World,* original cover. *Courtesy of Between the Covers Rare Books.*

all originated in letters, but these origins are not made equally visible. The title of *Letters of a Woman Homesteader* announces its genre. Stewart's exchange of personal news with Coney may be edited out, but each chapter includes salutations and valedictions like "Dear, dear Mrs. Coney" or the loaded send-off, "Your ex-washlady," and Stewart displays the letter writer's characteristic reflexivity. *The Stump Farm*'s epistolary identity is less signposted: the title offers no indication, recipients' names are excised, and no "Dears" or "Truly Yours" are on display. However, the text not only retains a large number of personal references but also intimates the other side of the correspondence, as when Rose comments on "the nomad life you speak of in your letters" (*SF* 16). Reading *The Stump Farm* can feel like eavesdropping on a private exchange.

In contrast, the prevailing inclination of Harrison's publishers was to present her text as travel journal rather than letter volume. Consequently, the excision of epistolary properties is comprehensive, if not total. The bulk of the entries are dated but not addressed, and Harrison does not appear to write to another person or respond to another text. She focuses on places and events, in a record that does indeed usually look like a journal.

In introducing Harrison's narrative, the *Atlantic* actually identifies it as correspondence: "These excerpts from her letters, which have been arranged for us by Miss Mildred Morris, are printed exactly as they were written." Yet within the space of a paragraph genre is reassigned, so that it concludes, "Whatever else the journal may be, it is certainly genuine." An advertisement for the book promises "the complete diary." Morris's disclosure, that her mother "suggested to Juanita that her written experiences might interest a larger public than her immediate friends" (*MP* xi), indicates personal letters, but not conclusively so. A *Los Angeles Times* reviewer complicates the generic picture by suggesting a miscellaneous composition: "Her Paris employer discovered Juanita Harrison's extraordinary gifts and persuaded her to publish the letters, notes and diary jottings." (Just which are the "jottings"?) Three letters, moreover, are included in the book as such, with full epistolary framing. Presenting only a select number of the entries as letters reinforces the impression that all the rest are journal, even as they appear so haphazardly as to feel like distracting intrusion. I used to just skip them. Elsewhere, the editors neglected to excise a valediction, so that an otherwise typical entry confusingly concludes, "Yours truly Juanita"

(*GWBW* 268). Harrison's writing partners are introduced only to be banished once more.[34]

With no records to draw on, the *Atlantic*'s rationale for the journal pretext can only be guessed at. By 1935 perhaps the guise of a "Life in Letters" seemed too old-fashioned to speak to the modernity of Harrison's experience, a quality that the book's original cover, at least, promotes. Or perhaps the editors did not want to call attention to her personal ties: she was to appear "self-dependent" (*HP* 200), as Sedgwick has it. They may even have looked to soften the incongruities of a text that, while celebrating personal liberty, is embedded in service relationships. "Journal" squares better than "letter" with Harrison's forceful arguments for autonomy.

Critical discussions of *My Great, Wide, Beautiful World* prove how easy it is to fall in line with the publishers and treat it as a travel journal, the ready evidence of its first iteration notwithstanding. Assessing Harrison's text as a diary certainly makes for the simpler critical enterprise. However, as Anne Bower argues, "delettering" an epistolary text impoverishes it, making over, in this instance, an intersubjective writing project into a less textured private record. While writing the letters may well have helped Harrison process her experiences in ways akin to a diary, they were addressed, and literally sent, to other people. Recuperating her book's generic origins restores its core identity as a narrative generated by women's relationships and textual exchange, knowledge that must inflect any reading. To adapt Stillinger's comments about collaborative writing, once we study epistolarity, "we may have to worry a little about the adequacy of our current theories. The reality of what authors actually do and how works are actually produced is often—perhaps usually—much more complex than our theories and practices allow." Our work is to recover these histories and then map the interpretive differences they make.[35]

As I hope the previous chapters have shown, for these *Atlantic* texts such work entails examining the influences of their first readers in concert with the choices of the editors and intermediaries who turned rough-hewn manuscripts into polished offerings. Editorial decisions ranged in scale from selecting which texts to publish to making line edits. Introducing his faraway cohort, Sedgwick maintained that "grammar could be overlooked, spelling come to heel, punctuation could be peppered and salted at will" (*HP* 197), but he routinely amended their prose nonetheless. The homesteading accounts Rose submitted include postscripts along the lines of "Mistakes in grammar, please correct," and her editors obliged. Whiteley's diary was purportedly printed solely in capital letters and "innocent" of punctuation, but the published book is otherwise.[36]

Harrison was accorded different treatment. While her manuscripts were culled and assembled for maximum narrative power, her writing itself was not touched. Alexander surmises that Sedgwick recognized the marketability of its untutored aspect, in that it "proclaimed its uncelebrated black author as a 'primitive': a lovable yet somewhat clownish Aunt Jemima or latter-day Uncle Remus, whose narrative was readily acceptable to white America as part of a traditional and popular black dialect genre."[37] Regulating her orthography would mute the minstrel performance. Yet while Sedgwick's judgment was undoubtedly racially informed, I am interested in results as well as motives: the preservation of Harrison's powerfully vernacular text. He took discursive liberties with her person but respected her writing, allowing her sentences to appear just as she wrote them. By way of contrast, consider his quibbling with Edith Wharton over her insistence on retaining British spelling in her 1912 *Atlantic* story, "The Long Run." Wharton won, with the compromise of having an *Atlantic* footnote call attention to her choice. (Although the archive proves her equanimity, Sedgwick, characteristically, maintained, "Mrs. Wharton was irritated, but after all, she had had her woman's way" [*AH* xxiv].) It is hard to conceive how Harrison's writing could survive standardization. We might think of the sea change Emily Dickinson's poetry underwent at the hands of her first editors, who altered punctuation, line breaks, grammar, and even diction.

Margo Culley's positive take, that the *Atlantic* "preserved the spelling and phrasing of the original manuscript," is an outlier in critical discussions of Harrison. Her prose is more usually figured as a roadblock to navigate, as in comments like "Reviewers were able to look past the lack of style in Harrison's writing and appreciate the realism of Harrison's personal record." Yet her very "lack of style" produces the text we "appreciate," potently rendering her experience and subjectivity. A 1936 *Time* review alludes to this effect in stating, "Readers of My Great Wide Beautiful World will admire not only Juanita's freedom from economic shackles but her impressionistic spelling, sometimes better than right." Her freedom from prescriptive rules does indeed make the text better—more vivid, more fresh, more representative of the sounds and rhythms of everyday speech.[38]

Such vernacular faithfulness, Gavin Jones has shown in *Strange Talk: The Politics of Dialect Literature in Gilded Age America*, was the gold standard during the last decades of the nineteenth century, when American literature was saturated with dialect.[39] Poised between orality and literacy, *My Great, Wide, Beautiful World* updates a long American tradition of depicting speech viewed as racial, ethnic, regional, or low. The greater the effort, the further the goal, and African American speech was deemed especially elusive, by black as well as white writers. Charles Chesnutt identified its transcription as a "despairing task" in a letter to his *Atlantic* editor, Walter Hines Page. We can add Harrison to Eric Sundquist's very short list of African American writers who successfully approximated it, composed of Zora Neale Hurston and Sterling Brown, both professional folklorists.[40]

Rather than depict the nonstandard speech of other people, as a linguistic insider Harrison proffers her rendition of the English language as she had once always heard it and as she continued to speak it. Thus, readers are spared the thicket of apostrophe marks that screen texts such as Mary Noailles Murfree's popular *Atlantic* serial, "In the Tennessee Mountains," signs that quantify the narrator's distance from the words transcribed. In *Cultures of Letters*, Richard Brodhead asks, "Where . . . is the literary output of semiliterate delinquent boys of the Mississippi River valley, or of unlettered black sharecroppers of the Deep South?"[41] He offers these examples facetiously, to emphasize that not every population had "literary output" to recover, continuing on to query, "[where] 'the mash'd fireman' whose sufferings Whitman superbly enters into." Yet Harrison intimates the potential of the "semiliterate" through replicating the language she had imbibed in Mississippi. She was not an unlettered sharecropper, but her parents or grandparents may well have been.

Within her book, as we have seen, Harrison references but does not emphasize her identity as an African American, choosing instead to portray herself as a newly minted world citizen. Her writing itself, however, broadcasts her racial and regional origins. She makes no attempt at concealment, issues no apologies or requests to "please correct." On the contrary, she hints it would be misguided to revise her prose. When urged to publish the letters "misteakes and all" (*GWBW* 243), she relays,

"I said that if the mistekes are left out there'll be only blank." At face value a humorous acknowledgment of shortcoming, the statement may signal real distress over the prospect of her words being tampered with. The outcome would be erasure; the word "blank" suggests a whitewashing. While Harrison does not adopt an open position of racial advocacy, her faith in her own writing can itself be read as political.

At just two installments, the relative brevity of her serial points to the *Atlantic*'s less than full commitment to Harrison. The magazine chose, moreover, not to foster the open-ended dialogue among writer, readers, and editors it made available for Stewart and Rose, both in the "Contributors' Column" and through Sedgwick's personal intervention. There were no calls for donations to support further travel or a new home, no forwarded cards, no gifts from readers or letters demanding her address—or if there were, this activity did not go on record.[42] The *Atlantic* instead showcased what white employers had to say about their black servants.

With fond familiarity, the letter that George Dickinson placed in the *Atlantic* testifies to the financial probity of his former maid:

> Juanita worked for us for four years prior to 1928, which were prosperous years prior to the crash of 1929. Domestic wages were very high and we paid her $75 a month, including room and board; and, as you know, Juanita never spent a cent unless she absolutely had to and saved every cent that she could get hold of. She always made friends with whomever she worked for and a great many gifts were given to her in the way of dresses and clothes. From time to time we purchased for her a $900 trust deed (mortgage) that bore 8 percent interest, a $450 trust deed at 8 per cent, a $650 trust deed at 8 per cent, and a $550 trust deed at 8 per cent. That made $51 interest quarterly, or $204 a year. After the crash in 1929 the trouble commenced; we reduced the interest rates. Two of the trust deeds fell down entirely. Now, instead of having her money invested in what we supposed were good mortgages, drawing good interest, she has but little interest, with vacant lots that at the present time are an expense to her.[43]

Dickinson did not hesitate to minutely delineate Harrison's portfolio. Even more egregious, the *Atlantic* published his letter, making thousands of readers privy to the details of her personal finances. The chummy "as you know" that Dickinson accords Sedgwick summons a scene of two wealthy white men familiarly discussing the economic strategies of an

African American woman whose labor—manual and intellectual—they each had contracted. On the letter's publication, the "you" Dickinson addresses becomes the *Atlantic* readership at large. As "we" (white, middle-class) readers know, this was how women like Harrison (black, working-class) behaved. This was exactly the concern of Arthur B. Spingarn, civil rights activist and future president of the National Association for the Advancement of Colored People (NAACP), as expressed in his brief review of *My Great, Wide, Beautiful World:* "A radiant and valiant personality shines through the book, but though highly touted, it is likely to thrill only those people who know 'colored people are like that.'"[44]

The nurse Harrison mentions meeting in Rome is the subject of another *Atlantic* letter, submitted by Joseph M. Marrone of Skaneateles, New York, who identifies her as "our Pearl, who has been in our family a great many years, and she is a black gem."[45] The comment is still another reminder of the racial climate within which Harrison's text circulated. The year's blockbuster, after all, was Margaret Mitchell's *Gone With the Wind,* with its fantasy of black devotion to place and mistress alike, and Mitchell's publisher was Harrison's own, Macmillan. Bizarrely, Marrone's letter—whose sole subject is Pearl—is prefaced with, "The travel notes of Miss Juanita Harrison have made many friends for this extraordinary colored woman. Here is a letter from one who knew her." The *Atlantic* literally positions African American women as interchangeable.

Still another "Contributors' Column" includes an employer's actual letter of reference, from Helen Rose to Mildred Morris. In introducing it, the *Atlantic* alludes to a slew of testimonials: "Of her many letters of reference we quote one from the English couple for whom she worked on the Cap d'Antibes":

> My husband and I are only too willing to give you references for Juanita. We were very fond of her and found her an amazing character, besides being a very good servant. We let her stay at the villa, knowing full well that she would look after it just the same as if we were there. Juanita is a really good woman in the finest sense of the word, and full of a wonderful humanity. I should be glad if you will tell her if she ever comes to London to write to us.[46]

The *Atlantic* chose to cast Harrison's editor as her prospective employer by reproducing this letter, and it may even have solicited it: Harrison had worked for the Morrises well before she worked for the Roses, which makes it hard to conceive why Mildred Morris should have asked them for references. The epistolary dialogue conducted in this popular *Atlantic* feature extends Harrison's writing project but shifts the terms. Rather than composed of letters written by her, it reproduces letters about her, and rather than develop her subjectivity, it flattens it. To promote an *Atlantic* contributor as "a very good servant" is a discursively violent act. Foregrounding Harrison's domestic skills, it obliterates her literary ones, a preview of Sedgwick's opening salvo in *The Happy Profession*, that "when the cook leaves and the other maids give notice, then like the needle to the pole, my thoughts turn to Juanita" (210).

To summarize, the editorial choices made in respect to Harrison are a mess. The modern cover of *My Great, Wide, Beautiful World* shows up as relics its old-fashioned title and epigraph, smacking of the schoolroom and normative American childhood. The book is assembled from letters even as it is (usually) identified as a diary. The employers to whom Harrison addressed her letters are evacuated from the body of the text, only to be restored in the epistolary revenants, the dedication and preface, and the "Contributors' Column" entries. In part this incoherence stems from the successive iterations of Harrison's text, from letters to magazine serial and finally to book. It also reflects the nature of her experience overseas, which little fit the usual categories of employment, tourism, or expatriation. And Harrison herself, of course, with her many actual and subjective locations, resists classification. But primarily, it is a consequence of deeply racialized social structures that did not support a language to accommodate her life, person, and text.

Harrison and Her "Unseen Sweetheart"

Harrison and Sedgwick met briefly in Hawaii in March 1936. Harrison had recently sailed from Japan to settle in Waikiki, while Sedgwick was beginning a voyage to the same country. By then Harrison was a local celebrity, and the *Honolulu Star-Bulletin* arranged for *Atlantic* author and editor to meet.

Sedgwick recollects the event in *The Happy Profession*. He begins innocuously enough, with an anecdote about assisting her in Argentina: "It was at Buenos Aires that my letters caught up with her. Then she needed my help, for her precious bankbook was on deposit in Boston and the South American Branch was not aware of its existence. A few Vice-Presidents set that right and Juanita moved on to Honolulu" (213). The time line is confusing, as Harrison went to Buenos Aires after, not before, Honolulu.[47] Yet obviously, she had trouble accessing her royalty income, which gave Sedgwick the opportunity to play his favorite role, that of rescuing editor-prince to the flock of faraway Cinderellas uplifted by *Atlantic* authorship. He goes on to gloss the main themes of her book, and he then announces that he had met Harrison in Hawaii. We, as readers, happily anticipate the meeting. Yet this suspense is released with something dreadful: "As I approached her tent, there was a mighty commotion within. 'Sakes alive!' I heard in a syrupy gurgle. 'I ain't got a mortal thing on me.' But things were found, the tent flap parted, and out came Juanita, her teeth shining under a carmine bandana, her big eyes bright as blobs of Mississippi molasses. 'Gord's sake,' she cried, 'did ever nigger see the likes of this!' and she bent double under the weight of her laughter. So I see her now" (215). Sedgwick's presentation of Harrison as "bent double" is a literal figure of his failure to offer a legible portrait of the sole African American in his memoir. Having come out all in a fluster, she immediately disappears from view. "So I see her now," he insists. A woman like Harrison was so outside his purview, he could scarcely focus.

Ten years prior to the memoir, Sedgwick had been criticized by Isadore Cecilia Williams, an *Atlantic* reader from Washington, D.C., for his use of the less noxious label "Negress." Williams wrote, "I assume that you do not realize the offense you give to your Negro readers and subscribers. Even the most ordinary newspapers north of the Mason-Dixon line no longer use the vile term." The *Atlantic* printed both her letter and the reply in which Sedgwick insists he "really did not know that the word 'Negress' carried a derogatory connotation." Implying his aversion to the conversation, he also states, "I am not sure that we care to take these subjects up, but it might be wise to print [your letter]." (H. L. Mencken characterized his response as "avoidance and confession.") Indicating that his depiction of Harrison little troubled his majority readership, none of the many positive reviews of *The Happy Profession*, and none of the many commendatory letters archived in his papers, objects to its racial caricature and epithet. In contrast, an oblique reference to an off-color story about Abraham Lincoln and an outhouse triggered outraged dispatches: "You gave space and time to dirt when there was a magnificent tree over head."[48]

In emphasizing Harrison's regional origins and race, Sedgwick acted on a ubiquitous critical impulse. Much of the impact of *My Great, Wide, Beautiful World* comes from the reader's knowledge of the enormous distance its author traveled from the world she was born into, and not a single contemporaneous or contemporary discussion neglects to mention that she was an African American woman from Mississippi. The problem was that Sedgwick denied her any change. Having enabled her to tell her transformative story to a national audience, he disavowed it in published statements of his own, discursively fixing this wanderer in place, race, and servitude. The memoir's final sentence about Harrison, which also concludes the "Faraway Women" chapter, states that she made the women she worked for "rejoice and be exceeding glad" (*HP* 215).

The *Honolulu Star-Bulletin* offers some relief with its own account of the Waikiki meeting that shows Sedgwick stepping into Harrison's world and evaluated on her terms. A front-page photograph, clearly staged, is of Harrison showing her passport stamps to Sedgwick outside her tent, offering proof she has been to the places she claims (see figure 1). Lettering on the picket fence that fronts the tent identifies it as "Villa Petit Peep," while the contrast between Sedgwick's natty three-piece white suit and Harrison's vaguely tropical print skirt and sleeveless top makes the encounter look near colonial. (Her clothes, incidentally, little resemble those Sedgwick describes. Where is that "carmine bandana"?) On first inspection, the image confirms racial and gender hierarchies. Yet it is Harrison who leans over Sedgwick, who sits perched on her fence (likely on account of his sciatica), and it was Harrison who named her home "Villa Petit Peep." As she explains in the last sentence of her book, "I let my callers sit on a seat in the yard and Peep in so I gave it this True name" (318).[49]

The newspaper headline, moreover, steers this potential scene of white authentication in a different direction, in referring to Sedgwick not by name but by Harrison's term for him: "Juanita, Unique Authoress, Meets 'Unseen Sweetheart.'" Sedgwick notes that Honolulu knew him as "the friend of Juanita Harrison" (*HP* 215), and while the comment is made in the spirit of an inside joke, this was just how he was positioned. He categorizes Harrison according to the other African American women he knew—as a servant—but reciprocally, Harrison categorizes him as still another of the generous, enamored men she regularly met on the road.

This makes for a rare instance in which a faraway woman represented Sedgwick in print outside the vetted arena of the *Atlantic*, a turning of the discursive tables. Reporter William Norwood, moreover, looked to enter into Harrison's subjectivity, relaying, "Juanita spends most of her time on the beach, where she has her kitchen and where she communes with her various muses."[50] For once, the focus is not her roguish ways but her creative work. The facetious tone notwithstanding, Norwood's intimation of artistic commitment stands out, given that the literary achievements of *Atlantic* life writers were usually figured as the product of urgent life experiences rather than musing communion.

Atlantic contributor and editor visited many of the same places. Sedgwick's and Harrison's paths crossed in Hawaii, as the start and end point for travel in Asia, and both lingered in Spain and toured South America, with Brazil their common point of entry. Their shared citizenship, moreover, led them to depend on many of the same services: travel agents, travel guides, money changers, American Express. That said, the disparity between their sensibilities as much as their incomes made for very differently textured experiences. To take their time in Japan as an example, Harrison's commenced with a ferry journey from Pusan, Korea, to Shimonoseki, during which a typhoon literally mixed the passengers all together: "It was Japanese matting floors we sat on stretched out as we liked and when the waves tosted the Ship on the side about 300 Bright Kimonos women and children Babies men suite cases Tea Trays all went to one side. we was as helpless as though we had neither hands or feet" (*GWBW* 285). On arrival, she settled in at the Kobe YWCA and made a habit of attending, in her words, "what I call a nude reseption The Public Baths at night with about 100 women I the only stray one" (*GWBW* 287). Sedgwick, in contrast, traveled on a complementary first-class Japan Rail pass, and he returned to Boston with a priceless Kamakura-era sculpture. Donated by a descendent to the Harvard Art Museums, the artifact is presently known as "The Sedgwick Statue of the Infant Shōtoku Taishi."

To date we have only trace evidence about Harrison's experiences in South America, but her book offers a reliable guide to imagining them. She ate market food and used public transportation. She had a private room in the thick of local life. She worked—especially in Buenos Aires, where she lived for many years. She closely observed the racial makeup of the people around her, just as she had in India, where she "had much joy noticing the difference" (*GWBW* 154) among the women she saw, or in Burma, which offered "a beautiful picture a few fair Europeans the Anglo Burmases girls in their cool short frocks some fair some light and some dark" (*GWBW* 150). And undoubtedly, she elicited special favors from high and low, all without the backing of illustrious name and institutional affiliation that Sedgwick enjoyed.

Her seeming ease wherever she found herself contrasts to Sedgwick's ready admission of the distress travel caused him, just as her alertness to the complexity of racial identity contrasts to his essentialist notions. During his 1923 voyage to Brazil, he plaintively confided to his journal, "When I don't sleep, I am sleepy, and when I do not think of home I think of almost nothing" (TJ March 12, 1923). On arrival, he juxtaposed his homesickness with the seeming rootlessness of young American expatriates: "They were pleasant and gay and lively and so detached. To a thoroughly domesticated animal like myself their lives seem hung in space" (TJ March 19, 1923). Pining for his regular class of associates, he had complained of his shipmates, "No ladies aboard, I think, and few enough gentlemen" (TJ March 4, 1923), and he went on to voice similar dismay about his guesthouse in Peru. Despite his reputation for coaxing stories from outliers, he was fastidious about the company he kept, acknowledging, "My social sense, active enough among people I like shrinks in an unfavorable environment to something less than nothing" (TJ March 7, 1923). But more serious are his racist comments. In alluding to a scandalous shipboard couple, a black man and a seemingly white woman, he asserted insider knowledge about American racial identity: "But any one who has traveled in our South would know at a glance that she is an octoroon, so there's no miscegenation about it though it's unpleasant enough to see the pair together" (TJ April 26, 1923). The journal's many racial slurs make the memoir's caricature of Harrison seem almost benign, even as it reveals the beliefs that produced it.

Sedgwick's reliance on stereotype and cliché to apprehend otherness, to conceptualize people, places, and activity outside his ken, seems directly linked to his endorsement of Franco. In January 1938, he toured Spain with his friend W. Cameron Forbes, former governor-general of the Philippines and diplomat to Japan; all expenses were paid by the regime. On their return, he "unleashed a blizzard of press releases" enthusing over nationalist Spain, which appeared in newspapers across the country. "Everything was well ordered and everyone appeared content," he averred. The *Atlantic* community erupted in outrage—and canceled subscriptions—accusing him of betraying core *Atlantic* values. One reader wrote, "I can no longer buy or read it. It is a far cry from the days when the defenders of liberalism—Emerson, Thoreau, Lowell, Dean Howells and such men molded American opinion through the pages of the Atlantic Monthly." Louise Pearson Mitchell looks to have made a death threat: "I am afraid, Mr. Sedgwick, that I shall look for you on the opposite side of the barricades, and that I shall get some better marksman than I on our side to take a shot at you." Hundreds signed a petition in protest, and it was reported that he supported the bombing of civilians. Sedgwick did not budge. To Mitchell, for example, he blandly replied, "It happens that I know something more about this matter than you do and I can assure you that the essence of the struggle is a fight between the alien virus of communism and the native Spanish culture." The controversy was a motivating factor in his decision to sell his controlling *Atlantic* shares the next year.[51]

Throughout each of the chapters in this study, I have looked to show that although culture, capital, and power were unevenly distributed between writers and readers, and between writers and editor, it was not all on one side. Who, after all, was the more worldly of the two, Sedgwick or Harrison? Outside his home environment, Harrison's editor can appear as "illiterate" as she (even literally as illiterate—his consistent spelling mistakes in Spanish, a language Harrison spoke, rival her spelling of English). Conceiving his move from Stockbridge to Boston as momentous, Sedgwick passed almost all of his adult life in "the Hub," to use the long since ironic nickname for this former colonial outpost, even as Harrison established herself in New York, Los Angeles, London, Paris, Madrid, Cairo, Kyoto, and Buenos Aires, to name only some of the world capitals she made home.

Pasadena Lap Desk

I conclude by returning to UCLA's Ann Cunningham Smith Collection, to consider the additional light it sheds on Harrison and her book. Along with the three letters to Alice Foster, the collection includes empty envelopes that once contained others, the small "lap desk" on which Foster wrote back, and writing appointments such as blotting paper, pencils, and sealing wax. Establishing a racial context for Harrison's experience overseas, there are also newspaper clippings about a gala in Paris held for African American gold-star mothers, a performance by Josephine Baker in the same city, and a "Parade of Kings" celebrated by Sevillians in blackface.[52] Finally, it includes materials from a 1936 exhibit about Harrison's journey and book organized by Miriam Matthews for the Vernon Branch of the Los Angeles Public Library. California's first African American professional librarian, Matthews was on her way to becoming the leading historian of black Los Angeles and a tremendously influential supporter of its literary and art movements. As an African American woman who curated Harrison's work and helped establish her archival foothold, she joins Foster, who preserved her letters, and Smith, who donated them. Their efforts counter mainstream institutional neglect, most notably Harrison's absence from the Ellery Sedgwick Papers.

Foster has her own story of writing, migration, and western reinvention. She was born in Mississippi, but her mother and father were from France and South Carolina, respectively. She and her husband reached California by way of Texas, where their first daughter was born in 1899. By 1902 they were in Pasadena, the birthplace of their second daughter, making them one of the city's earliest African American families. During Harrison's international travels, Foster (by then widowed) wrote to her from that city and from Los Angeles, where she lived with one of her daughters and her family. While the censuses do not identify an occupation for Foster herself, they indicate working-class households, as the occupations of the younger generations include that of chauffeur, janitor, maid, and office typist.[53]

If Harrison did know Foster in her home state, it was only as a child, given that she was not yet twelve when Foster left Mississippi. Perhaps her presence helped draw her to California, or perhaps home ties led to acquaintance upon arrival. Either way, the relationship suggests a different kind of western trajectory, connecting to one's place of origins even while venturing into new terrain. It also displays a distinct kind of literary effort, two friends supporting each other across the Atlantic and the Pacific. Foster elicited from Harrison potent commentary about her authorship along with her typical travel reports, and she also helped her get her passport in Los Angeles. Yet it should come as no surprise that the *Atlantic* shows no trace of her, or indeed of any other associate whose race and class status was closer to Harrison's. The magazine puts employers rather than friends on display, as when it reproduces the reference letter commending her as "a very good servant." White patronage was a familiar *Atlantic* topic that was easy to present. An enabling friendship between two African American women—including a shared writing project—was not.

In January 1931, Harrison contacted Foster to retrieve the letters she had sent her, another act, absent from the official record, that demonstrates how actively she participated in the making of her book. "Thanking you again for the well kept letters which you know not another woman could have done that she would have missed placed them and not found them," she wrote her two months later (FL2). It appears that Morris may not have returned the letters (despite Harrison's promise that she would), but Foster saved their envelopes nonetheless. And of course, she sent letters of her own. The "lap desk" that her family preserved, this economic, portable alternative to a private study, helps us imagine her activity. While not of the order of posting letters from around the globe, it too signifies writing agency and mobility, a reminder of her contribution to Harrison's enterprise.

The prospect that portions of the text were first addressed to personal friends opens up new interpretive possibilities for *My Great, Wide, Beautiful World*. With her working-class family, Foster could have identified far better than someone like Myra Dickinson with Harrison's satisfaction or dismay over her jobs and with her glee at moving on. Depending on whether they are directed to management or labor, as it were, the book's entries can be variously interpreted as compliant, resistant, familiar, or subversive. Readership inflects, for example, the previously quoted anecdote about the employer in Paris "looking at You in the mirrow and calling You such auful things." Was the intended reader a woman Harrison once worked for, making it pointed commentary about how not to treat one's maid? Or was the recipient perhaps a woman who herself had been in service, rendering it confiding and adding greater weight to that "You"?

Yet even as their existence opens up intriguing possibilities about the book's composition, the letters' primary subject is her generative relationship with the Dickinsons. Turning our critical gaze on Harrison's friend leads us right back to her patrons, checking efforts to discuss her work more fully in the context of African American women's alliances. Indeed, it turns out that the letters Foster returned did not make it into *My Great, Wide, Beautiful World*, after all. The package reached Paris only the day before Harrison left the city, and in any case, she informed Foster, she already had more than enough for the book. The reason? "My People in Lafayette had saved every one" (FL2). Those empty envelopes Foster carefully filed—from Nice, Paris, Rome, Naples, Brno, Colombia, Darjeeling, and London—speak to a regrettable absence in *My Great, Wide, Beautiful World,* the lost epistolary exchange of these two Mississippi transplants to California. However, Harrison's correspondence with Foster does increase the odds that her book includes other letters to other friends, a reminder that each entry has a range of possible first readers.

The set of letters also provides a more nuanced view of her relationship with the Dickinsons, a perspective that saves the couple from being reduced to faceless agents of white paternalism. It is certainly easy to view this relationship with cynicism, due to not only George Dickinson's paternalism and Harrison's avidity for perks but also, more fundamentally, its necessarily unequal nature. Yet Harrison herself identified the Dickinsons as the most important people in her life, cherished over her blood relatives. One of her letters to Foster, conventionally, states, "I am Glad your Family are well." However, she then immediately declares, "I am glad *I* have no one close to me glad I went out from my dozen of Kin before I were old enough to know all their names am sure I could never have trusted either of them my likes and dislikes from a tiny child were always so different. But in Mr. and Mrs. Dickinson I had an understanding friend" (FL2; emphasis added). That she was writing to Foster, as opposed to still another employer turned backer, lends credence to the sincerity of her claim. When she had to economize on stamps, she pared down her correspondence to only them (FL1).

"I never like to read any hard luck stories in a letter to me" (FL3), she once declared. More than just dispiriting, such missives check her own prose. While we can only guess at how the letters Stewart and Rose read inflected those they wrote, Harrison explicitly discusses this reciprocal process:

> Not another Two would have written me all these years so reagler and such kind encouraging letters as they did. Now when I was traveling in America in Canada and Cuba [before meeting the Dickinsons] I tried and they would wait a month or two and when they did write the first short Part would be excuses the next illness or death of ones that I knew nothing about and I am sure that they felt uneasy lest I would write and ask for a little money to get

back. People that are stay at home are narrow minded so that they would stop answering after a while. But not so with my Friends [the Dickinsons.] They wrote sweet letters and at each place or Country that I had written to them I would likely be on arriving it would be like getting home as a kind letter would be there to greet me so it made me happy and love the Country and its People and so it made The People love me and that's why there are joy in all of my letters which were sent to a Publisher in hopes that He will also for the joy that they express publish them. (FL2)

The "joy" in her letters, she argues—which induced the "Publisher" to accept them—can be credited to the Dickinsons. The tone and texture of their writing determined her own. To take this a step further, her narrative persona of the happy-go-lucky wanderer with her lusty world embrace has its source in her upper-middle-class employers. This is, of course, the inverse of the usual racial arguments that circulated in reviews like this one: "Miss Harrison is quite illiterate . . . but she more than makes up for this by her superabundant sense of life, by her capacity for the mere 'joy of living.' The rhythm of her race is in her blood, and she dances her way across continents."[54] Attributing her affect to the effusive Dickinsons, Harrison turns prevailing categories on their heads. In comparison to these real estate moguls in California, her "stay at home" kin in Mississippi were dreary and dour.

The letters also reveal her response to her new fame. That she had published a book became central to her identity: she identified herself as "escritoria" and "author" on official documents like her 1940 immigration card in São Francisco, Brazil, and her 1950 passport application in Buenos Aires.[55] However, various comments to Foster show she was just as ambivalent about authorship as she was about her other jobs— concerned about the labor it entailed, the attention it attracted, and, most especially, the social relationships it affected.

Relaying praise from Morris, she cleverly reanimates a collocation: "She said that I was a born writer. I thought how far I was from what I was born." Here she posits her book as a culminating life event, proof of her "faraway" achievement. But she unexpectedly continues, "Of course she was much pleased with me but I did not let it get into my life planes," elaborating, "I planned my life at 11 at 13 I began to live it a little like I had planned then at 21 I had it just right and at this moment am enjoying those planes and I have it all set up until I die and the two

Books are not included" (FL2). (I simply do not know what she means by "*two* Books.") Like enduring jobs, marriage, or a permanent home, authorship, too, threatened her liberty. At its onset, she indicates both her hopes for the project and her resentment of its demands, instructing her friend, "Please do not ask me any questions about the Book as I never count my chickens before T. A. H., and its not easy for the Writer to keep me as I am not interested although we have a contract and would like to be off for sunny Nice" (FL1). Suggesting that she resisted the idea of marketing herself, she also insists, "But like my traveling I did not do it for the Public it was for my own pleasure and I do not care weather the Public know who I am" (FL2). Writing Sedgwick in 1929, Whiteley had made the same assertion, in a more mournful register: "There was no need for the piecing nor for the public to have them."[56]

That the book was rooted in her relationship with the Dickinsons, and even dedicated to them, was a further source of anxiety for Harrison, as she fretted that "there would be something in it that wouldn't be just the proper reading." The death of "the gentle and kind Mr. Dickinson" just as it was published increased her unease. She refused to spend any more time in Los Angeles, dreaded writing the family, and did not want to even open her book. She asked, moreover, that it not be distributed to bookstores or libraries in Honolulu, her then city of residence. While her publisher thought she had been "troubled with publicity," in fact, she explained, "it was that Sadness that warned me of not wanting it." She "wept" on learning the family had approved the final result. Her only pleasure in the book came from her "true at heart" readers and the letters they sent her, she professed. To return to Kete's paradigm, she viewed *My Great, Wide, Beautiful World* as a "sentimental collaboration." The renown it brought mattered less than the social fabric it was fashioned from and potentially altered. "It isn't my Book its Mr. and Mrs. Dickinson its their Kindness and never failing faithfulness to me the 8 years why I wrote each line" (FL3). If we read the first clause about the Dickinsons literally, Harrison states that the book is theirs (or indeed *them*, given the lack of a possessive apostrophe). But even if assessed less literally, it is still a remarkable claim: that the Dickinsons motivated the entirety of her literary endeavor.

Holly Laird's discussion of Harriet Jacobs's *Incidents in the Life of a Slave Girl* as fostered by relationships that were "temporary and asymmetrical, yet not tyrannically hierarchical . . . mutually but not equivalently rewarding" helps us evaluate *My Great, Wide, Beautiful World* as a writing project with multiple participants. Laird shows how Jacobs's less than full control of her textual production, which was brokered by her illustrious editor, Lydia Maria Child, mirrored the legal, economic, and social restrictions she more largely endured: first as a slave in the South and a fugitive in the North and then as an overworked domestic servant. Yet Laird also shows how Child made the book possible, and she argues that her participation should be understood as empowering Jacobs rather than further oppressing her. She concludes, "The relationship between Jacobs and her editor only approximates coauthorship, yet Jacob's text itself shows how useful and how necessary for survival an approximate relationship may be."[57] This model of "approximate coauthorship" can be applied to Harrison's book, a text that was produced by, and inscribes, unequal but mutually beneficial relationships. While Harrison wrote each word, she was inspired and sustained by her correspondents' offerings and needs. Through their diligent correspondence, the Dickinsons structured her output, which they also scrupulously preserved. The Morris family recognized the letters' potential for a public readership and gave her a place to work on the book. Along with transcribing Harrison's oral history, Mildred Morris spent countless hours "arranging" the letters for publication; it may have been she, moreover, who first sounded the *Atlantic*. Foster not only saved her letters but also transferred the bulk of them to Harrison and Morris in Paris and the remainder to Miriam Matthews in Los Angeles, who exhibited them. Collectively, these women—and possibly others still unknown—helped both generate Harrison's text and ensure its history.

Finally, just as the *Atlantic* was invested in telling a certain story about Harrison, her associates in Los Angeles had a story of their own, as the exhibit at the city's Vernon Branch Library attests. A Carnegie library that opened in 1915, Vernon Branch first served a largely Jewish immigrant population before the neighborhood's demographic shifted. When Matthews became its director in 1934, 35 percent of its registered patrons were African American.[58] Thanks to her efforts, within two years the library was known for its Black History Collection: as it was reported then, its many "books by and about the Negro which is a very special attraction."[59] Identifying *My Great, Wide, Beautiful World* as "a book no one can afford to miss," the *California Eagle* directed readers to procure it at either Vernon or the Helen Hunt Jackson Branch.[60]

The poster for the library exhibit announces, "These original letters and postcards by Juanita Harrison, Author of 'My Great, Wide, Beautiful World,' are exhibited through the courtesy of Mrs. Alice Foster. They were written to her by the author and form part of the book." Photographs were on display, too, and while they are not extant, their captions include "The Author at La Riviera, France," "Juanita Harrison in Bethlehem Dress," and "The Author in Turkish Head Dress." (Also available for inspection: "Tea Leaves Sent from Burma, India by Juanita Harrison Six Years Ago.") In a brief letter, Matthews promised Foster, "If you could have seen the intense interest that was aroused at the library by Juanita Harrison's exhibit of letters, post cards and photographs you would realize how much we appreciate your great kindness in lending them to us. Although this exhibit has been in the glass case all summer, it continued to boost the circulation of 'My Great, Wide, Beautiful World' until the day it was removed. We still have a waiting list for the book."[61] The avidity of these library patrons intimates the enthusiasm with which ordinary African American readers responded to Harrison.

Iterating the erroneous claim on the exhibit poster, Matthews's newspaper review of *My Great, Wide, Beautiful World* imparts, "The letters which make up part of the book were originally written to Mrs. Alice M. Foster"; her assistance with the passport is also noted.[62] Did the misrepresentation originate with Foster or with Matthews? If the latter, perhaps it was deliberate, a bid to spotlight African American women's shared textual activity and aid. Matthews's letter to Foster intimates some pique that Harrison had not responded to her overture: "My letter to Miss Harrison remains unanswered although I am certain it was received since she sent a young man to take a picture of the exhibit to send to her."[63] Harrison was in Honolulu at the time, and there are of course many possible reasons she did not write back. However, she frequently indicated how selective she was about which writers and which letters merited a reply. We have also seen how she reveled in both her status as a citizen of the world who could assume manifold ethnic guises and, in respect to her suitors and employers, her ability to take what she needed without giving back what they thought she owed. Her neglect can thus be interpreted as an act of resistance. Just as she refused to play the role of faithful servant, and just as she insisted that authorship was not to disrupt her life plans, she may have balked at being made a character in a story purveyed by this promoter of black literary Los Angeles. "Its not easy," she had commented in respect to her work with her editor, "to keep me." Harrison continually eludes the narratives that would keep her, as construed by employers, editors, readers, and critics alike.

THE *ATLANTIC* ORIGINS

OF

THE AUTOBIOGRAPHY OF ALICE B. TOKLAS

"I Would Love to Write a Best Seller"

One of the Daughters is a writer and the mother said my travellers should be put into a Book. I told her I would come back after my trip to India and work for nothing if Miss Mildred, the Daughter would help me.

—Juanita Harrison, *My Great, Wide, Beautiful World*

Gertrude Stein sent the Atlantic Monthly some manuscripts, not with any hope of their accepting them, but if by any miracle they should, she would be pleased and Mildred delighted.

—Gertrude Stein, *The Autobiography of Alice B. Toklas*

F araway women," Sedgwick maintained, were proof of "an original *Atlantic* claim in the pleasantest of all the outlying territories of Literature" (*HP* 197). His recurring words of praise for their work included "genuine," "authentic," and "faithful," and he cherished the belief that intense experience drove ordinary women to write. Gertrude Stein's *The Autobiography of Alice B. Toklas*, which began as an *Atlantic* serial, seems to validate this view in proposing that Stein and Toklas's

extraordinary life together compelled Toklas—the couple's nonwrit-
er—to author a book. In what seems like an almost willful misreading,
Sedgwick happily announced that the memoir realized his "constant
hope that the time would come when the real Miss Stein would pierce
the smoke-screen with which she has always so mischievously surrounded herself."[1]

My contention is that Sedgwick's history with faraway women prepared him to accept the *Atlantic* submission that became *The Autobiography of Alice B. Toklas*. While most of Stein's offerings baffled or annoyed
him, this was just what he liked. His contentious correspondence with
Stein as she sought *Atlantic* entry is widely known, but it has yet to be
assessed from his perspective. I submit, moreover, that Stein's familiarity with the *Atlantic*'s faraway women informed the actual writing of
The Autobiography, which she strove to make a best seller. It is not just
that it is highly readable. It also displays a characteristic set of *Atlantic*
qualities, as a narrative kindled by women's relationships that transmits the author's history with the *Atlantic* itself. Faraway women modeled a different approach to the biographical project Stein had initiated
with *Three Lives*. To the worldly memoirs that Gabrielle Dean posits as
her inspirations (*Music at Midnight* and *My Nine Years with Picasso*), we
can add a text of the order of *The Stump Farm*.[2] Such texts prepared the
ground for *The Autobiography of Alice B. Toklas*, offering its publisher a
precedent and its author, a model.

My contribution to the critical conversation about this modernist
exemplar is to incorporate it within a less prestigious genre and movement, reading *The Autobiography of Alice B. Toklas* as one *Atlantic* life
narrative among others. Once situated thus, its genealogy looks very
different than usually conceived, entwined with the literary production of working-class American women. Stein proffers a deliberately
vernacular account of a relationship between two Californian women
that mirrors the "real" vernacular expression of these other *Atlantic*
contributors. In turn, placing Stein's autobiography within this group
helps us recognize the fictional qualities and generic hybridity they all
share: more performative, more staged, more "premeditated" (to adapt
Sedgwick's adjective) than first appearances indicate. Even Stein's
claim to genius distinguishes her only in degree. While these tales are
structured by emotional bonds between women, in each of them, the
author is the star.

Phoebe Stein Davis argues that to attract the popular readership she hungered for, the notoriously opaque Stein assumed "a distinctly plain-spoken American voice" that quashed her image as a continental aesthete. She states, "Stein at once ventriloquizes Alice's voice and a national voice, that of the plain-spoken American. With her adoption of a distinctly American aesthetic for her writing in *The Autobiography* . . . Stein demonstrates that nationality is an aesthetic that can be adopted."[3] As the circularity of the last sentence augurs, Davis never fully explains her reasoning. Why should American writers be associated with plainness? What is a "distinctly American aesthetic"? Rather than identify the qualities that constitute the national aesthetic of Stein's book, Davis catalogs the national assertions within it, as when Stein likens herself to George Washington. Stein herself claimed that she emulated not an American writer who wrote "simply" but an English one. "I am going to write it for you," she informs Toklas in the book's final reveal. "I am going to write it as simply as Defoe did the autobiography of Robinson Crusoe" (*AABT* 252).

We can refine Davis's argument in light of Sedgwick's practice: implementing a plain style made Stein appear like the kind of writer the *Atlantic* welcomed. She ventriloquizes Alice, ventriloquizes an American, ventriloquizes Defoe. To add another layer, she ventriloquizes faraway women, making for a recognizably *Atlantic* aesthetic as much as an American one. Through accessing a plain voice, she added to the *Atlantic*'s pool of reputedly plain narratives, texts that are further inscribed by the known and unknown women who as their original readers midwifed them.

Stein's keenness to level all manner of hierarchies is readily apparent. It is evident in her social practice. The guests she hosted at her Paris salon ranged from soldiers to tourists to art collectors, and she pontificated upon her egalitarian views: "It has always been rather ridiculous that she who is good friends with all the world and can know them and they can know her, has always been the admired of the precious" (*AABT* 80). It is evident in her catholic tastes. She relished detective novels, newspapers, movies, and advertisements, and she published in both avant-garde periodicals and *Vanity Fair*.[4] Most important, it is evident in her writing. *The Autobiography*, in respect to both style and affect, is flat. Its relentlessly paratactic prose, composed of independent clauses connected by "and," places everything on the same plane, and the actual subject matter has a similar horizontal quality. The text grants equal attention to Stein's great friend Picasso and her devoted cook, Hélène. It offers alternative stories about the First Battle of the Marne, including one that centers on the availability of a cab. Yet while all this is familiar to those conversant with Stein, *The Autobiography* is still mainly read in a high-literary context. For all the games the text plays with authorship, the identity of its author controls how it is approached.

Contrast this to the choice of Stein's agent, W. A. Bradley, to submit the manuscript to the *Atlantic* without identifying it as hers. Hinting only that the author was an "extremely well-known American writer living here in Paris," in promoting the text Bradley employed not Stein's reputation but that of Mildred Aldrich, former star *Atlantic* contributor. There was much to interest his readers, he promised Sedgwick, "the War section especially, and all that pertains to Miss Mildred Aldrich."[5] My intention is to carry over this initial emphasis in the following discussion: one, to *not* invoke "Gertrude Stein" and all its associations,[6] and, two, to direct attention to the other *Atlantic* writers and texts to which *The Autobiography* "pertains." By including it in this study, I place *The Autobiography* on the same level as the other life narratives it was published among, authored by writers who were not "consciously naive," but naive,[7] who did not "make it plain," but were always thus.[8] If, as Holly Laird puts it, Stein looks to interrogate "conventional divisions of writing," then let us examine *The Autobiography* in concert with texts from which it is usually divided.[9] If, as Catharine Stimpson maintains, Stein proffers a "joke about authorship," then let us take that joke at face value.[10] The converse holds true as well: that we grant these other authors serious critical attention, and not only in the service of better understanding Stein. I join her memoir with *Letters of a Woman Homesteader*, *The Stump Farm*, *My Great, Wide, Beautiful World*, and a text I have previously only referenced, Aldrich's *A Hilltop on the Marne*. Aldrich was Stein's close friend in Paris, and her *Atlantic* serial about the First Battle of the Marne was Sedgwick's commercial breakthrough. Teasing out the connections between them supports a reading of *The Autobiography* as Stein's response to the other woman's *Atlantic* success.

In his day Sedgwick was chided for his conservatism, for ignoring writers "at work on the frontiers of literary expansion and discovery."[11] Yet his stated aversion to "literature with a big 'L'" (*HP* 197) belies his prickly attention to modernist developments, a vexed interest that fueled enduring conversations with their proponents. Moreover, as I have argued, his backing of faraway women likewise attests to a certain receptivity to innovation. In ushering regional writers into authorship, he promoted both a different kind of writer and a different kind of genre: hybrid, vernacular, relational life narrative. This development found another iteration in Stein's book.

By the 1920s, Stein was widely recognized in both literary and popular forums, but the big sales and big readership she craved still eluded her, and she had yet to place a book with an important press. Consequently, she sought the confirmation of major stature she believed the *Atlantic* would confer, the discrepancy between its stodgy reputation and her experimental style notwithstanding. Starting in 1919, she sent Sedgwick a steady stream of poems, stories, and essays. Ironically, at the advent of his editorship she had produced (at her own expense) a text he might have favored, *Three Lives,* a set of fictional biographies that conveys the subjective experience of three working women in the United States. What she offered thereafter was more abstruse. This he turned down over the course of twelve years, in a series of artful rejection letters that display the same intellectual fencing evident in his debates with writers such as Amy Lowell. In the first of these, he avers, "My dear Miss Stein: Your poems, I am sorry to say, would be a puzzle picture to our readers. All who have not the key must find them baffling, and—alack! that key is known to very, very few." His string of rejections helped Stein sharpen her manifestos, starting with her reply to the previous: "I am sorry you have not taken the poems for really you ought to. I may say without exaggeration that my stuff has genuine literary quality, frankly let us say the only important literature that has come out of America since Henry James. After all Henry James was a picture puzzle but the Atlantic did not hesitate. . . . The Atlantic Monthly being our only literary magazine it really is up to it." He rejoined, "You misjudge our public. Here there is no group of literati or illuminati or cognoscenti or illustrissimi of any kind, who could agree upon interpretations of your poetry." "Not one of our readers in a thousand would understand your essay," he insisted five years later. Stein telegrammed him in 1926, asking if he would "CONSIDER CAMBRIDGE OXFORD ADDRESS FOR JUNE PUBLICATION." His answer: "UNFORTUNATELY NO." A scant year before accepting her memoir, he concluded, "We live in different worlds."[12]

Stein's persistence in the face of such rebuff indicates the legitima-tizing power of both the *Atlantic* as an institution and Sedgwick's per-sonal stamp of approval. "I always wanted two things to happen," she maintains in *Everybody's Autobiography*, "to be printed in the Atlantic Monthly and in the Saturday Evening Post."[13] Her protracted contest with Sedgwick also reflects the satisfaction both parties took from the actual exchange. This teasing, combative dialogue mattered enough to Stein to introduce into *The Autobiography* itself: "The Atlantic Monthly story is rather funny. As I said Gertrude Stein sent the Atlantic Monthly some manuscripts, not with any hope of their accepting them, but if by any miracle they should, she would be pleased and Mildred delighted. An answer came back, a long and rather argumentative answer from the editorial office" (202). By including it in her book, she both extends their conversation and gets the last word in.

The Autobiography also discloses her initial confusion about the edi-tor's identity: "Gertrude Stein thinking that some Boston woman in the editorial office had written, answered the arguments lengthily to Miss Ellen Sedgwick. She received an almost immediate answer meeting all her arguments and at the same time admitting that the matter was not without interest. . . . The letter ended by saying that the writer was not Ellen but Ellery Sedgwick" (202–3). After he corrected her, Stein pri-vately assured him, "Sorry I took you for a lady. I don't at all mind you being a man."[14] But she gave a rather different account in the *Atlantic* serial, transforming "not minding" into active pleasure: "Gertrude Stein of course was delighted with its being not Ellen."[15] And in the book, she clarified her response further: "Gertrude Stein of course was delighted with its being Ellery and not Ellen" (203). Her choice twice to revise her rendition of this small emotional event, from letter to serial to book, suggests the significance she attached to the gender dynamics of her dealings with Sedgwick. She never elucidates the "of course," but it points to the paradox of his faraway women texts. Even as they place female relationships center stage, they are brokered by a paternalistic editor for a venerable "gentlemen's magazine" — and their authors, like Stein, felt validated to number among his elect.

As we have seen, this group of writers supplied generically fluid texts, informed by close writer-editor-reader ties, which established puta-tively personal relationships within the *Atlantic* community. The cir-culation of their life narratives expanded and contracted — transmitted privately, in reading groups, in commercial forums, and then in private again. We see diaries bleeding into letters into essays into letters, *Atlantic* dialogue overflowing the boundaries of official contributions, serials contained in bound books but presenting as texts in process, writers discussing their *Atlantic* relations within their *Atlantic* texts. Stein's memoir furthers this distinctive *Atlantic* mode.

The *Atlantic* roots of *The Autobiography of Alice B. Toklas* can be traced twenty years back to the cluster of life narratives Sedgwick published at the onset of his tenure. Stewart's 1913 "Letters of a Woman Homesteader" initiated a fresh formula for the magazine, profiling women's friendship and shared writing projects. Aldrich's debut similarly offered, in the *Atlantic*'s words, "authentic letters of an American lady to a friend." "A Little House on the Marne" was sandwiched between Stewart's "Elk Hunt" letters—which concluded in the issue just before it—and Jean Kenyon Mackenzie's "Black Sheep," which commenced in the one that followed, "actual letters written from Africa by an American missionary." Annie Pike Greenwood's Idaho homesteading letters came out in 1919, and in 1927 "The Stump Farm" powerfully revised and expanded the form. A second Rose serial commenced in 1933, a banner *Atlantic* year for women's life narrative as it also saw "Letters of Two Woman Farmers," Nora Waln's "The House of Exile," Worth Tuttle Hedden's "Autobiography of an Ex-Feminist," Virginia Woolf's "Flush" (a fictional autobiography of Elizabeth Barrett Browning's dog), and "Autobiography of Alice B. Toklas."[16]

From among an array of *Atlantic* predecessors, Stein identified Aldrich as the impetus for her *Atlantic* bid, a process *The Autobiography* depicts. A former journalist, Aldrich left Boston for Paris in 1898, where she worked as a theater agent prior to her late-life career as a best-selling memoirist. She is now mainly known as Stein's friend, with a footnote as the American woman who joined Oscar Wilde's meager funeral procession and another as the first to publish a story by Willa Cather ("Peter"), in her short-lived literary weekly, the *Mahogany Tree*. Yet in her day, Aldrich was a celebrity author. Even as Stein struggled to place her work, *A Hilltop on the Marne* swiftly went through seventeen printings, and it was followed by three well-received sequels. Janet P. Stout's comments about the relative standing of Willa Cather and Dorothy Canfield apply equally well to that of Stein and Aldrich, respectively: Cather now occupies a "glowingly illuminated place on the modernist bright side," while Canfield is relegated to "the darkened side of literary history," but their stature was once much less disparate, and Canfield was the more widely and popularly read.[17] An even better analogy might be George du Maurier and Henry James: du Maurier's 1895 *Trilby* was the smash hit of the decade, to the envious dismay of his eminent friend. By the time of Aldrich's abrupt fame, Stein had made a name for herself as a stylist. However, she was frustrated to be more talked about than read, even as Aldrich, seemingly without effort, gained a mass following.

A collection of letters, *A Hilltop on the Marne* captures both Aldrich's response to the war and her relationship with the unnamed American woman to whom she writes, who pressures her to come home. In the spring of 1914, Aldrich had retired to Huiry-sur-Marne, a village thirty miles outside Paris. She had envisioned a "quiet refuge," her life's work "done." Yet a scant three months later, the First Battle of the Marne took place in the valley her house overlooked, and Aldrich meticulously recorded her impressions of the event and its aftermath. The book's most quoted passage is from her conversation with a British officer, which opens with his demanding, "I want to know how it happens that you—a foreigner, and a woman—happen to be living in what looks like exile—all alone on the top of a hill—in war-time?" "A sincere, lasting and graphic literary achievement," to use *Vanity Fair*'s assessment, *A Hilltop on the Marne* was said to have swelled American support for the French. Sedgwick's choice to publish Aldrich was integral to his "sw[inging] the full force of the magazine to the side of the Allies," which led to a circulation spike.[18]

Prior to *The Autobiography*, it was Stein's celebrity "portraits" that did most to bridge her critical and popular readerships. The subjects of these experimental sketches include Cézanne, Matisse, Picasso, and many others, but Stein identified her 1922 "Mildred's Thoughts" as one of the "most successful."[19] In a leisurely meditation, she enters into Aldrich's mind: "Mildred's thoughts are where. There with pear, with the pears and the stairs Mildred's thoughts are there with the pear with the stairs and the pears."[20] That Van Wyck Brooks and Lewis Mumford included the piece in their 1927 *The American Caravan* made it Stein's most widely circulated text to date.[21]

Having capitalized on Aldrich's fame with "Mildred's Thoughts," Stein went on to deploy her as a celebrity presence in *The Autobiography*, a tactic her agent replicated when he submitted the manuscript to the *Atlantic.* Referencing Aldrich by name a full sixty-seven times, she portrays her as generous, magnetic, and feckless—borrowing money, bestowing gifts, dropping keys. "It was largely to please Mildred that Gertrude Stein tried to get the Atlantic Monthly to print something of hers," she alleges. "Mildred always felt and said that it would be a blue ribbon if the Atlantic Monthly consented, which of course it never did" (*AABT* 202). However, elsewhere she more plausibly suggests motives of self-interest and competition. Regarding their mutual friend Henry McBride, she states that he was "enormously pleased when Mildred was successful and he now says he thinks the time has come when Gertrude Stein could indulge in a little success. He does not think that now it would hurt her" (*AABT* 130). With this allusion to how "success" can "hurt," Stein affirms her superior position as an artist, with higher standards than her crowd-pleasing friend. As a charismatic American writer, Aldrich has a different status in *The Autobiography* than its other secondary female characters, working women like Hélène and "the wives" of famous men. Stein does not exactly portray her as an equal. No bells ring for Alice on meeting Mildred. She does, however, appear as unexpected challenger as well as cherished friend. Within this tale of Stein and Toklas's love affair we can identity another story about another woman, one of professional rivalry.

Even as Stein figures her as one of her ardent admirers, "loyal and convinced that if Gertrude Stein did it it had something in it that was worth while" (*AABT* 129), she shows Aldrich, too, as producing narrative, with a riveted audience of her own: "No one in the world could tell stories like Mildred. I can still see her at the rue de Fleurus sitting in one of the big armchairs and gradually the audience increasing around her as she talked" (*AABT* 129). She reinforces their parallel positions by likening them both to George Washington and showing their mutual concern for each other's reputation. It "used to annoy Mildred dreadfully" that Stein was not in the American *Who's Who;* Stein was "very anxious" that Aldrich be awarded the Legion of Honor in France (*AABT* 202, 212). Aldrich introduced Stein to key supporters like McBride and Mabel Dodge, while Stein campaigned for the recognition of her war efforts.

Still, the balance of power and influence tips in Stein's favor. She claims, for example, that Aldrich's book originated in text she produced *for* her, a letter she received in London: "The first description that any one we knew received in England of the battle of the Marne came in a letter to Gertrude Stein from Mildred Aldrich. It was practically the first letter of her book the Hilltop on the Marne" (*AABT* 159). Scholars sometimes relay this statement as literal fact. Aldrich did write Stein and Toklas letters about the same events, but the actual letters published in the *Atlantic* were addressed to another friend in the United States. Aldrich's belief that the identity of her correspondent was intrinsic to "A Little House on the Marne" makes Stein's assertion especially egregious. Aldrich apprised Sedgwick, "The person to whom real letters are written in these times is even more important than the person who writes them," a sentiment that accords with what we know about the practice of faraway women. She confided, "There are only two people in the world who, as correspondents, are inspiring to me. One of the two is the person to whom the letters you have were written."[22] The other of the two was not Stein.

Having preempted the position of Aldrich's correspondent, Stein goes on to preempt the *Atlantic* by suggesting it was actually she and Toklas who first "published" her account of the battle: "We were delighted to receive it, to know that Mildred was safe, and to know all about it. It was passed around and everybody in the neighborhood read it." Of greater consequence, she undermines Aldrich's actual literary achievement. Aldrich's reputation rested exclusively on her Marne narrative, but Stein offers "two other descriptions of the battle of the Marne" (*AABT* 159), as relayed to her by eyewitnesses. One story is about seeing horse-drawn wagons haul gold out of Paris, while the other concerns the impossibility of getting a taxi that night, "and that was the battle of the Marne" (*AABT* 160). The implication is that all representations of the event must fall ludicrously short.

Perhaps most important, Stein shows herself assuming the role of Aldrich's patron. Despite her past success, by 1925 Aldrich was living in poverty, having abruptly lost the annuity that once supported her. In the midst of her debate with Sedgwick about publishing her work, Stein asked him to petition *Atlantic* readers to contribute to a fund for her: "She has been in the last year without an income and the little house which she has made immortal will be sold over her head unless this plan is quickly carried out." The alacrity with which he agreed confirms Aldrich's import to his *Atlantic* revival. "Atlantic readers owe a great debt to Miss Aldrich," he allowed, "and I am very glad indeed to be of some service in return for what she did for the magazine." *The Autobiography,* of course, reports on the deed, Stein's rescue of the friend who once led the way. It was perhaps the success of this project that convinced Sedgwick to participate in another charity drive a decade later, the "surprise party" that enabled Hilda Rose, too, to preserve the home and way of life "made immortal" in the *Atlantic.*[23]

Toklas characterized *The Autobiography* as "the only work Gertrude wrote for her." She had just learned of Stein's autobiographical manuscript, *QED,* which recounts a youthful affair. Consequently, Leigh Gilmore argues, *The Autobiography* "takes the form of a long love letter to Alice, a compensatory gift Gertrude wrote to appease her partner." (Twenty years on, Toklas tendered her reply to this "love letter" in the form of the similarly named *The Alice B. Toklas Cookbook,* which likewise chronicles her life with Stein.) Stein bypassed the process by which Aldrich's, Stewart's, Rose's, and Harrison's texts went through successive rhetorical iterations as they evolved from private letters to magazine serials to published books. From the start, she plotted *The Autobiography* as a book, and a popular one at that. "When it was all done I said to Alice B. Toklas, do you think it is going to be a best seller, I would love to write a best seller," she recalled. Yet despite not originating as an actual letter, *The Autobiography* conveys a sense of a dialogic, periodically produced text through commenting on its own history and prospects and through approximating epistolary features. The letter writer directs her work to a specific reader or readers in order to bring about distinct results. Her assumption of shared knowledge results in a text that to the uninitiated appears riddled with gaps and omissions, even as it is highly self-reflexive. She does not feel constrained to order events chronologically, and she admits to faulty memory and incomplete facts. She is likely to employ everyday language, to repeat and contradict herself, to stall or rush forward, and to cast stories across a series of texts. And a letter, once sent, cannot be revised. *The Autobiography of Alice B. Toklas* is multiply situated: as serial and book; letter and memoir; collaboration, manifesto, gift, and joke.[24]

Finally, a few words about Harrison's *My Great, Wide, Beautiful World,* to suggest that even as Stein's memoir was advanced by the "faraway women" genre, her recasting of the form helped perpetuate it. Another life narrative of an American woman largely produced in, and submitted from, Paris, a portion of Harrison's book was serialized in the *Atlantic* just two years after Stein's. Publishing an African American woman was a near-singular event in Sedgwick's editorship. Despite his racial biases, Harrison's text—just like Stein's—passed muster due to the qualities it shared with faraway women predecessors. Yet I would submit that Harrison's likeness to *Stein* further prepared him to see her text as appropriate *Atlantic* fare. Thanks to the colloquial register, simple sentences, and blithe orthographic disregard of *The Autobiography of Alice B. Toklas*, a prose style like Harrison's was already within his purview. Sedgwick's choice to leave her nonstandard spelling and grammar intact is usually viewed as either indulgent or racially motivated, supporting a promotion of a stock African American rustic. But the choice was instead (or as well) an aesthetic one.

Like Stein's memoir, *My Great, Wide, Beautiful World* records its own conception. In the dedication to Dickinson in Los Angeles, Harrison maintains, "If You hadnt been interested in me I never would have tryed to explain my trips," and she identifies the crucial role of the Morrises in Paris, who insisted her "travellers should be put into a Book" (16). And once more, the impact of *Atlantic* publication is folded within the text: "That cheque from the Atlantic Monthly for my article gave joy" (315). Some passages in Harrison's book read as near interchangeable with some in Stein's. The default assumption is that her vernacular prose simply represents the everyday speech of an uneducated servant, whereas Stein's is the harvest of deliberate method. Yet Harrison, too, had formative writing experiences and models. Carl Van Vechten, at least, intimated Stein's affinity with Harrison in urging her, "If there are any Atlantic Monthlies handy around your parts, please read Juanita Harrison's My Great, Wide, Beautiful World."[25] (He made the same recommendation to Langston Hughes, adding, "I LOVE her."[26])

The *Atlantic* office is said to have been "astonished" to learn that *The Autobiography*, submitted anonymously, was authored by Stein; Sedgwick was "stunned."[27] Given her long history with the *Atlantic*, this strains credulity. However, the story does accord with Sedgwick's template in representing faraway women, the "twists of fate" that led to felicitous submissions. More complete knowledge of his editorial practice makes his characterization of *The Autobiography* as revealing "the real Miss Stein" seem less risible. Taking Stein's self-described joke at face value, he conceived of it as still another of the "unpremeditated record[s] of interesting happenings by an interesting person" (*HP* 197) he had long favored.

In turn, *The Autobiography* puts into focus the generic complexity and relational aspects of the so-called records it was published among. Responding to, and infused by, the voices of partners, friends, employers, and patrons, these texts all stage relations between differently placed and empowered women. They also acknowledge the pivotal role played by their eminent editor, Sedgwick, and map their creative and material conditions. The subject of *Letters of a Woman Homesteader* is both Stewart's Wyoming exploits and her productive friendship with Coney in Denver. *The Stump Farm* portrays Rose's life in northern Alberta in conjunction with the network of epistolary relationships that quite literally sustained it. *The Story of Opal* exhibits the beginnings of Whiteley's rejection of family and domestic life in favor of a legion of benefactors and a public career, while *My Great, Wide, Beautiful World* preserves its author's connections to the women who fostered her travels and her writing alike. Just so, the rationale for *The Autobiography of Alice B. Toklas* is not Toklas's life, or even Stein's, but the life that they shared, coupled with the case Stein makes for her significance as a major writer. The critical work of breaking down generic hierarchies in connecting these texts mirrors their own controlling dynamic: generative relationships between unequal women and men and with the *Atlantic Monthly* itself.

NOTES

INTRODUCTION: "OUTLYING TERRITORIES OF LITERATURE"

1. Evelyn Harris and Caroline Henderson, "Letters of Two Women Farmers, I," *Atlantic*, August 1933, 242. Harris first contacted Henderson after reading her *Atlantic* essay about harvesting wheat at the onset of the Depression. Alvin O. Turner, introduction to *Letters from the Dust Bowl*, by Caroline Henderson (Norman: University of Oklahoma Press, 2001), 17–18.

2. I follow theorist Margaret Beetham's lead in applying Anderson's concept of the "imagined community" to that network of loose affiliations formed by a magazine's editors, contributors, and readers. Beetham, "Periodicals and the New Media: Women and Imagined Communities," *Women's Studies International Forum* 29, no. 3 (2006): 232.

3. Donald Clifford Gallup, "Gertrude Stein and the Atlantic," *Yale University Library Gazette* 28, no. 3 (1954): 111.

4. Hilda Rose to Jack Jensen, n.d., ESP.

5. Clifford Geertz, *The Interpretation of Cultures: Selected Essays* (New York: Basic Books, 1973), 25.

6. Jean Marie Lutes, "Beyond the Bounds of the Book: Periodical Studies and Women Writers of the Late Nineteenth and Early Twentieth Centuries," *Legacy: A Journal of American Women Writers* 27, no. 2 (2010): 349.

7. Holly A. Laird, *Women Co-authors* (Urbana: University of Illinois Press, 2000), 5.

8. Jack Stillinger, *Multiple Authorship and the Myth of Solitary Genius* (Oxford: Oxford University Press, 1991), 24.

9. Linda Karell, *Writing Together/Writing Apart: Collaboration in Western American Literature* (Lincoln: University of Nebraska Press, 2002), xxxi.

10. As Victoria Lamont trenchantly formulates it, western women's literary criticism was once located at "the margins of a marginal field," and scholars long lacked the resources and critical paradigms to analyze western women's lives and texts. Lamont identifies the mentoring of senior scholars such as Melody Graulich and Ann Ronald as foundational to the discipline, along with early

critical anthologies, Annette Kolodny's *The Land Before Her*, and Jane Tompkins's *West of Everything*. Other monographs in her survey include those by Krista Comer, Janet Floyd, Brigitte Georgi-Findlay, Susan J. Rosowski, and myself. Her own *Westerns: A Women's History* belongs on the list, and Nina Baym's *Women Writers of the American West, 1833–1927* makes a useful resource. Lamont additionally glosses work on Indigenous, Mexican, African American, and Asian American writers by scholars including Cynthia Davis and Verner D. Mitchell, Kathryn Zabelle Derounian-Stodola, Eric Gardner, Hsuan L. Hsu, Erin Murrah-Mandril, Paul B. Wickelson, and Kay Yandell, studies that while not necessarily foregrounding a regional critical context create a more complete account of western women's writing. Lamont, "Big Books Wanted: Women and Western American Literature in the Twenty-First Century," *Legacy: A Journal of American Women Writers* 31, no. 2 (2014): 311.

11. See Nathaniel Lewis, *Unsettling the American West: Authenticity and Authorship* (Lincoln: University of Nebraska Press, 2003).

12. Quoted in Lutes, "Beyond the Bounds of the Book," 339.

13. Jerome J. McGann, *The Textual Condition* (Princeton, NJ: Princeton University Press, 1991), 9, 11; John Kevin Young, *Black Writers, White Publishers: Marketplace Politics in Twentieth-Century African American Literature* (Jackson: University Press of Mississippi, 2006), 23; Gabrielle Dean, "Make It Plain: Stein and Toklas Publish the Plain Edition," in *Primary Stein: Returning to the Writing of Gertrude Stein*, ed. Janet Boyd and Sharon J. Kirsch (Lanham, MD: Lexington Books, 2014), 31; Gérard Genette, "Introduction to the Paratext," *New Literary History* 22, no. 2 (1991): 261.

14. Robert Scholes and Clifford Wulfman, *Modernism in the Magazines: An Introduction* (New Haven, CT: Yale University Press, 2010), viii; Susan L. Johnson, *Roaring Camp: The Social World of the California Gold Rush* (New York: W. W. Norton, 2000), 311.

15. In "The American Genteel Tradition in the Early Twentieth Century," Ellery Sedgwick III, for example, introduces a group of once prominent but now forgotten women contributors only to delineate their shortcomings, while Susan Goodman's study discusses just a handful of women. Sedgwick, *American Studies* 25, no. 1 (1984): 49–67; Goodman, *Republic of Words: The "Atlantic Monthly" and Its Writers, 1857–1925* (Lebanon, NH: University Press of New England, 2011).

16. Ellery Sedgwick III, *A History of the "Atlantic Monthly," 1862–1909: Yankee Humanism at High Tide and Ebb* (Amherst: University of Massachusetts Press, 1994), 2; Sean Latham and Robert Scholes, "The Rise of Periodical Studies," *PMLA* 121, no. 2 (2006): 520.

17. Anne E. Boyd, "'What! Has She Got into the "Atlantic"?': Women Writers, the *Atlantic Monthly*, and the Formation of the American Canon," *American Studies* 39, no. 3 (1998): 9.

18. Richard Brodhead, *Cultures of Letters: Scenes of Reading and Writing in Nineteenth-Century America* (Durham, NC: Duke University Press, 1995), 117.

CHAPTER ONE: ELLERY SEDGWICK AND THE DISTAFF

1. Carolyn See, *Making a Literary Life: Advice for Writers and Other Dreamers* (New York: Random House, 2007), 93.
2. Annie Winslow Allen to Ellery Sedgwick, December 6, 1919, ESP.
3. George F. Whicher, "An Editor's Final Choice," *New York Herald Tribune*, September 28, 1947, scrapbook, ESP; Frederick Lewis Allen, "Sedgwick of the *Atlantic*," *Saturday Review of Literature* (September 28, 1946), 8.
4. Nancy Glazener, *Reading for Realism: The History of a U.S. Literary Institution, 1850–1910* (Durham, NC: Duke University Press, 1997), 235–36.
5. Ellery Sedgwick III, *A History of the "Atlantic Monthly," 1862–1909: Yankee Humanism at High Tide and Ebb* (Amherst: University of Massachusetts Press, 1994), 314.
6. F. Allen, "Sedgwick of the *Atlantic*."
7. Mark Antony De Wolfe Howe, *The "Atlantic Monthly" and Its Makers* (Boston: Atlantic Monthly Press, 1919), 99.
8. Walter Prichard Eaton, "Editor Who Made the 'Atlantic' Famous," *New York Herald Tribune Weekly Book Review*, September 29, 1946, vii.
9. Howe, *"Atlantic Monthly" and Its Makers*, 97.
10. Bonnie James Shaker, *Coloring Locals: Racial Formation in Kate Chopin's Youth Companion, 1891–1902* (Iowa City: Iowa University Press, 2003), 128n26.
11. Angela Gianoglio Pettitt and Bonnie James Shaker, "'Her First Party' as Her Last Story: Recovering Kate Chopin's Fiction," *Legacy: A Journal of American Women Writers* 30, no. 2 (2013): 393n9.
12. Shaker, *Coloring Locals*, 28.
13. "Interesting People Ellery Sedgwick Met," *Chicago Tribune* (Sunday, n.d.), scrapbook, ESP; Yone Noguchi, *Collected English Letters*, ed. Ikuko Atsumi (Tokyo: Yone Noguchi Society, 1975), 60–61; *Current Literature* 36 (April 1904), Edward Marx Noguchi Collection, privately owned; Julia Ehrhardt, *Writers of Conviction: The Personal Politics of Zona Gale, Dorothy Canfield Fisher, Rose Wilder Lane, and Josephine Herbst* (Columbia: University of Missouri Press, 2004), 62.
14. Greg Gross, "The Staff Breakup of *McClure's Magazine*: 'The Explosions of Our Fine Idealistic Undertakings,'" *Allegheny College* (1997): n.p., http://sites.allegheny.edu/tarbell/mcclurestaff/chapter-ii. They "assumed this hideous debt," Sedgwick recalled. "Relieved me of these shackles round my neck." "Talks with Ellery Sedgwick Shortly before He Died, February 1960," ESP.
15. Gross, "Staff Breakup of *McClure's Magazine*"; Peter Lyon, *Success Story: The Life and Times of S.S. "McClure"* (New York: Scribner's, 1963), 121.
16. Sedgwick, *History of the "Atlantic Monthly*," 313.
17. Howe, *"Atlantic Monthly" and Its Makers*, 97–98.
18. Sedgwick, "Talks with Sedgwick."
19. Howe, *"Atlantic Monthly" and Its Makers*, 66; Sedgwick, *History of the "Atlantic Monthly*," 317; Sedgwick, "Talks with Sedgwick"; Sedgwick, *History of the "Atlantic Monthly*," 313.
20. Sedgwick, *History of the "Atlantic Monthly*," 314.
21. Sedgwick, "Talks with Sedgwick."

22. Edward Weeks, "Ellery Sedgwick: Eighth Editor of the *Atlantic*, 1872–1960," *Atlantic* (June 1960): 126.

23. David E. Sumner, *The Magazine Century: American Magazines since 1900* (New York: Peter Lang, 2010), 77.

24. "Ellery Sedgwick, Editor, 88, Dead," *New York Times*, April 22, 1960.

25. Merrill F. Clarke to "Atlantic Monthly editors," February 16, 1938, ESP; Richard Badlian to Ellery Sedgwick, n.d., ESP.

26. Alfred R. McIntyre to Sedgwick, October 23, 1945, ESP.

27. Sedgwick to Juliet B. Rublee, May 23, 1941, ESP.

28. Glazener, *Reading for Realism*, 261.

29. Werner Sollors, introduction to *The Promised Land*, by Mary Antin (New York: Penguin, 2012), xiv.

30. Glazener, *Reading for Realism*, 239.

31. Howe, *"Atlantic Monthly" and Its Makers*, 13; Mary Ellen Chase to Sedgwick, Monday, n.d., ESP; Dorothy Canfield to Sedgwick, September 29, 1915, ESP; Robert Frost to Sedgwick, September 20, 1916, and February 29, 1936, ESP; Elinor Frost to Sedgwick, March 8, 1935, ESP; Nora Waln, "Contributors' Column," *Atlantic*, October 1936, n.p. Waln was a Quaker and *Atlantic* contributor who wrote about her experiences in China and Germany.

32. Amy Lowell to Sedgwick, February 8, 1919, and October 9, 1914, ESP; Willa Cather to Sedgwick, August 6, 1932, ESP; Ann Hulbert, *The Interior Castle: The Art and Life of Jean Stafford* (Amherst: University of Massachusetts Press, 1992), 260.

33. Gertrude Bogart to Sedgwick, February 3, 1947, ESP. The letter is actually one of protest, triggered by an allusion in *The Happy Profession* to an off-color story about Lincoln; Bogart felt herself on sure ground morally, if not culturally.

34. Everett E. Pettigrew and Mattie W. Knight, 1920, "Maine Vital Records, 1670–1921," FamilySearch, https://familysearch.org/ark:/61903/1:1:Q24N-TMMP; Gertrude K. Bogart, U.S. Census, 1930, FamilySearch, FHL microfilm 2,341,193, https://familysearch.org/ark:/61903/1:1:X78L-QFD; Gertrude K. Bogart, U.S. Census, 1940, FamilySearch, NARA digital publication T627, https://family search.org/pal:/MM9.3.1/TH-1961–27842–2669–99?cc=2000219.

35. Amy Blair, *Reading Up: Middle-Class Readers and the Culture of Success in the Early Twentieth-Century United States* (Philadelphia: Temple University Press, 2011), 4; Susan Goodman, *Republic of Words: The "Atlantic Monthly" and Its Writers, 1857–1925* (Lebanon, NH: University Press of New England, 2011), 251; Margaret Beetham, "Periodicals and the New Media: Women and Imagined Communities," *Women's Studies International Forum* 29, no. 3 (2006): 235.

36. See Glazener, "Addictive Reading and Professional Authorship," chap. 3 of *Reading for Realism*.

37. Henrietta Ellery Sedgwick to Marjorie Russell, May 1, 1960, ESP; Sedgwick to Elizabeth J. Woodward, March 26, 1920, ESP.

38. Annie Winslow Allen to Sedgwick, December 6, 1919; Canfield to Sedgwick, April 15, 1915, ESP; Chase to Sedgwick, January 30, 1933, ESP.

39. Opal Whiteley to Sedgwick, February 20, 1920, ESP; L. Adams Beck to Sedgwick, September 23, 1920, ESP; Betty Smith to Sedgwick, June 18, 1942, ESP.

40. Chase, Monday, n.d.

41. Ellery Sedgwick III, "The American Genteel Tradition in the Early Twentieth Century," *American Studies* 25, no. 1 (1984): 49–67.
42. Eaton, "Editor Who Made the 'Atlantic' Famous"; Harold J. Laski, review of *The Happy Profession,* by Sedgwick, *New England Quarterly* 20, no. 1 (1947): 116.
43. Beulah Rector, review of *The Happy Profession,* by Sedgwick, October 4, 1946, scrapbook, ESP.
44. Weeks, "Ellery Sedgwick," 126.
45. Edward Weeks, *My Green Age: A Memoir* (Boston: Little, Brown, 1973), 208–9.
46. Bogart to Sedgwick, February 3, 1947, ESP.
47. Quoted in Anne E. Boyd, "'What! Has She Got into the "Atlantic"?': Women Writers, the *Atlantic Monthly,* and the Formation of the American Canon," *American Studies* 39, no. 3 (1998): 12.
48. For an overview of scholarship on women and periodicals, see Jean Marie Lutes, "Beyond the Bounds of the Book: Periodical Studies and Women Writers of the Late Nineteenth and Early Twentieth Centuries," *Legacy: A Journal of American Women Writers* 27, no. 2 (2010): 336–56.
49. Shirley Marchalonis, "Women Writers and the Assumption of Authority: The *Atlantic Monthly,* 1857–1898," in *In Her Own Voice: Nineteenth-Century American Women Essayists,* ed. Sherry Lee Linkon (New York: Garland, 1997), 8.
50. Lutes, "Beyond the Bounds of the Book," 339.
51. Howe, *"Atlantic Monthly" and Its Makers,* 17, 23; Joan D. Hedrick, *Harriet Beecher Stowe: A Life* (Oxford: Oxford University Press, 1995), 289.
52. Quoted in Boyd, "'What! Has She Got into the "Atlantic"?,'" 27.
53. Ibid., 12.
54. Susan Coultrap-McQuin, *Doing Literary Business: American Women Writers in the Nineteenth Century* (Chapel Hill: University of North Carolina Press, 1990), 125–28.
55. Sedgwick, *History of the "Atlantic Monthly,"* 78.
56. Hedrick, *Harriet Beecher Stowe,* 294.
57. Willa Cather, "The House on Charles Street," *Literary Review* 3 (November 4, 1922): 173–74.
58. Annie Fields to Sedgwick, July 12, 1911, ESP.
59. Mary Antin to Sedgwick, June 7, 1911, ESP.
60. Sedgwick, *History of the "Atlantic Monthly,"* 88, 79, 143.
61. Sedgwick to Antin, June 19, 1911, ESP.
62. Keren R. McGinity, "The Real Mary Antin: Woman on a Mission in the Promised Land," *American Jewish History* 86, no. 3 (1998): 288. In reference to Sedgwick and Antin's work together, McGinity has shown there is no record of "how and why certain edits were made to the autobiography," or by whom (289).
63. Sedgwick to Antin, July 17, 1911, ESP.
64. Smith to Sedgwick, June 24, 1942, ESP.
65. Frank Luther Mott, *Golden Multitudes: The Story of Best-Sellers in the United States* (New York: Macmillan, 1947), 8.
66. May Sarton, *Plant Dreaming Deep* (reprint, New York: W. W. Norton, 1996), 126.
67. Laski, review of *The Happy Profession,* by Sedgwick, 117; Frederick Lewis Allen, quoted in Goodman, *Republic of Words,* 224.
68. Peter Davison, "Robert Frost: The Long Road to Acceptance," *"Atlantic" Ideas*

Tour, http://www.theatlantic.com/ideastour/contributors/frost.html; Newton Arvin, review of *Atlantic Harvest: Memoirs of the "Atlantic,"* by Sedgwick, *Nation* (October 11, 1947): 385.

69. Willa Cather, *The Selected Letters of Willa Cather,* ed. Andrew Jewell and Janis Stout (New York: Alfred A. Knopf, 2013), 168; Florence Wheelock Ayscough MacNair and Amy Lowell, *Florence Ayscough and Amy Lowell: Correspondence of a Friendship,* ed. Harley Farnsworth MacNair (Chicago: University of Chicago Press, 1945), 127; Lowell to Sedgwick, October 9, 1914, ESP; Donald Clifford Gallup, "Gertrude Stein and the *Atlantic,*" *Yale University Library Gazette* 28, no. 3 (1954): 111; May Sarton to Marjorie and Ellery Sedgwick, May 25, 1953, ESP.

70. Christine Holbo, "'Industrial & Picturesque Narrative': Helen Hunt Jackson's California Travel Writing for the *Century,*" *American Literary Realism* 42, no. 3 (2010): 245.

71. F. Allen, "Sedgwick of the *Atlantic.*"

72. Edward T. James, Janet Wilson James, and Paul S. Boyer, eds., *Notable American Women, 1607–1950: A Biographical Dictionary* (Cambridge, MA: Harvard University Press, 1971), 3:470. Sedgwick himself promoted Mackenzie at the onset of her career (to Roger L. Scaife, November 23, 1915, Houghton Mifflin Collection, Houghton Library, Cambridge, MA).

73. Ellery Sedgwick, introduction to *The Story of Opal: The Journal of an Understanding Heart,* by Opal Whiteley (Boston: Atlantic Monthly Press, 1920), vi.

74. Opal Whiteley to Sedgwick, September 16, 1919, ESP.

75. Hilda Rose, "Long Distance Calling: New Letters from the Stump Farm," *Atlantic* 156, no. 5 (1935): 551.

76. Sedgwick resumes narrative control in an afterword that likewise reads as a knowing allusion to the interplay of these different accounts, commencing, "Here her *Atlantic* story closes, but not her own" (*AH* 417). He employs a favorite *Atlantic* theme—the magazine's far-reaching effects—to reveal that her husband was saved from a jail sentence in California when the judge learned of her *Atlantic* connection.

77. John M. Rosenfield, "The Sedgwick Statue of the Infant Shōtoku Taishi," *Archives of Asian Art* 22 (1968–69): 56.

78. Ellery Sedgwick, "A Chinese Printed Scroll of the Lotus Sutra," *Quarterly Journal of Current Acquisitions* 6, no. 2 (1949): 6.

79. *American Magazine* (July 1936): 78.

CHAPTER TWO: ELINORE PRUITT STEWART AND HER SILENT PARTNERS

1. *Atlantic,* December 1913, 97.

2. Alvin O. Turner, introduction to *Letters from the Dust Bowl,* by Caroline Henderson (Norman: University of Oklahoma Press, 2001), 12.

3. "The Incomplete Letter-Writer," *Atlantic,* January 1912, 139.

4. Elinore Pruitt Stewart, U.S. Census, 1930, FamilySearch, FHL microfilm 2,342,359, https://familysearch.org/ark:/61903/1:1:X7WH-31J.

5. Bloomfield did not find definitive evidence that Stewart fabricated Rupert's death, and her children contested the theory. I know this because Bloomfield generously donated the research materials she gathered for *The Adventures of*

the Woman Homesteader to the Sweetwater County Historical Museum in Green River, Wyoming. In addition to the material that appears in the biography, the Bloomfield collection includes many transcribed letters to and from Stewart and transcripts of Bloomfield's interviews with her adult children. I cite *Adventures* as my source for all the letters it reprints.

6. Elinore Pruitt Stewart, "Letters of a Woman Homesteader," serial, *Atlantic,* October 1913, 433–43; November 1913, 589–98; December 1913, 820–29; January 1914, 17–26; February 1914, 170–77; April 1914, 525–32.

7. *Christian Science Monitor,* quoted in back matter of *LWH.*

8. Doubleday, Page & Company to Elinore Pruitt Stewart, October 3, 1913, SBC.

9. *Atlantic,* October 1913, 433; *Atlantic,* April 1914, 532; Sedgwick to Stewart, April 27, 1914, SBC; "The Joys of Homesteading," review of *Letters of a Woman Homesteader,* by Stewart, *Dial,* July 1, 1914, 22; *Boston Transcript,* quoted in *AWH* 32.

10. V. Poovey, review of *Letters of a Woman Homesteader,* by Stewart, *Mississippi Valley Historical Review* 2, no. 3 (1915): 451; "*Atlantic Monthly* Advertiser," 56, insert in *Atlantic,* November 1913.

11. The glancing attention her book accords the domestic sphere is always attributed to Stewart herself, so intent on an intrepid self-portrait that she subordinates her family life. However, it might instead be the outcome of editorial intervention, the excision of prosaic detail deemed irrelevant to frontier narrative. Recognizing the generic iterations and collaborative dimension of this text, and of the others in this study, calls into question many of our assumptions about them.

12. Susan J. Rosowski and Helen Winter Stauffer, *Women and Western American Literature* (Albany, NY: Whitson, 1982), 45.

13. Linda Karell, *Writing Together/Writing Apart: Collaboration in Western American Literature* (Lincoln: University of Nebraska Press, 2002), xxvii.

14. Elizabeth Hewitt, "The Networks of Nineteenth-Century Letter Writing," preface to *The Edinburgh Companion to Nineteenth-Century American Letters and Letter-Writing,* ed. Celeste-Marie Bernier et al. (Edinburgh: Edinburgh University Press, 2016), 5.

15. William Merrill Decker, *Epistolary Practices: Letter Writing in America before Telecommunications* (Chapel Hill: University of North Carolina Press, 1998), 21, 19; Anne Bower, *Epistolary Responses: The Letter in Twentieth-Century American Fiction* (Tuscaloosa: University of Alabama Press, 1997), x.

16. "*Atlantic Monthly* Advertiser."

17. Victoria Lamont, "Li(v)es of a Woman Homesteader: Silence, Disclosure, and Self in the Letters of Elinore Pruitt Stewart," *a/b: Auto/Biography Studies* 16, no. 2 (2001): 227; Sherry L. Smith, "Single Women Homesteaders: The Perplexing Case of Elinore Pruitt Stewart," *Western Historical Quarterly* 22, no. 2 (1991): 164; Natalie A. Dykstra, "The Curative Space of the American West in the Life and Letters of Elinore Pruitt Stewart," in *Portraits of Women in the American West,* ed. Dee Garceau-Hagen (New York: Routledge, 2005): 209–32. Coney is unnamed in Floyd's study, named only in a footnote in Lynn Z. Bloom's analysis of frontier autobiographies, and thrice misnamed, as "Mrs. Elizabeth Coney," in Peter C. Rollins's essay about the film adaptation. It is symptomatic of Coney's position in the scholarship that Bloomfield did not turn her

formidable research skills her way, in contrast to her thorough investigation of a later correspondent, Mariah Wood.

18. Hewitt, "Networks of Nineteenth-Century Letter Writing," 5.

19. Lamont, "Li(v)es of a Woman Homesteader," 224.

20. Susanne George Bloomfield, interview with Clyde Stewart Jr., October 1985, SBC.

21. Walter Prichard Eaton, "Editor Who Made the 'Atlantic' Famous," *New York Herald Tribune Weekly Book Review,* September 29, 1946, vii.

22. Thomas W. Baldwin, *Vital Records of Reading Massachusetts, to the Year 1850* (Boston: New England Historic Genealogical Society, 1912), n.p. Transcribed by Dave Swerdfeger. http://dunhamwilcox.net/ma/reading_d2.htm.

23. In 1850 Graves's real estate was valued at $2,000, in 1860 at $3,000, and in 1870 at $6,000. Ebenezer Graves, U.S. Census, 1850, FamilySearch, citing family 93, NARA microfilm publication M432, https://familysearch.org/ark:/61903/1:1 :MDSM-RTG; Ebenezer Graves, U.S. Census, 1860, FamilySearch (no record cited), https://familysearch.org/ark:/61903/1:1:MZHX-8S1; Ebenezer Graves, U.S. Census, 1870, FamilySearch, FHL microfilm 552,130, https://familysearch.org /ark:/61903/1:1:MD3B-B94.

24. The 1870 and 1880 Censuses identify the occupation of Mary Hannah Graves as that of preacher and minister, respectively; her 1908 death certificate, less willing to grant such a title, simply states "Religious." Ibid.; Mary Hannah Graves, U.S. Census, 1880, FamilySearch, FHL microfilm 1,254,539, https://familysearch.org/ark:/61903/1:1:MH6R-DLB; Mary Hannah Graves, death, December 5, 1908, FamilySearch, FHL microfilm 2,217,886, https://familysearch.org/ark:/61903/1:1:NWTL-V45.

25. Jeremiah Coney, U.S. Census, 1850, FamilySearch, family 146, NARA microfilm publication M432, https://familysearch.org/ark:/61903/1:1:MD92-YNJ.

26. Edwin S. Coney and Sarah Juliette Graves, marriage, March 31, 1858, FamilySearch, FHL microfilm 1,433,016, https://familysearch.org/ark:/61903/1:1: NWR8-KTF.

27. Eben Putnam, *Lieutenant Joshua Hewes, a New England Pioneer, and Some of His Descendants* (New York: J. F. Tapley, 1913).

28. John H. Perkins, U.S. Census, 1870, FamilySearch, FHL microfilm 552,131, https://familysearch.org/ark:/61903/1:1:MDQM-KH3.

29. Paul G. Faler, *Mechanics and Manufacturers in the Early Industrial Revolution: Lynn, Massachusetts, 1780–1860* (Albany: State University of New York Press, 1981), 23.

30. Sarah J. Coney, pension, 1916, "United States Veterans Administration Pension Payment Cards, 1907–1933," FamilySearch, FHL microfilm 1,634,480, https://familysearch.org/ark:/61903/1:1:K6H6-C5Z.

31. Christine Stansell, *City of Women: Sex and Class in New York, 1789–1860* (New York: Alfred A. Knopf, 1986), 106.

32. Perkins, U.S. Census, 1870.

33. *Register and Circular of the State Normal School at Salem, Mass., Spring and Summer Term, 1878* (Digital Commons at Salem State University), n.p.

34. This misconception may have originated with Jerrine Rupert (Wire), only nine

when Coney died, who in at least one interview transposed the profession of the daughters onto the mother (Bloomfield, March 22, 1986).

35. Jeremiah Coney, U.S. Census, 1880, FamilySearch, FHL microfilm 1,254,526, https://familysearch.org/ark:/61903/1:1:MH6W-GBZ.

36. Frank H. Allen, U.S. Census, 1880, FamilySearch, FHL microfilm 1,254,558, https://familysearch.org/ark:/61903/1:1:MHX5–97J. Jeremiah Coney had previously taken in Pamelia after she lost her parents. Jeremiah Coney, Massachusetts State Census, 1855, FamilySearch, FHL microfilm 953,980, https://familysearch.org/ark:/61903/1:1:MQ4B-NY7. Florence Allen's marital family closely resembled her natal one. Frank was a grocer from Wakefield, and his father had been a shoemaker. His older brothers were also shoemakers, and one of his sisters worked in Wakefield's Rattan Works.

37. Frank H. Allen, Colorado State Census, 1885, FamilySearch, FH microfilm 498,503, https://familysearch.org/ark:/61903/1:1:K8WZ-8NF.

38. Putnam, *Lieutenant Joshua Hewes*, 177.

39. Juliet Coney, U.S. Census, 1900, FamilySearch, FHL microfilm 1,240,119, https://familysearch.org/ark:/61903/1:1:MQMS-8NH.

40. Putnam, *Lieutenant Joshua Hewes*, 177; *Boston Daily Globe*, September 7, 1902.

41. Bloomfield, interview, March 22, 1986.

42. My thanks to Melissa Homestead for suggesting this possibility.

43. Dora L. Costa, *The Evolution of Retirement: An American Economic History, 1880–1990* (Chicago: University of Chicago Press, 1998), 197.

44. Sophia Coney, pension, 1907–33, FamilySearch, NARA microfilm publication M850, https://familysearch.org/pal:/MM9.3.1/TH-1–17559–22674–4?cc=1832324.

45. In 1900 Coney lived with her daughters and grandchildren at 357 Grant Avenue. In 1908 her residence was 1010 Seventeenth Avenue, room 10 (*AWH* 9), but by 1910 she and Florence were at 122 Acoma Street. Juliet Coney, U.S. Census, 1900, FamilySearch, FHL microfilm 1,240,119, https://familysearch.org /ark:/61903/1:1:MQMS-8NH; Juliet Coney, U.S. Census 1910, FamilySearch, FHL microfilm 1,374,129, https://familysearch.org/ark:/61903/1:1:MKW1-XTQ. Florence continued to live with her mother until the latter's death in 1915. By 1930 she resided in a boardinghouse in Berkeley, in the same city as her daughter Ethelind and her family. Ten years later, she was living alone in Berkeley in her own home. Florence E. Allen, U.S. Census, 1930, FamilySearch, https://familysearch.org/ark:/61903/1:1:XCXV-595; Florence E. Allen, U.S. Census, 1940, FamilySearch, (ED) 1–140, sheet 8B, family 310, NARA digital publication T627, https://familysearch.org/ark:/61903/1:1:K9QQ-6XF.

46. Bloomfield, interview with Jerrine Rupert Wire, September 1986, SBC.

47. "*Atlantic Monthly* Advertiser."

48. Stewart to Josephine Harris, May 18, 1933, SBC.

49. Mary Louise Kete, *Sentimental Collaborations: Mourning and Middle-Class Identity in Nineteenth-Century America* (Durham, NC: Duke University Press, 2000), 17; Decker, *Epistolary Practices*, 22.

50. Lamont, "Li(v)es of a Woman Homesteader," 230.

51. Mary Hannah, the preacher, never married. Caroline Wellington worked as a teacher, although late in life she did marry a prosperous farmer, having

relocated to Earlville, Illinois, with or before her sister Hellen M., who remained single and had a teaching career in the same town. At twenty-four, Elizabeth J. was still living at home with her mother. Carrie W. Graves, U.S. Census, 1870, FamilySearch, FHL microfilm 552,130, https://familysearch.org /ark:/61903/1:1:MD3B-B9Z; Caroline Wellington (Graves) Burlingame, U.S. Census, 1900, FamilySearch, FHL microfilm 1,240,315, https://familysearch.org/ark: /61903/1:1:MSWY-R2C; Helen M. Graves, death, January 1, 1919, FamilySearch, FHL microfilm 1,544,470, https://familysearch.org/ark:/61903/1:1:N36P-PVG; Elizabeth J. Graves, U.S. Census, 1880, FamilySearch, FHL microfilm 1,254,539, https://familysearch.org/ark:/61903/1:1:MH6R-DL1.

52. J. David Hacker, Libra Hilde, and James Holland Jones, "The Effect of the Civil War on Southern Marriage Patterns," *Journal of Southern History* 76, no. 1 (2010): 17.

53. Victoria Lamont, *Westerns: A Women's History* (Lincoln: University of Nebraska Press 2016), 21.

54. Florence E. Allen, U.S. Census, 1920, FamilySearch, FHL microfilm 1,820,160, https://familysearch.org/ark:/61903/1:1:MX2K-34T; Clara J. Coney, U.S. Census, 1920, FamilySearch, FHL microfilm 1,820,159, https://familysearch.org/ark: /61903/1:1:MX2X-FP3.

55. Mary C. C. Bradford, *Colorado Educational Directory, School Year 1917–1918* (Denver: Colorado Department of Public Instruction, 1917), 40, 39, http://archive .org/stream/coloeduc18colo/coloeduc18colo_djvu.txt.

56. Decker, *Epistolary Practices*, 27.

57. Bloomfield, interview, September 1986.

58. Houghton Mifflin to Elinore Pruitt Stewart, April 25, 1914, SBC.

59. *Atlantic*, April 1914, 532.

60. Sedgwick to Jerrine Rupert, May 20, 1922, SBC.

61. Stewart's January 1914 letter forecasts the sequel: "Some women and myself went on an elk-hunt not long since, and I shall shortly send you an account of it" (*Atlantic*, April 1914, 532). It is unclear if she truly had just returned from such a hunt, if she was pitching a new book project, or if she was referencing an idea bruited by Sedgwick. *Letters on an Elk Hunt* chronicles the expedition she took seven months later—its sole woman—in July 1914.

62. Display ad 231, no title, *Los Angeles Times*, December 5, 1915.

63. Kete, *Sentimental Collaborations*, 53.

64. Sedgwick to Mariah Wood, January 12, 1914, SBC; Stewart to Wood, December 15, 1917, and November 26, 1929, SBC; Bloomfield, interview, September 1986; Stewart to Wood, August 4, 1915, SBC; Mary Antin to Stewart, August 29, 1919, SBC; Stewart to Wood, July 29, 1919, SBC.

65. In *Twenty Thousand Roads: Women, Movement, and the West* (Berkeley: University of California Press, 2003), Virginia Scharff describes Hebard as promoting a "new regional legend, that the West was a place where men—and women!—could be free" (94).

66. Bloomfield, interview, September 1986; Stewart to Wood, February 8 (no year) and April 27, 1914, SBC; Bloomfield, interview with Jerrine Rupert Wire, October 1986, SBC.

67. Stewart to Mr. Zaiss, January 26, 1931, SBC.

68. Stewart to Wood, November 22, 1924, SBC.

69. Lamont, "Li(v)es of a Woman Homesteader," 224.

70. *Letters of a Woman Homesteader* is, in fact, structurally and thematically akin to two antebellum predecessors, Caroline Kirkland's *A New Home: Who'll Follow?* and Louise Clappe's *The Shirley Letters*. Kirkland and Clappe, newcomers to frontier Michigan and a California gold camp, respectively, comically staged their misadventures in personal letters that were later published. Even as Sedgwick looked to stake a new claim, he revived an established mode of western women's periodical writing.

71. Stewart to Wood, July 29, 1919. With less than her usual deference, she remarked, "Our Letter put Sedgwick in such a sweet temper that I expected to send him a few more letters while he was in an 'acceptable' mood, but alack and alas! His acceptable moods don't last as long as my lacharynoise [*sic*] moods do."

72. Bloomfield, interview, March 22, 1986.

73. Stewart to Grace Raymond Hebard, December 6, 1926, Hebard Papers, box 45, folder 25, American Heritage Center, University of Wyoming, Laramie.

74. Stewart to Wood, February 26, 1929, SBC.

75. Bloomfield, interview, March 22, 1986. Bloomfield recounts Stewart's unfruitful turn to plot-driven, sentimental fiction and a discouraging failure to place a novel.

76. The Atlantic Monthly Press bought *House Beautiful* in 1915, and Sedgwick was actually its editor in 1922.

77. Ellen Moers, "The Tradition of *McClure*," *Commentary* 37, no. 4 (1964): 71.

78. Sterling Brown has a number of dialect poems in the same 1932 *Folk-Say* volume that features Stewart, including "A Bad, Bad Man," "Call Boy," "Puttin' on Dog," "Rent Day Blues," "Slim in Hell," and "Long Track Blues."

79. Elinore Pruitt Stewart, "Snow: An Adventure of the Woman Homesteader," *Atlantic*, December 1923, 782–83.

80. Still another of Jerrine's letters captures the defining elements of her mother's writing philosophy: "Dear Mr. Sedgwick, I am so glad you will let me write to you once in a while. I have been wanting to do something real very good for a long time but it seems I cant. One morning I rised very early and went for a long walk trying to think what I could do to show you I liked you" (n.d., ESP). Genuine feeling is conveyed by locating an apt subject and giving it its due, in a text expressly composed for a superior friend.

81. Charles Johanningsmeier, "Sarah Orne Jewett and Mary E. Wilkins (Freeman): Two Shrewd Businesswomen in Search of New Markets," *New England Quarterly* 70, no. 1 (1997): 57–82; Willa Cather to Sedgwick, August 6, 1932, ESP.

82. Sedgwick to Stewart, April 27, 1914, SBC.

83. Sedgwick, *Atlantic*, October 1913, 433.

84. Margaret Lynn, *A Stepdaughter of the Prairie* (New York: Macmillan, 1914), 19.

85. Ellery Sedgwick, "Recent Reflections of a Novel-Reader," *Atlantic*, October 1914, 531.

86. Dorothy Anne Dondore, review of *Grandmother Brown's Hundred Years: 1827–1927*, by Harriet Connor Brown, *Mississippi Valley Historical Review* 17, no. 1 (1930): 168.

87. Ellery Sedgwick III, "The American Genteel Tradition in the Early Twentieth

Century," *American Studies* 25, no. 1 (1984): 49–67. Surveying these writers, Sedgwick argues for how "constricted" they appear compared to the progressive male essayists they appear among (50). Perhaps they will find a larger place within studies of the middlebrow, which prioritize women's cultural production. Joan Shelley Rubin's *The Making of Middlebrow Culture* (Chapel Hill: University of North Carolina Press, 1992) includes a rare discussion of Agnes Repplier as well as an account of how Sedgwick encouraged Stuart P. Sherman to write *My Dear Cornelia*, a book composed of fictional conversations between a woman of the cultural old guard and her up-to-date friend.

88. Discussions to date are confined to my own "'A Reading Problem': Margaret Lynn, Jean Stafford, and Literary Criticism of the American West," *Legacy* 33, no. 1 (2016): 127–49; and Ellen Gruber Garvey's references to Lynn's scrapbook activity in *Writing with Scissors: American Scrapbooks from the Civil War to the Harlem Renaissance* (Oxford: Oxford University Press, 2012).

CHAPTER THREE: COLLABORATIVE ALCHEMY AND ACRIMONY

1. Jill Lepore, "Historians Who Love Too Much: Reflections on Microhistory and Biography," *Journal of American History* 88, no. 1 (June 2001): 135; Ava Chamberlain, *The Notorious Elizabeth Tuttle: Marriage, Murder, and Madness in the Family of Jonathan Edwards* (New York: New York University, 2012), 10.

2. Holly A. Laird, *Women Co-authors* (Urbana: University of Illinois Press, 2000), 5, 4; Melissa Homestead, "Willa Cather, Edith Lewis, and Collaboration: The Southwestern Novels of the 1920s and Beyond," *Studies in the Novel* 45, no. 3 (2013): 408–41.

3. *Eugene (OR) Daily Guard*, 1915, quoted in Benjamin Hoff, introduction to *The Singing Creek Where the Willows Grow: The Mystical Nature Diary of Opal Whiteley*, by Whiteley (New York: Penguin, 1994), 21–22; Maurice Van Slaten to "Cora," June 10, 1919, ESP; Maud Harwood Bales to Sedgwick, November 25, 1920, ESP.

4. Kathrine Beck, *Opal: A Life of Enchantment, Mystery, and Madness* (New York: Viking, 2003), 38. Beck met with numerous Whiteley scholars (and even called me in Japan). She gained access to private collections and, in addition to the usual fine-combed archives, worked with the Opal Whiteley Papers in London. Consequently, she offers the best record available for Whiteley's time in New York, India, and London. However, that she writes for a general audience makes it hard to build on her work. Quotations lack dates and provenance, small errors are evident, and the book has no footnotes, works cited, or index.

5. Bales to Sedgwick, November 25, 1920, ESP.

6. Elbert Bede, *Cottage Grove (OR) Sentinel*, May 5, 1915, ESP.

7. Sedgwick to Whiteley, November 10, 1919, ESP; Whiteley, "The Story of Opal," serial, *Atlantic*, March 1920, 289–98; April 1920, 445–55; May 1920, 639–50; June 1920, 772–82; July 1920, 56–67; August 1920, 201–13; Sedgwick to Opal Whiteley, September 14, 1920, ESP.

8. Bede to Sedgwick, November 6, 1920, ESP.

9. Edith B. Acken to Sedgwick, March 3, 1920, ESP.

10. Sedgwick to anonymous, July 7, 1920, ESP; Sedgwick to Richard C. Cabot, March 23, 1921, ESP.

11. Sedgwick to Mrs. Oscar R. Howard, December 1, 1920, ESP; Sedgwick to Alfred McIntyre, October 23, 1945, ESP.

12. Opal Whiteley, U.S. Census, 1910, FamilySearch, FHL microfilm 1,375,295, https://familysearch.org/ark:/61903/1:1:MLB4-QC8.

13. Edna Whipple to Sedgwick, February 8, 1920, ESP.

14. James E. Denton to Sedgwick, January 5, 1921, ESP.

15. G. Evert Baker, "Statement," n.d., ESP.

16. Quoted in Elbert Bede, *Fabulous Opal Whiteley: From Oregon Logging Camp to Princess in India* (Portland, OR: Binfords and Mort, 1954), 11.

17. Ellery Sedgwick, "Record of Opal Whiteley," June 1920, 7, 8, 9, ESP.

18. April 1917, quoted in Steve McQuiddy, "The Fantastic Tale of Opal Whiteley," Intangible, 1996, http://www.intangible.org/Features/Opal/OpalHome.html, 10.

19. Sedgwick, "Record," 11.

20. Ibid.

21. Bales to Sedgwick, November 25, 1920, ESP.

22. Dennis Harbach, "Harbach and the House Book," *Autry Museum of the American West,* July 23, 2013, https://autrylibraries.wordpress.com/2012/07/23/harbach-and-the-housebook-4/.

23. Quoted in Inez Fortt, "The Education of an Understanding Heart," *Call Number* 18, no. 1 (1952): 8.

24. Bales to Sedgwick, November 25, 1920, ESP.

25. Rose L. Ellerbe, "History of the Southern California Woman's Press Club, 1894–1929," *Southern California Woman's Press Club* (1930): n.p., transcribed by Jeanne Sturgis Taylor, 2011, http://freepages.genealogy.rootsweb.ancestry.com/~npmelton/scnw.htm.

26. Opal Whiteley, *The Fairyland around Us* (Los Angeles: Opal Stanley Whiteley, 1918; Durham, NC: Duke University Libraries, 2014), 216, https://archive.org/details/fairylandarounduoowhit; Deborah Garfield, "The Heir Unapparent," in *Women's Experience of Modernity, 1875–1945,* ed. Ann L. Ardis and Leslie W. Lewis (Baltimore: John Hopkins University Press, 2003), 84.

27. Charles F. Lummis, foreword to *The Fairyland around Us,* by Whiteley, 9; Bales to Sedgwick, November 25, 1920, ESP; Gentle to Sedgwick, June 17, 1920, ESP; James to Sedgwick, February 11, 1920, ESP.

28. Alice Roon Platen to Sedgwick, February 8, 1920, ESP.

29. Marie Rose Mullen to Sedgwick, February 11, 1920, ESP.

30. Whiteley to Sedgwick, September 16, 1919, ESP; Sedgwick, introduction to *The Story of Opal: The Journal of an Understanding Heart,* by Whiteley (Boston: Atlantic Monthly Press, 1920), x.

31. Ora Read Hemenway to Sedgwick, June 15, 1920, ESP; Bede, "Parentage," n.d., ESP; Sedgwick, "Record," 9; Bede, "Parentage"; Opal Whiteley to Pearl Whiteley, February 3, 1920, ESP.

32. Whiteley to Bede, March 30, 1920, ESP; Hemenway to Sedgwick, June 15, 1920, ESP.

33. Garfield, "The Heir Unapparent," 88.

34. Helen Carson to Sedgwick, September 1, 1920, ESP.

35. Sedgwick, "Statement," November 23, 1920, 1, ESP.

36. Sedgwick to McIntyre, November 19, 1919, ESP.

37. Beck, *Opal*, 89.

38. Bede, *Fabulous Opal Whiteley*, 30; invoice, Boston & Albany Railroad, March 30, 1920, ESP; Sedgwick, introduction to *Story of Opal*, by Whiteley, x.

39. Whiteley to Sedgwick, October 30 and November 12, 1919, ESP; Sedgwick to Whiteley, October 30, 1919, ESP.

40. Sedgwick, *Atlantic*, March 1920, 290.

41. Judith Plotz, review of *The Child Writer from Austen to Woolf*, by Christine Alexander and Juliet McMaster, *Victorian Studies* 49, no. 1 (2006): 118. Whiteley's reports are composed of flat statements such as "Across the track and to the left was a house like ours but with additions—a shed kitchen and an eat woodshed. Almost at the other end of the pond and on the same side as our house was the cookhouse." Whiteley to Sedgwick, October 30, 1919, ESP.

42. Bede, "Copy of diary [March 14, 1911] found by Mrs. Lou M. Thompson put away in a notebook and forgotten," notes, n.d., ESP.

43. John Kevin Young, *Black Writers, White Publishers: Marketplace Politics in Twentieth-Century African American Literature* (Jackson: University Press of Mississippi, 2006), 23; Cathryn Halverson, "Opal Whiteley and the Disappearing Region," in *Western Subjects: Autobiographical Writing in the North American West*, ed. Kathleen A. Boardman and Gioia Woods (Salt Lake City: University of Utah Press, 2005), 247–76.

44. Sedgwick to Bede, February 7, 1921, ESP; Sedgwick to Constant Huntington, November 22, 1920, 13, 7, 8, ESP; Frances Lee to Whiteley, September 9, 1920, ESP; Sedgwick to Lee, May 5, 1920, ESP; Sedgwick to Mr. Caswell, July 14, 1920, ESP.

45. Sedgwick to Huntington, November 22, 1920, 13, ESP; Sedgwick to Bede, February 7, 1921, ESP.

46. Whiteley to Mark Howe, n.d., ESP.

47. Sedgwick to Dr. Stone, November 25, 1919, ESP; Sedgwick to Edmund Conklin, March 15, 1920, ESP.

48. Sedgwick, "Contributors' Column," *Atlantic*, March 1920, 429; Sedgwick, introduction to *Story of Opal*, by Whiteley, xv.

49. Advertisement, *Littell's Living Age* 307, no. 3990 (1920): back cover; Patricia Okker, *Social Stories: The Magazine Novel in Nineteenth-Century America* (Charlottesville: University Press of Virginia, 2003); Michael Lund, *America's Continuing Story: An Introduction to Serial Fiction, 1850–1900* (Detroit: Wayne State University Press, 1992).

50. "Jane Doe" to Sedgwick, August 4, 1920, ESP.

51. Sarah Elizabeth Forbush Downs to Sedgwick, October 11, 1920, ESP.

52. Sedgwick to Bede, November 8, 1920, ESP.

53. Sedgwick to Huntington, November 22, 1920, 14, ESP.

54. Sedgwick to Bede, September 14, 1920, ESP.

55. Sedgwick, "Statement," 6.

56. Reed Tucker, "Step Inside the Mansion Built for Jesus' Return," *New York Post*, December 27, 2015; Whiteley to Sedgwick, September 27, 1929, ESP.

57. Sedgwick to Bede, November 8, 1920, ESP; Sedgwick to Raymond H. Oveson, July 23, 1920, ESP; Sedgwick to Bede, November 8, 1920, ESP.

58. Don E. Fehrenbacher, *The Minor Affair: An Adventure in Forgery and Detection* (Fort Wayne, IN: Louis A. Warren Lincoln Library and Museum, 1979), 13. Teresa S. Fitzpatrick, the *Atlantic*'s circulation manager, eventually extracted a signed confession from Minor, having taken a train all the way to Los Angeles to get it. Minor explained that the letters were transcriptions of messages that her mother, a medium, had received from "the spirits of Ann and Abe" ("Confession," July 3, 1929, ESP). Its channeling of presidential thoughts notwithstanding, "Lincoln the Lover" displays some features of a Sedgwick "faraway woman" exchange, composed of letter and diary supplied by an unusual, ambitious westerner. An aspiring fiction writer who worked as a freelance journalist for the *San Diego Union*, Minor had published profiles of women like "Mrs. J. C. Hawkesworth, an eighty-six-year-old painter . . . Der Ling, a visiting Manchu princess, [and] Mrs. Francis M. Hinkle, author of 'Wild Ginger,' a narrative poem about army life in Honolulu" (Fehrenbacher, *Minor Affair*, 11). After her Boston visit, Sedgwick wrote her, "Isn't it strange that sometimes one feels as though they have known a person a long time, although their hours together may have been very brief?" (September 17, 1928, ESP). He also wrestled with his conscience over whether to accept her offer of "any one of the original Lincoln letters that appeals to you most" (Minor to Sedgwick, August 29, 1928, ESP). Once it was published, scholars convened to debunk the find, while the magazine belatedly hired the J. B. Armstrong Detective Agency to investigate Minor and her mother, discovering evidence of marriages, divorce, alibis, and acting (Opr. W.H.C. #10, "Report," January 16 and 17, 1929, ESP; Agent W-3, "Report," January 19, 1929, ESP).

59. Sedgwick to Bede, March 16, 1945, ESP.

60. Henry Savage, *The New Witness*, October 29, 1920, n.p., scrapbook, ESP; Sedgwick to Ernest Harold Baynes, March 31, 1920, ESP.

61. Sedgwick to Nellie Hemenway, September 14, 1920, ESP.

62. Bede to Sedgwick, May 3, 1921, ESP.

63. Bede to Sedgwick, August 17, 1920, ESP.

64. Sedgwick to Bede, November 19, 1920, ESP.

65. Whiteley to Charles Edward Whiteley, n.d., ESP.

66. Sedgwick to Whiteley, September 14, 1920, ESP; Whiteley to Sedgwick, September 16, 1920, ESP.

67. Ibid.; Sedgwick to Bede, June 7 and May 26, 1921, ESP.

68. Whiteley to Willard James, February 11, 1920, ESP.

69. Bede to Sedgwick, October 17, 1920, ESP.

70. Bede to Sedgwick, February 15 and March 7, 1921, ESP.

71. Sedgwick to Bede, March 15, 1921, ESP.

72. Bede to Sedgwick, October 17, 1920, ESP.

73. Bede to Sedgwick, December 5, 1920, ESP.

74. Whiteley, "Letters, 1922–1923," Amy Lowell correspondence, Houghton Library, Cambridge, MA; Whiteley, "Notes on Novel," n.d., Richard Clark Cabot Papers, Harvard University Archives, Cambridge, MA.

75. Whiteley to Richard and Ella Cabot, April 9, 1923, Cabot Papers.
76. Beck, *Opal*, 178–79.
77. Ibid., 185–203.
78. Whiteley to Sedgwick, September 17, 1929, ESP.
79. Whiteley to Sedgwick, October 14, 1929, ESP.
80. Sedgwick to Whiteley, September 17, 1929, ESP.
81. Sedgwick, note to Teresa S. Fitzpatrick, September 27, 1929, ESP. The minutely itemized guide to the Opal Whiteley Papers at the Senate House Library documents her frenetic epistolary activity; recipients include Pope Pius XI. Even the bare finding aid is a poignant document, as in the description of MS 949/4A/2, "Diary style notes": "They are particularly concerned with her feelings about various priests," or MS 949/4G, "Code writings": "Whiteley spent time working out complex numerical codes and calculations using published sources, often religious or biblical" (http://archives.ulrls.lon.ac.uk/detail.aspx). Running to fourteen boxes, most of the material was generated in London. However, it also includes papers Whiteley brought with her from the United States, including some pertaining to *Fairyland*. Little studied relative to its American counterparts, the collection is sure to reward scholars with further insights.

CHAPTER FOUR: *ATLANTIC* EXCHANGE

1. Hilda Rose to Ellery Sedgwick, July 20, 1927, ESP.
2. Hilda Rose, "The Stump Farm," serial, *Atlantic*, February 1927, 145–52; March 1927, 334–42; April 1927, 512–18. Chronologically, Annie Pike Greenwood's 1919 "The Sage-Brush Farmer's Wife" and "Letters from a Sage Brush Farm" bridge Rose and Stewart's *Atlantic* serials, although her memoir, *We Sagebrush Folks,* was only published in 1934. Raised in Provo, Utah, in an upper-class family, Annie Pike worked as a teacher and a reporter prior to marrying Charles Greenwood. The couple began homesteading in 1913 near Hazleton, Idaho—scarcely one hundred miles from Rose's "stump farm"—and Greenwood depicts an even more severe cultural dislocation as she chronicles her family's deepening poverty and debt. They gave up on farming in Idaho in 1928, not long after the Roses did the same. In *We Sagebrush Folks* (New York: D. Appleton–Century, 1934), Greenwood refers to Sedgwick as "my ever kind and patient friend"; she also comments that her *Atlantic* check saved her teeth (362). Although Sedgwick does not mention Greenwood in *The Happy Profession,* her authorship resembles that of his nominal faraway women. In an effort to place work in "the better magazines," she explains, she had "the frantic thought of carbon-copying my letters to my folks" (370); the serial that anticipates the book is composed of letters to her "Dear Sister," "Dear Cousins," and "Dear Folks." *We Sagebrush Folks* relays responses to her *Atlantic* debut: "A professor of English in Columbia University came striding into his classroom. . . . He bore in his hand a copy of the Atlantic, and holding the magazine up before the class he began: 'My wife is a college graduate. She has been trying for years to get into the *Atlantic Monthly* . . . and yet here is a mere farmer's wife who has done it!'" (361). When asked how she "managed to break into the Atlantic," Greenwood replied, "I took an ax" (236).

3. *Atlantic*, February 1927, 145.

4. Rose to Margaret Emerson, June 11, 1927, EFP.

5. *Atlantic*, February 1927, 145.

6. Rose, *Atlantic*, September 1927, 296–97; Sedgwick, "Contributors' Column," *Atlantic*, September 1927, 429.

7. Sedgwick, "Contributors' Column," *Atlantic*, September 1927, 429; Samuel A. Eliot, foreword to *The Stump Farm*, by Hilda Rose (Boston: Little, Brown, 1928), viii; "Books of All Types," *Kansas Industrialist* 55, no. 17 (1929); Hilda Rose, "Long Distance Calling: New Letters from the Stump Farm," *Atlantic*, November 1935, 551–59.

8. Rose to Emerson, n.d., EFP.

9. "A Look Back," *Rock River Times* (Rockford, IL), July 1, 1993, http://rockriver times.com/1993/07/01/a-look-backthe-story-of-rockford-furniture.

10. Hilda M. Gustafson, U.S. Census, 1900, FamilySearch, FHL microfilm 1,240,355, https://familysearch.org/ark:/61903/1:1:MSCC-NDV.

11. Rose to Emerson, n.d., EFP; Rose, "Christmas at the Ranch," *Atlantic*, December 1933, 672.

12. Rose to Emerson, March 6, 1945, EFP.

13. Rose to Jack Jensen, n.d., ESP.

14. Rose to Jensen, September 17, 1933, and n.d., ESP; Hilda M. Gustavson [*sic*], U.S. Census, 1910, FamilySearch, FHL microfilm 1,374,238, https://family search.org/ark:/61903/1:1:MLHG-M6F.

15. Charles W. Rose and Hilda M. Gustafson, marriage, 1911, "Idaho, County Marriages, 1864–1950," FamilySearch, FHL microfilm 1,548,243, https://family search.org/ark:/61903/1:1:F3Y4–5LN.

16. Charles W. Rose, U.S. Census, 1900, FamilySearch, FHL microfilm 1,240,233, https://familysearch.org/ark:/61903/1:1:MM55-DNN.

17. Rose, "Christmas," 676; Charles W. Rose, U.S. Census 1880, FamilySearch, FHL microfilm 1,254,628, https://familysearch.org/ark:/61903/1:1:MZ9N-GF7.

18. Charles W. Rose, U.S. Census, 1900; Charles W. Rose, U.S. Census, 1910, FamilySearch, FHL microfilm 1,374,238, https://familysearch.org/ark:/61903 /1:1:MLHG-Q7G.

19. Simeon C. Rose, U.S. Census, 1920, FamilySearch, FHL microfilm 1,820,291, https://familysearch.org/ark:/61903/1:1:MDCG-Y9F.

20. Will Ferguson, *Beauty Tips from Moose Jaw: Excursions in the Great Weird North* (Edinburgh: Canongate, 2006), 44; Edward L. Affleck, "Steamboating on the Peace River," *British Columbia Historical News* 33, no. 1 (1999–2000): 2–7. http:// www.library.ubc.ca/archives/pdfs/bchf/bchn_1999-00_winter.pdf.

21. Rose to Jensen, August 8, 1932, ESP.

22. Eliot, foreword to *The Stump Farm,* by Rose, vii; Rose to Sedgwick, May 11, 1928, ESP; Rose to Edward Weeks, February 10, 1933, ESP. Rose eventually became a Canadian citizen.

23. Eliot, foreword to *The Stump Farm,* by Rose, ix.

24. Rose to Jensen, n.d., ESP.

25. Charles B. Driscoll, "Are You Discouraged?," *New Castle (PA) News*, May 4, 1928.

26. There were two Mrs. T's, both a neighbor and the middle-class woman Charles feared offending.

27. Anne Ruggles Gere, *Intimate Practices: Literacy and Cultural Work in U.S. Women's Clubs, 1880–1920* (Urbana: University of Illinois Press, 1995), 1.
28. Rose to Mrs. Austin, April 6, 1925, ESP.
29. *Kansas City Times,* August 27, 1952.
30. Barbara Brackman, "The Fisk Sanitary Commission Quilt," July 25, 2015, http://civilwarquilts.blogspot.jp/2015/07/the-fisk-sanitary-commission-quilt.html.
31. Conant K. Halsey, "Grace Mullen and the Prosellis," *Fortnightly Club of Redlands, California* (April 13, 1995), http://www.redlandsfortnightly.org/papers/Proselis.htm; Florence Fisk White, "Contributors' Column," *Atlantic,* March 1927, 405.
32. Rose to Jensen, n.d. and August 8, 1932, ESP.
33. Peter C. Holloran, *Boston's Wayward Children: Social Services for Homeless Children, 1830–1930* (Madison, NJ: Fairleigh Dickinson University Press, 1989), 207; Mary Hannah Graves, death, December 5, 1908, FamilySearch, FHL microfilm 2,217,886, https://familysearch.org/ark:/61903/1:1:NWTL-V45.
34. Rose to Sedgwick, January 2, 1928, ESP.
35. Laurel Thatcher Ulrich, *A Midwife's Tale: The Life of Martha Ballard, Based on Her Diary, 1785–1812* (New York: Alfred A. Knopf, 1990), 346, 346, 349, 350.
36. Rose to Sedgwick, July 20, 1927, ESP; Rose to Mary F. Hobart, October 17, 1929, ESP; Rose to Sedgwick, July 18, 1931, ESP.
37. Rose to Sedgwick, May 11, 1928, ESP.
38. Rose to Jensen, n.d., ESP.
39. Rose to Jensen, September 8, no year, ESP.
40. Rose typically uses "Indian" to refer to men and "squaw" to refer to women.
41. Rose to Jensen, n.d., ESP.
42. Rose to Emerson, September 20, 1933, and May 14, 1937, EFP.
43. Willa Cather, *O Pioneers!* (Boston: Houghton Mifflin, 1913), 124.
44. Rose to Emerson, January 11, 1929, EFP.
45. Rose to Emerson, n.d. [ca. May 1930], EFP.
46. "The *Atlantic Monthly* Has Discovered a New Canadian Writer of Heart," *Carp Review* (October 6, 1927): 4.
47. Rose to Sedgwick, January 2, 1928, ESP. Rose noted that *The Stump Farm* was excerpted for "school readers" in Canada (to Christine Fowler, October 1, 1942, EFP), and she at one point believed Houghton Mifflin would publish her second book as "a school-book supplementary to the study of Canada" (to Emerson, September 16, no year, EFP).
48. Edward Weeks, *My Green Age: A Memoir* (Boston: Little, Brown, 1973), 208–9.
49. Leon Jackson, *The Business of Letters: Authorial Economies in Antebellum America* (Stanford, CA: Stanford University Press, 2008), 28.
50. Rose to Jensen, June 6, 1932, ESP; Rose to Emerson, February 6, 1935, EFP.
51. Christine Holbo, "'Industrial & Picturesque Narrative': Helen Hunt Jackson's California Travel Writing for the *Century,*" *American Literary Realism* 42, no. 3 (2010): 245; Annie Bartom to J. C. Bitterman, January 16, 1929, http://homepages.rootsweb.ancestry.com/~bartom/annie/year1934.txt; Will Rogers, *Will Rogers' Weekly Articles,* vol. 5, *The Hoover Years, 1931–1933,* ed. Steven K. Gragert (Norman: Oklahoma State University Press, 1982), 168.

52. Nancy Glazener, *Reading for Realism: The History of a U.S. Literary Institution, 1850–1910* (Durham, NC: Duke University Press, 1997), 193; Rose, "Long," 555; Rose to Clara and Blanche, May 20, 1925, ESP.
53. Chris Baldick, *The Oxford Dictionary of Literary Terms*, 3rd ed. (Oxford: Oxford University Press, 2008), 157; Charles Johanningsmeier, "Understanding Readers of Fiction in American Periodicals, 1880–1914," in *U.S. Popular Print Culture, 1860–1920*, ed. Christine Bold, the Oxford History of Popular Print Culture, vol. 6 (Oxford: Oxford University Press, 2012), 598; Janice Radway, "American Studies, Reader Theory, and the Literary Text: From the Study of Material Objects to the Study of Social Processes," in *American Studies in Transition*, ed. David E. Nye and Christen Kold Thomsen (Odense: Odense University Press, 1985), 37.
54. Rose to Jensen, n.d., ESP.
55. For example, her letters were avidly read by the "Old Timers Club" affiliated with the W. D. Allen Manufacturing Company in Chicago, which assured her, "You have a group of warm friends and admirers in this section of the country" (W. H. Symons to Rose, August 29, 1927, EFP).
56. Rose to Sedgwick, January 2, 1928, EFP; Rose to Margaret Emerson, May 14, 1929, EFP; "Contributors' Column," *Atlantic*, December 1933, 49; Rose to Weeks, February 10, 1933, ESP; Rose to Jensen, April 29, 1934, ESP.
57. Rose to Emerson, June 11, 1927, EFP; Rose to Jensen, June 6, 1932, June 30, 1935, and n.d., ESP.
58. Rose, "Long," 556.
59. Thomas Wentworth Higginson, "Letter to a Young Contributor," *Atlantic*, April 1862, 402; Rose to Jensen, June 28, 1933, and n.d., ESP.
60. Rose to Jensen, June 6, 1932, and n.d., ESP.
61. Rose, "Long," 557; Rose to Jensen, July 30, no year, and July 30, 1935, ESP; Rose to Emerson, August 24, 1936, ESP.
62. Margaret Emerson, "Lafcadio Hearn's Funeral," *Critic* 46, no. 1 (1905): 34–38; Stewart to Emerson, November 18, 1915, EFP.
63. Rose, statement, August 30, 1938, EFP.
64. Rose to Emerson, July 29, 1927, spring 1941, and March 4, 1944, EFP.
65. Fowler to Emerson, February 10 and March 25, 1945, EFP.
66. Rose, "Christmas," 670.
67. Rose, "Long," 557, 556, 557, 559.
68. Hilda Rose, "Pioneering on the Peace River," *Atlantic*, January 1934, 96.
69. Rose, "Contributors' Column," *Atlantic*, November 1927, 718–19; "Contributors' Column," *Atlantic*, December 1933, 50; "Contributors' Column," *Atlantic*, November 1927, 718.
70. Margaret Beetham, "Periodicals and the New Media: Women and Imagined Communities," *Women's Studies International Forum* 29, no. 3 (2006): 235.
71. "Contributors' Column," *Atlantic*, October 1929, 573; "Contributors' Column," *Atlantic*, August 1933, 17.
72. Donald Clifford Gallup, "Gertrude Stein and the *Atlantic*," *Yale University Library Gazette* 28, no. 3 (1954): 118.
73. "Contributors' Column," *Atlantic*, October 1935, 40.

74. "Contributors' Column," *Atlantic*, November 1935, 46; Rose to Emerson, February 6, 1935, EFP; Rose to Sedgwick, December 15, 1936, ESP; Rose, note, n.d., ESP.

75. Rose to Emerson, October 3, 1944, EFP.

76. We can contrast the money and goods Rose received with the more sentimentally freighted, actual Christmas presents that *Atlantic* associates sent Stewart, inventoried in one of her private letters: "A Doctor-Lady in Denver sent me a box of candy, a little stenographer in Chicago sent me a box of candy. A dear little Woman in Oklahoma whom I never saw sent me a year's subscription to a little paper called Comfort, cards came from many. . . . Miss Emerson sent Jerrine 'The Journal of an Understanding Heart' [*The Story of Opal*]. Mr. Segewick [*sic*] sent her 'Lorna Doone.' A little Swede sent her 'the Other Wise Man' and Miss Prindle who wrote you, sent her 'Prince and Pauper'" (to Mariah Wood, December 29, no year, SBC).

77. Rose to Sedgwick, January 10, 1936, ESP.

78. Rose to Sedgwick, December 15, 1936, ESP.

79. It was all a little more complicated, of course. Rose's bounty filled the postmaster's tiny kitchen, giving her neighbors ample opportunity to review it and to pilfer small items like candy. The display made some so enviously resentful that they considered writing to the senders to inform them that they, too, were hard up (Fowler to Emerson, February 10, 1945, EFP). Patriotic Canadians, conversely, did not appreciate the implication that one of their own was in need of American rescue. Most important, the flow of all these goods across the border attracted the attention of Canadian officials. As a homesteader, Rose was, after all, participating in a federal program in another nation. Sedgwick reported that the Canadian government both investigated Rose's situation and asked him to forbear from "further immediate steps" (to Emerson, September 8, 1936, EFP). Thus, he turned down Emerson's proposal that they repeat the venture the following year, as likely to draw state ire. In 1938 Emerson took matters into her own hands, writing out to a group of associates for further help: "Hilda would be horrified at my writing in this way to you. My only excuse is my feeling that this is no time to keep back from her friends her great need" (letter draft, n.d., EFP). Among other responses, Blanche Randolph arranged, through E. Phanz at the "Imperial Store" in Edmonton, to have a load of groceries freighted to Fort Vermilion. Helen A. Lee in Chicago sent Phanz ten dollars to purchase "treats" (to E. Phanz, October 1, 1940, EFP), an order to which Ada Fitts contributed five dollars more, while John B. Weston attempted to ship her a box of dates from India. Inquiring after his dates, Weston reminded Emerson of her proposal that "each of us send a dollar or two to Mrs. Rose" (February 7, 1941, EFP).

80. Rose to Sedgwick, September 2 and August 15, 1933, ESP.

81. Rose to Jensen, December 27, 1933, August 19, 1934, n.d., and December 9, 1934, ESP; Rose, "Long," 553; Rose to Jensen, June 30, 1935, ESP.

82. Rose to Jensen, June 12 and August 19, 1934, September 17, 1933, and June 30, 1935, ESP.

83. Rose to Jensen, June 28 and December 27, 1933, n.d., and June 28, 1933, ESP.

84. Rose to Jensen, August 19, 1934, ESP.

85. Rose to Jensen, June 28, 1933, ESP.

86. Rose to Jensen, n.d., ESP; Rose to Emerson, May 23, 1931, EFP.

87. Rose to Hobart, December 28, 1930, ESP; Rose to Jensen, n.d., ESP.

88. Rose to Jensen, n.d., ESP; Rose to Sedgwick, July 18, 1931, ESP; Rose, "Christmas," 670.

89. Rose to Jensen, June 28, 1933, ESP; Rose to Emerson, February 19, no year, EFP; Eliot, foreword to *The Stump Farm*, by Rose, viii.

90. Rose to Sedgwick, September 2, 1933, ESP; Richard Brodhead, *Cultures of Letters: Scenes of Reading and Writing in Nineteenth-Century America* (Durham, NC: Duke University Press, 1995), 81; Rose to Jensen, n.d., ESP.

91. Rose to Emerson, September 16, no year, EFP.

92. Rose, "Pioneering on the Peace" (m.s.), EFP.

93. Rose to Emerson, n.d., EFP.

94. Clarence Karr, *Authors and Audiences: Popular Canadian Fiction in the Early Twentieth Century* (Montreal: McGill-Queen's University Press, 2000), 64.

95. Rose to Hobart, December 28, 1930, ESP.

96. Rose to Sedgwick, July 14, 1933, ESP.

97. Rose to Emerson, December 12, 1935, EFP.

98. Rose to Emerson, March 10, 1930, EFP. *Asia: The American Magazine on the Orient* originally focused on culture, business, and travel in Asia. It became more political at the helm of editors Richard J. Walsh and Pearl Buck, adopting anti-colonialist positions.

99. Rose to Sedgwick, July 14, 1933, ESP; Rose to Jensen, December 27, 1933, ESP; Rose to Emerson, August 28, 1933, EFP.

100. Rose to Emerson, May 20 and August 5, 1934, EFP; Emerson, letter draft to Weeks, n.d. (ca. 1937), EFP; Weeks to Emerson, December 2, 1937, EFP; Sedgwick to Emerson, October 25, 1938, EFP; Rose to Emerson, February 6, 1938, and n.d., EFP; Weeks to Emerson, November 27, 1942, EFP.

101. Rose to Jensen, December 9, 1934, and January 6, 1935, ESP.

102. Weeks to Emerson, March 23, 1939, EFP; Rose, "Contributors' Column," *Atlantic*, May 1939, n.p.; "Contributors' Column," *Atlantic*, March 1941, n.p.

103. Rose to Emerson, December 10, no year. Emerson's papers include a reference letter that this employer wrote for Rose.

104. Rose to Emerson, May 10, 1943, EFP.

105. Rose to Fowler, September 12, 1945, EFP. Associate of Harriet Monroe, Kathleen Foster was an active member of the University of Chicago Poetry Club. Since Rose knew her as Mrs. Donald Campbell, she may not have been aware of the extent of her accomplishment.

106. Rose to Emerson, n.d., EFP.

107. Rose to Emerson, July 5, 1944, EFP.

108. Rose to Emerson, September 11, 1934, March 6, 1945, February 6, 1946, March 6, 1945, n.d. (ca. 1946), and May 27, 1940, EFP.

CHAPTER FIVE: JUANITA HARRISON AND
MY GREAT, WIDE, BEAUTIFUL WORLD

1. Cathryn Halverson, *Playing House in the American West: Western Women's Life Narrative, 1839–1987* (Tuscaloosa: University of Alabama Press, 2013), 158.

2. Samuel A. Eliot, foreword to *The Stump Farm*, by Hilda Rose (Boston: Little, Brown, 1928), vii.

3. Juanita Harrison, "My Great, Wide, Beautiful World," serial, *Atlantic*, October 1935, 434–43; November 1935, 601–12; "Miss Harrison's Book in Fifth Printing," *California Eagle*, August 14, 1936.

4. *Atlantic*, November 1935, 601; Virginia Kirkus, quoted in advertisement, *Publishers Weekly* (April 25, 1936): 1670; Martha Gruening, "Natural," *New Republic* (June 3, 1936): 111; Katherine Woods, "Juanita Harrison Has Known Twenty-Two Countries," *New York Times*, May 17, 1936.

5. Carolyn Steedman, *Dust: The Archive and Cultural History* (New Brunswick, NJ: Rutgers University Press, 2002), 8; Eric Gardner, "Sowing and Reaping: A 'New' Chapter from Frances Ellen Watkins Harper's Second Novel," *Common-place: The Interactive Journal of Early American Life* 13, no. 1 (2012), www.common-place.org; John Kevin Young, *Black Writers, White Publishers: Marketplace Politics in Twentieth-Century African American Literature* (Jackson: University Press of Mississippi, 2006), 22; Lois Brown, "Death-Defying Testimony: Women's Private Lives and the Politics of Public Documents," *Legacy* 27, no. 1 (2010): 138.

6. Lizzie Crigler, census, 1870, FamilySearch, FHL microfilm 552,243, https://familysearch.org/ark:/61903/1:1:MFSL-T55. The spelling variants appear on Harrison's 1940 immigration card, 1950 passport application, and 1953 Social Security application, respectively.

7. Oktibbeha County, Mississippi," transcribed by Tom Blake, 2001, http://freepages.genealogy.rootsweb.ancestry.com/%7Eajac/msoktibbeha.htm; Adele Logan Alexander, introduction to *My Great, Wide, Beautiful World*, by Juanita Harrison (New York: G. K. Hall, 1996), xv.

8. Bridget Smith Pieschel, "The History of Mississippi University for Women," *Mississippi History Now* (Mississippi Historical Society) (March 2012): n.p.

9. Patricia Yaeger, *Dirt and Desire: Reconstructing Southern Women's Writing, 1930–1990* (Chicago: University of Chicago Press, 2000), 59; *Atlanta Constitution*, September 2, 1902, http://www3.gendisasters.com/alabama/814/berry,-al-train-wreck,-sept-1902.

10. James R. Grossman, *Land of Hope: Chicago, Black Southerners, and the Great Migration* (Chicago: University of Chicago Press, 1991), 35.

11. David M. Katzman, *Seven Days a Week: Women and Domestic Service in Industrializing America* (Urbana: University of Illinois Press, 1981), 212–13.

12. Juanita Harrison, application for passport renewal, February 17, 1950; Juanita Harrison, 1925, "Hawaii, Honolulu Passenger Lists, 1900–1953," FamilySearch, NARA microfilm publication A3422, https://familysearch.org/pal:/MM9.3.1/TH-1971–36723–34012–40?cc=2141044; Juanita Harrison, 1925, "California, San Francisco Passenger Lists, 1893–1953," FamilySearch, FHL microfilm 2,380,987, https://familysearch.org/ark:/61903/1:1:KX4R-6JY.

13. Juanita Harrison, death, 1967, FamilySearch, "United States Social Security Death Index," https://familysearch.org/ark:/61903/1:1:JG3V-6Q3.

14. George Dickinson, "Contributors' Column," *Atlantic,* October 1935, 39.

15. Harrison lived there for a full four years, on affectionate terms with the Tadas. To commemorate Sedgwick's 1936 visit, she proposed that they name their newborn daughter Lillian Ellery instead of Lillian Shizuyo, an incident reported by the *Nippu Jiji,* a local Japanese newspaper.

16. W. E. B. Du Bois, *Dusk of Dawn: An Essay toward an Autobiography of a Race Concept* (New York: Harcourt, Brace, 1940), 153; Yaeger, *Dirt and Desire,* 59.

17. Gayle Wald, *Crossing the Line: Racial Passing in Twentieth-Century U.S. Literature and Culture* (Durham, NC: Duke University Press, 2000), ix, 6.

18. Gene Andrew Jarrett, introduction to *African American Literature beyond Race: An Alternative Reader,* ed. Gene Andrew Jarrett (New York: New York University Press, 2006), 3 (quote), 14.

19. Julia Ehrhardt, *Writers of Conviction: The Personal Politics of Zona Gale, Dorothy Canfield Fisher, Rose Wilder Lane, and Josephine Herbst* (Columbia: University of Missouri Press, 2004), 43; Sedgwick, "Contributors' Column," *Atlantic,* December 1935, 80; Jean Marie Lutes, "Beyond the Bounds of the Book: Periodical Studies and Women Writers of the Late Nineteenth and Early Twentieth Centuries," *Legacy: A Journal of American Women Writers* 27, no. 2 (2010): 339.

20. The piece was written by editor Ben Burns, who published it under one of his pseudonyms, Wallace Lee. Burns, *Nitty Gritty: A White Editor in Black Journalism* (Jackson: University Press of Mississippi, 1996), 32.

21. Richard Yarborough, "Strategies of Black Characterization in *Uncle Tom's Cabin* and the Early Afro-American Novel," in *New Essays on "Uncle Tom's Cabin,"* ed. Eric J. Sundquist (Cambridge: Cambridge University Press, 1986), 67.

22. Harrison to John Mason Brown, n.d., John Mason Brown Papers, Houghton Library, Harvard University, Cambridge, MA. While likely written shortly after Burns broadcast Brown's comments, the letter is undated and gives no indication of where it was sent from.

23. Claire Garcia, "'For a Few Days We Would Be Residents in Africa': Jessie Redmon Fauset's 'Dark Algiers the White,'" *Ethnic Studies Review* 30, nos. 1–2 (2007): 111.

24. William Norwood, "Juanita, Unique Authoress, Meets 'Unseen Sweetheart,'" *Honolulu Star-Bulletin,* March 25, 1936.

25. Myra K. Dickinson, U.S. Census, 1940, FamilySearch, (ED) 60–987, sheet 13A, family 499, https://familysearch.org/ark:/61903/1:1:K9ZW-JNS.

26. "Dickinson Rites Set: Octogenarian Realty Man Will Be Paid Final Honor Tomorrow," *Los Angeles Times,* May 11, 1936.

27. Myra K. Dickinson, U.S. Census, 1920, FamilySearch, FHL microfilm 1,820,108, https://familysearch.org/ark:/61903/1:1:MHQL-XJT; Myra K. Dickinson, U.S. Census, 1930, FamilySearch, FHL microfilm 2,339,884, https://familysearch.org/ark:/61903/1:1:XCVP-6CH.

28. Kevin Lane Dearinger, *Clyde Fitch and the American Theatre: An Olive in the Cocktail* (Lanham, MD: Rowman & Littlefield, 2016), 92; "Pretty Good Remarks by the Press," *Theater* 5 (1888): 423.

29. Bruce K. Hanson, *Peter Pan on Stage and Screen, 1904–2010* (Jefferson, NC: McFarland, 2011), 59.

30. Harrison indicates she and Morris had once planned a serialized biography, with her identity shielded: "So my story will be cut up in many stories for magazines with another name as I wished" (FL2).

31. Carolyn Steedman, "Servants and Their Relationship to the Unconscious," *Journal of British Studies* 42, no. 3 (2003): 320.

32. Franco Moretti, *Distant Reading* (London and New York: Verso, 2013), 181; Kate Douglas Wiggin, *Rebecca of Sunnybrook Farm* (New York: William Morrow, 1994), 119; Angela Sorby, *Schoolroom Poets: Childhood, Performance, and the Place of American Poetry* (Durham: University of New Hampshire Press, 2005), 37.

33. Alexander, introduction to *My Great, Wide, Beautiful World*, by Harrison, xvii.

34. *Atlantic*, October 1935, 434; advertisement, *Publishers Weekly* (April 25, 1936): 1670; Wilbur Needham, "A Book to End Pessimism and Renew Joy in Life," *Los Angeles Times*, May 7, 1936.

35. Anne Bower, *Epistolary Responses: The Letter in Twentieth-Century American Fiction* (Tuscaloosa: University of Alabama Press, 1997), 99; Jack Stillinger, *Multiple Authorship and the Myth of Solitary Genius* (Oxford: Oxford University Press, 1991), vi.

36. Hilda Rose to Sedgwick, September 2, 1933, ESP; Sedgwick, introduction to *The Story of Opal: The Journal of an Understanding Heart*, by Opal Whiteley (Boston: Atlantic Monthly Press, 1920), xi.

37. Alexander, introduction to *My Great, Wide, Beautiful World*, by Harrison, xvii.

38. Margo Culley, ed., *A Day at a Time: The Diary Literature of American Women from 1764 to the Present* (New York: Feminist Press, 1985), 223; Kelly A. Squazzo, "Juanita Harrison," in *African American Autobiographers: A Sourcebook*, ed. Emmanuel Sampath Nelson (Westport, CT: Greenwood Press, 2002), 177; "'Gelorious!,'" review of *My Great, Wide, Beautiful World*, by Harrison, *Time*, May 18, 1936, 83–85.

39. Gavin Jones, *Strange Talk: The Politics of Dialect Literature in Gilded Age America* (Berkeley: University of California Press, 1999), 7.

40. Quoted in Eric J. Sundquist, *To Wake the Nations: Race in the Making of American Literature* (Cambridge, MA: Belknap Press, 1998), 309.

41. Richard Brodhead, *Cultures of Letters: Scenes of Reading and Writing in Nineteenth-Century America* (Durham, NC: Duke University Press, 1995), 108.

42. That is not to say that Harrison didn't receive fan mail. She reported, "Since the Book came out I have read letters from dozon of fine unseen friends of Americans best" (FL3).

43. Dickinson, "Contributors' Column," 38–39. Dickinson's reported dates for her time in their employ do not quite tally. Harrison spent the first half of 1925 in Hawaii, and a passenger manifest for the journey out identifies Denver as her city of residence. She also held a job in New York City just before sailing for England. Moreover, she worked in at least one other Los Angeles household, that of Mary Ann Tufts. Intriguingly in light of Harrison's authorship, Tufts was a book reviewer for the *Los Angeles Times*. Harrison mentions she was the first person in Los Angeles to receive a copy of her book (FL3), and she was one

of her visitors in Honolulu. "Mrs. Edward Tufts on Honolulu Vacation," *San Bernardino Sun* 43, no. 4 (1937): 8.

44. Arthur B. Spingarn, "Books by Negro Authors in 1936," *Crisis* 44, no. 2 (1937): 48.

45. Joseph M. Marrone, "Contributors' Column," *Atlantic*, November 1935, 78.

46. Helen Rose, "Contributors' Column," *Atlantic*, November 1935, 48. The couple's involvement in her life, while scarcely visible in the historical record, must have been considerable. Harrison housesat for them for more than a year on the Cap d'Antibes, and the book includes a grateful letter to Helen Rose, penned in Japan.

47. Nor could this refer to her later return to Honolulu, since she was still living in Buenos Aires when *The Happy Profession* was published.

48. Isadore Cecilia Williams, "Contributors' Column," *Atlantic*, December 1935, 79–80; Sedgwick, "Contributors' Column," *Atlantic*, December 1935, 80; H. L. Mencken, "Designations for Colored Folk," *American Speech* 19, no. 3 (1944): 165; William J. Cox to Sedgwick, February 17, 1947, ESP.

49. Harrison also met with William Pickens, writer, activist, and NAACP director of branches ("Juanita Harrison, Author, Fetes Pickens in Waikiki Tent," *California Eagle*, August 28, 1936, 174). Pickens casually mentions reading her book on his onward voyage to Latin America, suggesting he assumed his readers were familiar with it ("Wm. Pickens, Nearing Home, Writes Impressions of Trip 'below Gulf of Mexico,'" *California Eagle*, September 18, 1936, 229). Pickens espoused a "theory of race progress that hinges on the physical movement of peoples across continents," so we can see why he admired Harrison. Marlon Bryan Ross, *Manning the Race: Reforming Black Men in the Jim Crow Era* (New York: New York University Press, 2004), 35.

50. Norwood, "Juanita, Unique Authoress."

51. Michael E. Chapman, "Pro-Franco Anti-communism: Ellery Sedgwick and the *Atlantic Monthly*," *Journal of Contemporary History* 41, no. 4 (2006): 649; Ellery Sedgwick, "Franco Is Shrewd in Political Acts," *New York Times*, February 15, 1938; Ethel M. Alper to Sedgwick, February 13, 1938, ESP; Louise Pearson Mitchell to Sedgwick, February 15, 1938, ESP; Sedgwick to Mitchell, March 28, 1938, ESP.

52. "Negro Mothers Forget Sorrows at Music Gala" (ca. July 1930); "Miss Josephine Baker's Pet Panther"; "La Cabalgata de los Reyes Magos." While the clippings do not show provenance, Harrison had likely sent them to Foster to give her insight into black experience in Europe: one of them is in Spanish, and she had a habit of sending her "some papers that you may enjoy the news" (*FL3*). An essay by Rebecca Jo Plant and Frances M. Clarke discusses the pilgrimage program that "Negro Mothers" references: "'The Crowning Insult': Federal Segregation and the Gold Star Mother and Widow Pilgrimages of the Early 1930s," *Journal of American History* 102, no. 2 (2015): 406–32.

53. Alice M. Foster, U.S. Census, 1930, FamilySearch, FHL microfilm 2,339,903, https://familysearch.org/ark:/61903/1:1:XC8L-MB; Alice F. Cunningham, U.S. Census, 1940, FamilySearch, ED 60–477, sheet 4B, line 57, family 121, https://www.familysearch.org/ark:/61903/1:1:K9C1-K26.

54. John Cournos, "Exploring We Go," *Yale Review* 25 (1936): 840.
55. Juanita Harrison, immigration, 1940, FamilySearch, "Brasil, Cartões de Imigração, 1900–1965," citing 1940, Arquivo Nacional, Rio de Janeiro, https://familysearch.org/ark:/61903/1:1:KCXW-WCT.
56. Whiteley to Sedgwick, September 17, 1929, ESP.
57. Holly A. Laird, *Women Co-authors* (Urbana: University of Illinois Press, 2000), 58, 59.
58. Claudia Maureen Horning, "Trailblazing Librarian in the Golden State: A Look at the Life and Career of Miriam Matthews" (master's thesis, University of California–Los Angeles, 2012), 39, https://escholarship.org/uc/item/8nx1v57d.
59. "Anniversary of Library Is Celebrated," *California Eagle*, September 18, 1936, 229.
60. Review of "*My Great, Wide, Beautiful World*," by Harrison, *California Eagle*, June 26, 1936, 60. Matthews had previously worked at the Helen Hunt Jackson Branch. Horning, "Trailblazing," 74.
61. Matthews to Alice M. Foster, October 6, 1936, Charles E. Young Research Library, University of California–Los Angeles.
62. Matthews, review, newspaper clipping, n.d., ibid.
63. Matthews to Foster, October 6, 1936, ibid.

EPILOGUE: THE *ATLANTIC* ORIGINS
OF *THE AUTOBIOGRAPHY OF ALICE B. TOKLAS*

1. Donald Clifford Gallup, "Gertrude Stein and the *Atlantic*," *Yale University Library Gazette* 28, no. 3 (1954): 126.
2. Gabrielle Dean, "Make It Plain: Stein and Toklas Publish the Plain Edition," in *Primary Stein: Returning to the Writing of Gertrude Stein*, ed. Janet Boyd and Sharon J. Kirsch (Lanham, MD: Lexington Books, 2014), 18.
3. Phoebe Stein Davis, "Subjectivity and the Aesthetics of National Identity in Gertrude Stein's *The Autobiography of Alice B. Toklas*," *Twentieth Century Literature* 45, no. 1 (1999): 18, 38–39.
4. Karen Leick, *Gertrude Stein and the Making of an American Celebrity* (New York: Routledge, 2009), 4–24.
5. Gallup, "Gertrude Stein and the *Atlantic*," 126.
6. Catharine R. Stimpson, "Gertrude Stein and the Lesbian Lie," in *American Women's Autobiography: Fea(s)ts of Memory*, ed. Margo Culley (Madison: University of Wisconsin Press, 1992), 152. Serendipitously, this influential essay is published in Culley's volume adjacent to the first critical discussion of Hilda Rose, Lynn Z. Bloom's "Utopia and Anti-utopia in Twentieth-Century Frontier Autobiographies."
7. Ralph Thompson, review of *The Autobiography of Alice B. Toklas*, by Gertrude Stein, *Current History* (January 1934): n.p.
8. Gertrude Stein, *Four in America* (New Haven, CT: Yale University Press, 1947), 125.

9. Holly A. Laird, *Women Co-authors* (Urbana: University of Illinois Press, 2000), 186.

10. Stimpson, "Gertrude Stein and the Lesbian Lie," 157.

11. Newton Arvin, review of *Atlantic Harvest: Memoirs of the "Atlantic,"* by Ellery Sedgwick, *Nation* (October 11, 1947): 385.

12. Gallup, "Gertrude Stein and the *Atlantic*," 110, 111, 111, 117, 121, 125.

13. Gertrude Stein, *Everybody's Autobiography* (New York: Random House, 1937), 46.

14. Gallup, "Gertrude Stein and the *Atlantic*," 112.

15. Gertrude Stein, "Autobiography of Alice B. Toklas," *Atlantic*, August 1933, 198.

16. *Atlantic*, July 1915, 1; October 1915, 433.

17. Janis P. Stout, "Dorothy Canfield, Willa Cather, and the Uncertainties of Middlebrow and Highbrow," *Studies in the Novel* 44, no. 1 (2012): 28.

18. Mildred Aldrich, *A Hilltop on the Marne: Being Letters Written June 3–September 8, 1914* (Boston: Houghton Mifflin, 1915), 1, 152; Frederick James Gregg, "Good and Bad Writing about the War," *Vanity Fair*, November 1915, 67; Edward Weeks, "Ellery Sedgwick: Eighth Editor of the *Atlantic*, 1872–1960," *Atlantic*, June 1960, 126. Jean Gallagher's *The World Wars through the Female Gaze* (Carbondale: Southern Illinois University Press, 1998) offers the most sustained discussion of Aldrich.

19. Leick, *Gertrude Stein*, 114.

20. Gertrude Stein, *A Stein Reader*, ed. Ulla E. Dydo (Evanston, IL: Northwestern University Press, 1993), 358.

21. Leick, *Gertrude Stein*, 114.

22. Mildred Aldrich to Sedgwick, Oct. 15, 1915, ESP.

23. Gallup, "Gertrude Stein and the *Atlantic*," 118, 119.

24. Davis, "Subjectivity and the Aesthetics of National Identity," 42; Leigh Gilmore, *Autobiographics: A Feminist Theory of Women's Self Representation* (Ithaca, NY: Cornell University Press, 1994), 199, quoted in Davis, "Subjectivity and the Aesthetics of National Identity," 42.

25. Gertrude Stein and Carl Van Vechten, *The Letters of Gertrude Stein and Carl Van Vechten, 1913–1946*, ed. Edward Burns (New York: Columbia University Press, 1986), 471.

26. Langston Hughes and Carl Van Vechten, *Remember Me to Harlem: The Letters of Langston Hughes and Carl Van Vechten*, ed. Emily Bernard (New York: Vintage, 2002), 135.

27. Gallup, "Gertrude Stein and the *Atlantic*," 126; Bryce Conrad, "Gertrude Stein in the American Marketplace," *Journal of Modern Literature* 19, no. 2 (1995): 225.

INDEX

CATHRYN HALVERSON is the author of *Maverick Autobiographies: Women Writers and the American West, 1902–1936* (University of Wisconsin Press, 2004) and *Playing House in the American West: Western Women's Life Narrative, 1839–1987* (University of Alabama Press, 2013). Her current book is a cultural biography of writer and world traveler Juanita Harrison.

She was previously associate professor of American studies at the University of Copenhagen, Denmark, and prior to that English professor at a liberal arts college in Kobe, Japan. She continues to divide her time between Europe, Asia, and North America, the last in respect to her current position as assistant professor of English at Minot State University in Minot, North Dakota.